writing metrical poetry

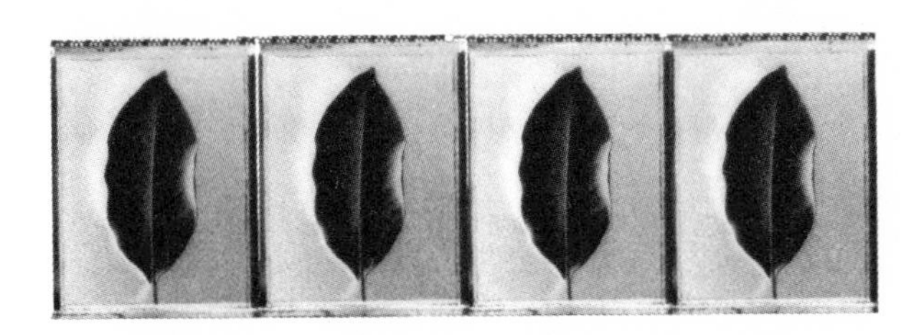

Contemporary Lessons
for Mastering Traditional Forms

WILLIAM BAER

writersdigestbooks.com
Cincinnati, Ohio

 Published by Writer's Digest Books, an imprint of F+W Publications, Inc., 4700 East Galbraith Road, Cincinnati, Ohio 45236. (800) 289-0963. First edition.

10 09 08 07 06 6 5 4 3 2 1

Distributed in Canada by Fraser Direct
100 Armstrong Avenue
Georgetown, ON, Canada L7G 5S4
Tel: (905) 877-4411

Distributed in the U.K. and Europe by David & Charles
Brunel House, Newton Abbot, Devon, TQ12 4PU, England
Tel: (+44) 1626 323200, Fax: (+44) 1626 323319
E-mail: mail@davidandcharles.co.uk

Distributed in Australia by Capricorn Link
P.O. Box 704, Windsor, NSW 2756 Australia
Tel: (02) 4577-3555

Library of Congress Cataloging-in-Publication Data
Baer, William.
Writing metrical poetry / by William Baer.
p. cm.
Includes index.
ISBN-13: 978-1-58297-415-6 (pbk.: alk. paper)
ISBN-10: 1-58297-415-2
1. English language--Versification. 2. English language--Rhythm. 3. Poetry--Authorship. 4. Poetics. I. Title.
PE1505.B16 2006
808.1--dc22 2005032795

Editor: Jane Friedman
Designer: Claudean Wheeler
Cover Photograph: Ann Cutting
Production Coordinator: Robin Richie

dedication

For my family and friends

[ACKNOWLEDGMENTS]

I am especially grateful to my editor, Jane Friedman, and to my generous readers: Michael Carson, Samuel Maio, and Rob Griffith. I would also like to thank the many students who have contributed to my Introduction to Poetry Writing classes at the University of Evansville.

[ABOUT THE AUTHOR]

William Baer is the author of ten books, including *Borges & Other Sonnets*; *Fourteen on Form: Conversations with Poets*; and *Luís de Camões: Selected Sonnets*. For fifteen years (1990-2004), he was the editor of *The Formalist: A Journal of Metrical Poetry*, and he is currently the consulting editor for *Measure: An Annual Review of Formal Poetry*. A past recipient of the T.S. Eliot Poetry Prize, a National Endowment for the Arts fellowship, a Fulbright, and the Jack Nicholson Screenwriting Award, he is a professor of creative writing and cinema at the University of Evansville in southern Indiana.

TABLE OF CONTENTS

APPENDICES

ASSIGNMENTS

PREFACE

In his short but brilliant essay "The Pleasure Principle," the distinguished British poet Philip Larkin (1922–1985) discusses the three stages in the writing of a poem. According to Larkin, the writing begins (1) when the poet becomes obsessed with a concept; then (2) the poet proceeds to construct a "verbal device" that will reproduce that concept; and, finally, (3) "in different times and places," people will be found "setting off the device and re-creating what the poet felt when he wrote it."

In this book we will naturally refer to parts one and three of the process, but we'll focus on the creation of the *device*—or what W.H. Auden has referred to as the *contraption*. All poets, of course, wish to be artists, but all art begins with craft, and this book is about the craft of writing poetry in the great tradition of English-language poetry, which extends from Geoffrey Chaucer to Larkin and Richard Wilbur.

As Larkin points out in his essay:

> If the second stage has not been done well, the device will not deliver the goods, or will deliver only a few goods to a few people, or will stop delivering them after an absurdly short while.

In this book we'll study the craft of poetry writing with an eye to delivering the goods. Writing poetry, of course, is a creative challenge—one that's sometimes frustrating—but it's also a great pleasure that should, as Larkin points out in his essay, create pleasure for the reader. Fortunately, the more one develops one's craft, the more satisfying it becomes for both the writer and the reader.

This book is intended to set aspiring poets on exactly that path.

CHAPTER I | INTRODUCTION

Since poetry is a specific type of literature, which is something we often take for granted, it's useful to begin by asking some basic questions about the fundamental nature of literature itself.

WHAT IS LITERATURE COMPOSED OF?

Literature, as we know, is composed of words—of language—and language is often considered the greatest tool of human beings, if not the greatest of all human inventions. As the biblical story of the Tower of Babel reminds us, little can be achieved in this life without language. In the best literature, we always have the sense that the language is being used in the most powerful and sophisticated manner—that the author has a remarkable command of the language, and thus of the craft of his art.

WHAT DOES IT DEAL WITH?

Literature covers the entire range of human experience, which, of course, also includes the endless speculations and fantasies of the human mind. There is *nothing* that literature cannot attempt to explore or discuss. It can, unlike any other human activity, take its writer and readers to the furthest limits of the human mind, and it can focus on anything that seems important, interesting, or significant.

WHAT IS ITS PURPOSE?

It's generally agreed that literature should *move* us in some way, either emotionally, intellectually, or spiritually. But as Horace has correctly pointed out, literature should also *teach* and *entertain*. In modern times, many writers and critics have become wary of both of these terms, but all honest writers will admit that they have personal opinions and points of view that affect their work. They will also admit that they want to have their say (thus *teach*), even if not in an overt or aggressive manner. As for entertainment, this is another term that makes many modern writers nervous, but it's a simple fact that if one's work doesn't entertain its readers in some way, it will soon be unread and forgotten.

Thus, great literature can be described as the most sophisticated use of man's greatest tool to consider the most important human subjects with the purpose of moving the reader to serious thought while also affecting the emotions of the human heart. No wonder writers are held in such high esteem in every human culture.

WHAT IS POETRY?

Poetry is the Queen of the Arts where there is no king. The definitions of poetry are endless, but it's helpful to consider a few.

> Poetry is the mother tongue of mankind.
>
> —JOHANN GEORG HAMANN

> Poetry is the music of the soul, and, above all, of great and feeling souls.
>
> —VOLTAIRE

> Poetry is truth dwelling in beauty.
>
> —GEORGE GILFILLAN

> Poetry is the blossom and the fragrance of all human knowledge, human thoughts, human passions, emotions, language.
>
> —SAMUEL TAYLOR COLERIDGE

> Poetry is the best words in the best order.
>
> —SAMUEL TAYLOR COLERIDGE

> Poetry is the attempt which man makes to render his existence harmonious.
>
> —THOMAS CARLYLE

> Poetry is simply the most beautiful, impressive, and widely effective mode of saying things, and hence its importance.
>
> —MATTHEW ARNOLD

> Poetry is the search for the inexplicable.
>
> —WALLACE STEVENS

> Poetry is a way of taking life by the throat.
>
> —ROBERT FROST

Great poetry is universally respected for its power to affect its readers and even to change their lives.

WHAT DISTINGUISHES POETRY FROM PROSE?

The fundamental medium of prose (language) is the same as for poetry, as is its subject matter (human experience) and its purpose (to move, teach, and entertain). So the difference clearly lies in poetry's unique form or format—in the way a poem is crafted—and there are three main differences that distinguish the poem from prose.

1. **Emphasis on the line.** Poetry emphasizes the line over the sentence, and this is immediately clear when we observe its placement on the page. The lines of poetry seldom extend to the right-hand margin. While the sentences of prose naturally flow into visual blocks or paragraphs, the poetic line is much more focused, intense, and unique. This seemingly small but fundamental difference creates enormous potential for the poet.
2. **Emphasis on rhythm.** Although creative prose can be highly melodic, poetry *is* rhythm. In most great poetry—in various languages and metrical systems—this sonic quality is enhanced by an underlying metrical rhythm. Even modern writers of nonmetrical

poetry (*vers libre*) work extremely hard to create melodic motifs in their poetic writings.

3. **Emphasis on compression.** The compressed nature of poetry is, of course, the most debatable of the three differences, since some prose can be very "tight," and some poetry can be rather wordy (prolix). But, in general, the language of poetry is more specific and compressed than that of prose, and even the most verbose epic or the densest of blank verse passages are still constrained by the limits of the line and its underlying rhythm.

SOUND IS THE KEY

In poetry, sound is where the power comes from. Even the "best words" (in Coleridge's terms) will be further enhanced by the power of the poem's sound, whether by meter, rhyme, or the various other sonic devices. Sound is how we tend to identify poetry, and it's how we remember it. Children, especially, have a natural attraction to the power of sound, but everyone finds it hard to forget rhythmic poetry.

> Was this the face that launched a thousand ships
>
> —CHRISTOPHER MARLOWE

> But, soft! what light through yonder window breaks?
>
> —WILLIAM SHAKESPEARE

> They also serve who only stand and wait.
>
> —JOHN MILTON

> A little learning is a dangerous thing
>
> —ALEXANDER POPE

> Once upon a midnight dreary, while I pondered, weak and weary
>
> —EDGAR ALLAN POE

> Listen, my children, and you shall hear
>
> —HENRY WADSWORTH LONGFELLOW

> Whose woods these are I think I know.
>
> —ROBERT FROST

In this book, we will write poems with a constant awareness of sound, rhythm, and meter. Metrical poetry has been written for thousands of years, from Homer to Dante to Shakespeare to William Butler Yeats, and we will learn to craft our poems within that great tradition. As an apprentice of poetry, it's crucial for you to learn your craft, and before we begin, it would be helpful to consider a few comments made by a number of distinguished modern writers about the importance of sound—and the importance of learning the craft of sound. The Nobel laureate Derek Walcott, for example, is particularly appalled by the notion of diminishing sound in contemporary poetry.

> I don't know any other culture in the history of the world that has ever said that [a poem] has too much melody!

The Pulitzer winner Anthony Hecht is equally appalled by aspiring but lazy poets.

> No one would dream of trying to be a Metropolitan basso or soprano if one were born tone-deaf, or without years of painstaking private practice. But no such decent humility deters great hordes of "poets" who could not, to save their lives, compose some formal neck-verses.

Even poets who generally write in open forms, like the Pulitzer winner Stanley Kunitz, acknowledge the necessity of learning the basic craft of poetry.

> So many young poets today don't find it of value to study metrics. But a close knowledge of prosody is helpful, even if you're going to move away from it. You have to know what you're rejecting.

Similarly, all the great prose writers of the twentieth century have recognized the necessity of learning poetic craft, and it's important to remember that James Joyce, William Faulkner, Jorge Luis Borges, and many other writers began as poets. The following comes from an undated letter (probably circa 1940) from F. Scott Fitzgerald to his daughter, Scottie.

> I don't think anyone can write succinct prose unless they have at least tried and failed to write a good iambic pentameter sonnet.

Maybe it's best to end this section of the first chapter with a quote from Yeats, who's generally considered the greatest poet of the twentieth century. The following lines come from one of the master's final poems, "Under Ben Bulben," which was written in 1938, the year before he died. One of Yeats's purposes in the poem was to give advice to the young Irish poets who would follow in his wake. It's sound advice for all aspiring poets.

> Irish poets, learn your trade,
> Sing whatever is well made

[A BRIEF SURVEY]

In order to get our bearings straight, it would be helpful to recollect the entire history of Western poetry! Such a thing is, of course, impossible, but we can't know where we're going if we don't know where we've been. So the following, despite its numerous omissions, will remind us of certain literary landmarks in Western history.

B.C.

Western literature is rooted in the Jewish-Christian Bible, which contains both prose and poetry, and which was composed over more than a millennium, from approximately 1200 B.C. (the Pentateuch) until St. John's Revelation, which was written on the Greek island of Patmos near the end of the first century A.D. Within that millennium, the other foundational literary sources of the West also rose from the Aegean, these being the seminal epics of Homer (*The Iliad* and *The Odyssey*) and the plays of the great Greek tragedians: Aeschylus, Sophocles, and Euripides. Approaching the birth of Christ, the Romans, the cultural heirs of the Greeks, would produce Virgil (*The Aeneid*), Catullus, Horace, Ovid, and others.

A.D.

As a result of the gradual unraveling of the Roman Empire (sacked by Alaric in 410) and nearly a thousand years of barbarian invasions, creative literature declined in the West. Although many of the great works of the ancient world were preserved in monasteries, the rise of Christianity (especially after Constantine's victory at the Milvian Bridge in 312) naturally shifted the literary emphasis to treatises and sermons (from Augustine and Athanasius to Aquinas), and away from more imaginative works. In time, allegorical medieval plays and various epics would appear, including the Nordic *Beowulf* and the two epics about the defense of Western Europe from the Iberian Islamic invasion (initially thwarted by Charles Martel's victory at Poitiers near Paris in 732): the French *Song of Roland* and the Spanish *El Cid*. The later Middle Ages would produce the highly popular *Romance of the Rose* and Dante's masterpiece, the *Commedia* (*The Divine Comedy*).

After the Crusades (1095–1291) and the resultant opening of the Mediterranean trade routes, the Italian Renaissance, close on the heels of Dante, would blossom forth. This exciting rebirth was flush with art and architecture and masterful literary works, as exemplified by Petrarch and Boccaccio. In England, Chaucer, the great father of English literature, was clearly affected by the distant Renaissance, but he's still, quite appropriately, considered a late-medieval figure. Eventually, as the Renaissance moved north, it culminated in the greatest of all writers, William Shakespeare, whose work would overlap with the publication of the extremely influential King James Version of the Bible. It's reasonable to accept the notion that both our modern English language and our English and American literatures were founded on Shakespeare and the King James Bible.

In England, the brief Puritan era would produce John Milton, and the subsequent Restoration and Augustan periods would produce John Dryden and Alexander Pope. In 1798, the "Advertisement" of the *Lyrical Ballads* (expanded as a preface for the 1800 edition) would usher in the Romantic era of William Wordsworth, Coleridge, Percy Bysshe Shelley, Lord Byron, and John Keats, and the subsequent and equally fertile Victorian era would lead to Robert Browning and Alfred, Lord Tennyson. The twentieth century, despite all its chaos and turmoil, would produce Yeats, Frost, Auden, and many other distinguished poets.

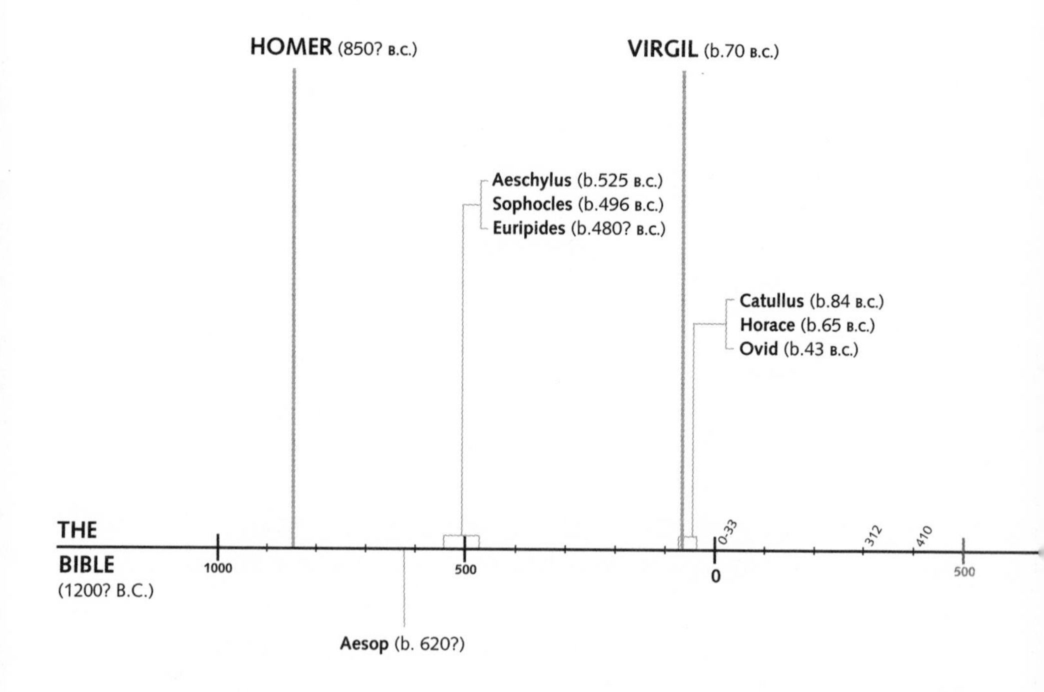

In the historical sweep of more recent times, it's important to note several significant landmarks, beginning with the creation of the novel (initiated by the gothics of Horace Walpole and the epistolaries of Samuel Richardson) at the end of the eighteenth century. The new form would soon be mastered by Jane Austen, followed by Charles Dickens, Herman Melville in the United States, Fyodor Dostoyevsky in Russia, and Faulkner in the American South. Also extremely important was the development of the modern short story under the impetus of Poe (and, later, Guy de Maupassant in France). This popular format would allow for the genius of Nathaniel Hawthorne, Nikolai Gogol in Russia, and Borges in Argentina. Another influential new form of creative writing would arise at the very end of the nineteenth century, namely

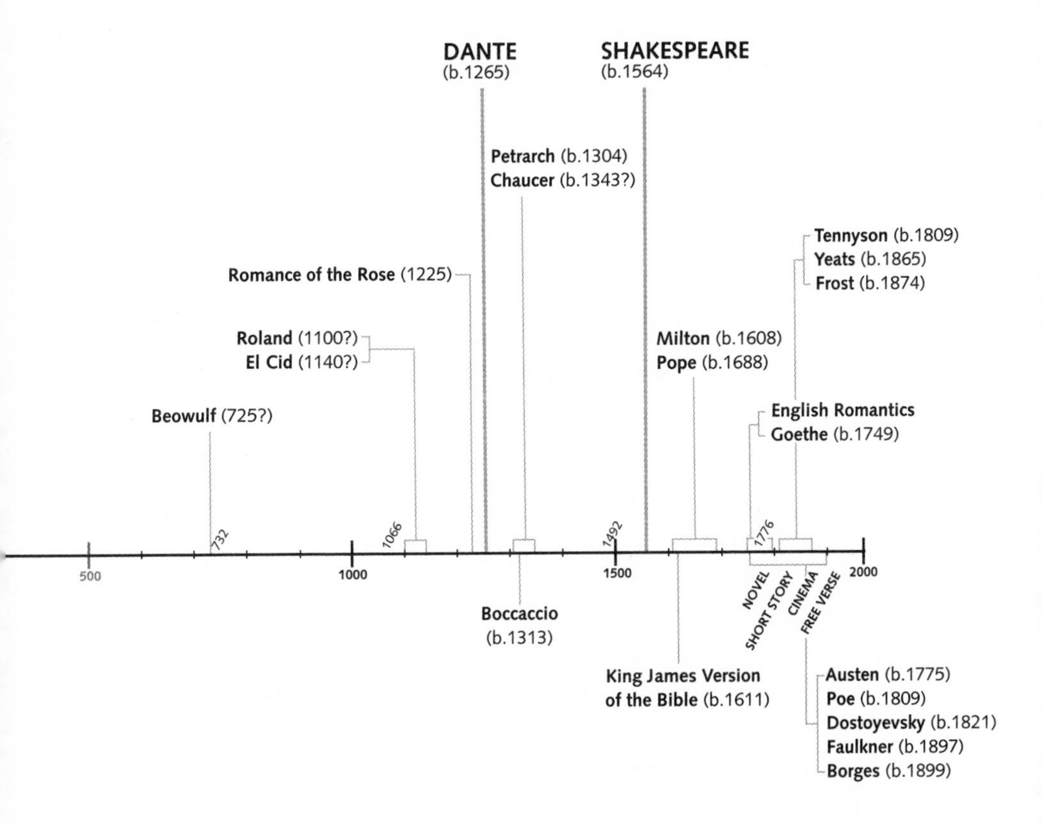

scenarios (screenplays) for the significant new medium of the cinema, which would inspire many great writers, including Graham Greene and Sweden's Ingmar Bergman.

Finally, there's Ezra Pound. In 1914, the American expatriate published *Des Imagistes* in London, championing a new mode of nonmetrical verse (free verse) that borrowed from earlier experiments by Walt Whitman and several of the latter French Symbolists.

So what does this terribly brief and incomplete survey reveal?

1. **The domination of poetry.** With few exceptions—mostly modern—the history of Western literature is also the history of poetry. Everything placed above the timeline is a work written in poetry (or the name of a poet). There have been, of course, many exceptional writings in prose (Aesop's *Fables*, *The Decameron*, *Don Quixote*, and the more recent novels and short stories), but the fact remains that most of the great literary achievements of the West have been written in poetry.
2. **The domination of metrical poetry.** With only recent exceptions, all of the significant literary works of the West have been written within the metrical systems of their various languages. This is a truly glorious and amazing tradition that includes the Homeric epics, the Greek tragedies, *The Aeneid*, *Beowulf*, *The Song of Roland*, *El Cid*, Dante, Petrarch, Chaucer, Luís de Camões, Shakespeare, Milton, Dryden, Pope, Goethe, Aleksandr Pushkin, the Romantics, Robert and Elizabeth Browning, Tennyson, Emily Dickinson, Yeats, Frost, Borges, Auden, and many more.

In order to actively participate in this great tradition, it's crucial to understand the metrics of our extraordinary language. Even the modern experimenters understood their metrics. Ezra Pound (my doctoral focus, see appendix III) wrote over a hundred sonnets, and T.S. Eliot was continually obsessed with rhythms, often tapping a little drum to discover new melodic beats. As Pulitzer winner Mary Oliver writes in her book *Rules for the Dance*, "Without it [an understanding of metrics], one is uneducated, and one is mentally poor." She also writes:

Every poem is music—a determined, persuasive, reliable, enthusiastic, and crafted music.

Without an understanding of this music, Shakespeare is only the sense we can make of him; he is the wisdom without the shapeliness, which is one half of the poem.

[HAMLET]

In the previous section, we briefly scanned the literary history of the West; in this section, we'll focus on the single most famous line in world literature—which comes from act 3, scene 1 of Shakespeare's *Hamlet*.

> To be, or not to be: that is the question.

Although Shakespeare wrote thousands of other lines of poetry, this is the one that most resonates in the human consciousness. It's the great poetic line that every actor wants to perform—Sir John Gielgud, Laurence Olivier, Paul Scofield, Kenneth Branagh, Mel Gibson, and even Dame Judith Anderson, who starred as Hamlet in the early 1970s. Given the line's unique significance and power, it's fair to ask why it's so unforgettable.

IS THE SUBJECT UNIQUE?

Not really. A troubled young man is considering taking his own life; and, although this is certainly a serious matter, it's hardly unique in the annals of literature, or even within *Hamlet*—since the Danish prince has already considered suicide in an earlier passage (act 1, scene 2).

IS THE SITUATION UNIQUE?

Actually, most people who are familiar with the line will be unable to remember the exact situation leading up to Hamlet's famous soliloquy. At that point in the narrative, Claudius and Gertrude are extremely concerned about Hamlet's peculiar behavior, and they wonder if he's gone mad. Since the prince's friends, Rosencrantz and Guildenstern, haven't been able to figure out the reason for Hamlet's odd behavior,

Claudius and Polonius, with the help of Ophelia and the assent of the queen, decide to determine if Hamlet's altered demeanor is caused by his love for Ophelia. So the two men hide themselves, planning to listen to Hamlet's conversation with Ophelia. Then the prince enters the scene and reflects his internal thoughts in his famous monologue. Thus, there's nothing very unique about Shakespeare's narrative set-up for his classic line.

IS THE SIGNIFICANCE OF THE MESSAGE UNIQUE?

Most people will be unable to remember Hamlet's specific conclusion that suicide is best avoided, given his fears of the unknown (of what will happen after death). Clearly, it's not the conclusion of Hamlet's celebrated soliloquy that makes the line so memorable. Thus, it must be compelling because of the unique *way* in which Hamlet says what he says—the way in which Shakespeare has crafted the line. So let's take a closer look at the most famous line in literary history and see what we can learn from it. We'll begin by focusing on the first half of the line.

TO BE, OR NOT TO BE:

Word Types and Sounds

Up to the colon, which creates a marked pause within the line (known as a *caesura*), the poet chooses to use only monosyllabic words. Such a rare string of one-syllable words tends to slow down a poetic line, since each word must be individually enunciated. This is particularly effective at this moment in the play because Hamlet is engaged in a serious and thoughtful consideration about life and its worth and its aftermath.

What else slows down the line?

- the comma—punctuation can be used most effectively by the skillful poet
- the back-to-back *t*s—the letter *t* demands careful enunciation
- the *o* in *to*—this double *o* vowel heightens the sense of duration

- the long *e* in *be*—these vowels also emphasize the sense of duration

The long *e* sounds are particularly crucial because they're part of the word *be*, which stands for *life* and *duration*, and this sense of duration is further reinforced by the repetition of the words *to be*.

What About *not*?

The word *not*, given its short *o* and its final sharp *t*, is extremely abrupt. It's also a very powerful word with great cultural impact, especially given its prominence in the Ten Commandments. *Not* is the authoritative word of negation (containing the word *no*), and every child knows it well. It's both emphatic and effective.

The Diction

Diction is a writer's individual word choice, and Shakespeare chooses to use (and then reuse) the word *be*. He could, of course, have used other words (like *exist*, or *subsist*, or *live*), but his preference for the word *be* has two marked advantages: (1) it has the sound and sense of duration, and (2) it's much more fundamental, having less connotative baggage. He also might have used, for example, a word like *breathe*, but such a word would have been much more narrow and confining.

Similarly, Shakespeare could have easily avoided the word *not*. He could have written something like "Existence or oblivion: that is the question." But he chose to employ the undeniable power of the word *not*—the no, the negation, the negative.

The Syntax

Syntax is how an individual writer orders or structures the words in his sentences. In the first part of Hamlet's unforgettable line, Shakespeare carefully crafts a marvelous three-part symmetry with various repetitions.

To be, | or not | to be:

The comma and the natural pause after the word *not* create a three-part structure, which is enhanced by its various repetitions, symmetries, and reversals.

- the two *o* sounds in the middle section
- the single *o* sounds in parts one and three
- the reversal of letters at the end of part two and the beginning of part three (*not* and *to*)
- the middle section ending with a *t* sound, which initiates the other two sections

The Meter

English-language meter (discussed further in chapter two) is the ordered placement of accents within a poetic line. The first six words of Hamlet's classic line are written in an iambic pattern, meaning that an unaccented syllable is immediately followed by an accented syllable.

> Tŏ bé, | ŏr nót | tŏ bé:

Thus, Shakespeare masterfully structures these initial six words so that his three accents fall perfectly on the three most important words (*be*, *not*, and *be*). This is no coincidence! Shakespeare is carefully using the power of his accents to highlight his key words and to stress the duration of his two *be*s and the firmness of his *not*. Notice also that each of the unstressed sounds are *o* vowels, and that the middle stress falls on the word *not*, which is a different and sharper (shorter) *o* sound.

Now let's continue to examine the rest of Shakespeare's famous line, proceeding word by word.

THAT IS THE QUESTION

that

After the heavy caesura of the colon, Shakespeare alters the dominant meter of his line by emphasizing the word *that* over the subsequent *is*. This reversal of the iamb is called a trochee (an accented syllable followed by an unaccented syllable). Some readers and performers might still prefer to read the line as entirely iambic.

> Tŏ bé, | ŏr nót | tŏ bé: | thăt ís | thĕ quéstion.

But most readers will substitute a trochee after the first three iambs by giving more emphasis to the referent pronoun *that*.

> Tŏ bé, | ŏr nót | tŏ bé: | thát ĭs | thĕ quéstion.

Such a reading emphasizes the crucial word *question* as well as the word's previous referent, *To be, or not to be*. The strength of the word *that* is also enhanced by the word's initial and final *t*s—and it's worth noting that there are seven *t*s in Shakespeare's line.

is

In English-language poetry, the verb *is* is generally unaccented, but Shakespeare carefully crafts his line to make this crucial word far more powerful than it usually is. First of all, the word *is* is quite appropriately known as "the verb to be"! Thus it's the verb of being and duration—of existing and existence—and it's fundamental to Hamlet's primary subject. Also, a lingering effect from the previous iambs in the line will encourage most readers to give the word more emphasis, even though it seems that the word *that* is more highly stressed.

the

The definite article *the*, which is rather dull-sounding and almost always unaccented in English poetry, is also given enhanced weight in Hamlet's line. It initiates with another *t*, and it repeats the *th* in the word *that*. But much more important is the word's semantic usage in the line. Hamlet's question is not just *any* question; it's *the* question! It's a crucial matter relating to life and death, and many performers will tend to give extra weight to this unexpectedly significant little word.

question

After all the monosyllables in the line, Hamlet's *question* seems truly gigantic, and this is perfectly appropriate. Again, this is not just *any* question; this is *the* question, and the word's length and mass indicate its significance. Semantically, the word *question* comes from the word *quest*, which, of course, relates to both life itself (being) and to Hamlet's current quest for answers. Soundwise, the word *question* contains another *t* as well as the unique and attention-getting *q* sound. Finally, this disyllabic word ends with the suffix *-ion*, which creates an extra, light syllable at the end of the line.

> To be, or not to be: that is the questiŏn.

This additional unstressed sound at the end of an iambic line is called a *feminine ending*. Feminine endings are light and delicate, and they often provide a brief moment of respite. After all of Hamlet's slow monosyllabic words and the heavily accented *quest* of *question*, Shakespeare gives his readers (and listeners) a moment of pensive rest before Hamlet reiterates his question, "Whether 'tis nobler in the mind to suffer...."

Now that we've moved, rather slowly, through this famous line of poetry, we can step back and admire its marvelous symmetry!

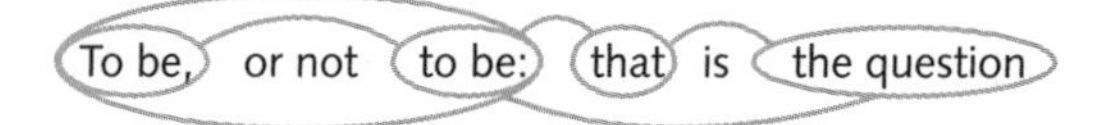

Naturally, the aspiring poet will question whether Shakespeare, in the actual process of creation, consciously considered all the amazing effects that occur within Hamlet's famous line. Surely he did not. But, just as surely, he sensed them all—and more. After years and years of hard work at his craft, and now working at the peak of his poetic powers, Shakespeare sensed and carefully crafted each of the sounds, meanings, and symmetries that make his line so memorable. This is truly genius in action, but it's also genius tempered by years of hard work.

This is the payoff.

> To be, or not to be: that is the question:
> Whether 'tis nobler in the mind to suffer
> The slings and arrows of outrageous fortune,
> Or to take arms against a sea of troubles,
> And by opposing end them? To die: to sleep;
> No more; and, by a sleep to say we end
> The heart-ache and the thousand natural shocks

That flesh is heir to, 'tis a consummation
Devoutly to be wished. To die, to sleep;
To sleep: perchance to dream: aye, there's the rub[1];
For in that sleep of death what dreams may come
When we have shuffled off this mortal coil,
Must give us pause. There's the respect[2]
That makes calamity of so long life;
For who would bear the whips and scorns of time,
The oppressor's wrong, the proud man's contumely[3],
The pangs of disprized love, the law's delay,
The insolence of office, and the spurns
That patient merit of the unworthy takes,
When he himself might his quietus[4] make
With a bare bodkin[5]? who would fardels[6] bear,
To grunt and sweat under a weary life,
But that the dread of something after death,
The undiscovered country from whose bourn
No traveler returns, puzzles the will,
And makes us rather bear those ills we have
Than fly to others that we know not of?
Thus conscience[7] does make cowards of us all;
And thus the native hue of resolution
Is sicklied o'er with the pale cast of thought,
And enterprises of great pith[8] and moment
With this regard their currents turn awry,
And lose the name of action.

[1] impediment [2] consideration [3] scorn [4] full discharge [5] dagger [6] burdens [7] introspection [8] height

CHAPTER 2 | METER

The fundamental nature of every language determines its meter (the underlying rhythmic structure of its poetry), and the study of meter is called *prosody*. Different languages use different methods to create their sonic patterns; for example, accent is used in German, duration in Latin, and syllable-counting in Japanese. Whatever the specific method, the purpose is always the same: to create a comforting sense of structural order and, if possible, a recognizable up-and-down or back-and-forth rhythm or beat. For millennia, poets and literary theorists have generally assumed that the natural pleasure derived from this underlying rhythm relates to various aspects of the natural world: the waves of the ocean, the inhale and exhale of the human breath, and, most significantly, the human heartbeat. Modern scientific studies, reported by Frederick Turner and Ernst Pöppel in their famous essay "The Neural Lyre: Poetic Meter, the Brain, and Time," reveal that the human body has a physiological response to a regular beat, releasing endorphins, the body's pleasure-producing peptides, into the listener's brain. Whatever the specific reasons human beings respond so instinctively (and pleasurably) to poetic meter, sophisticated poets have been using this biological fact to their advantage for several millennia.

THE ENGLISH LANGUAGE

The English language is an accentual language that was gradually formed in the wake of the Battle of Hastings in 1066. After his victory, William the Conqueror, a Norman from the west coast of France, brought the French language into England, where it dominated the royal court. Eventually, French, the lovely Romance language derived from Latin, combined with the harsher Saxon words and phrases of the English people to create our extraordinarily versatile language. Thus, it was the language's Germanic roots that first brought accentuated syllables into the language, and English poets from William Langland to the present time have used this formidable feature of the language to give their poetry both power and melodic beauty.

SCANSION

The method of determining the meter of a poem is called *scansion*. This is done rather simply by marking the accents, recognizing the metrical feet (see below), and counting the feet. As the distinguished poet John Hollander has pointed out, each individual poem creates a "metrical contract" with its reader. Once the poem's meter has been established in its first few lines, the reader will then expect the meter to continue in the same pattern, and he will derive great pleasure from its continued presence. Of course, sophisticated poets will intentionally make slight variations from their established meter to achieve certain poetic effects; thus, very few poems are perfectly regular from beginning to end. But all such changes must be executed carefully and subtly, with the full awareness that too many alterations will be discomforting for the reader.

Scansion is not an exact science, and there will often be points of disagreement among readers. Nevertheless, scansion is extremely helpful because it allows us to recognize the poet's methodology and determine his poetic variations. Pulitzer winner Karl Shapiro and his colleague Robert Beum have suggested in their excellent book, *A Prosody Handbook*, that the best way to read a line of English poetry is a subtle compromise between a "natural" reading of the words and a metrical reading of the lines.

THE METRICAL FEET

Following the Greek and Latin traditions, English poets and prosodists recognize a number of poetic *feet*, which are short combinations of stressed and unstressed syllables that create a distinctive metrical beat. There are numerous and varied feet in the classical tradition; but, in truth, there are only five feet that are crucial to an understanding of metrical English poetry.

The Iamb *(thĕ heárt)*

Over 90 percent of English verse is written in iambic meter, which is the pattern that is most like our normal, informal speech. Iambs create a constantly rising rhythm, moving from light syllable to stressed syllable, and they have remarkable adaptability, being effective for any type of poetry. The iamb is also a rather intense foot, being 50 percent stress. Over the centuries, there have been numerous studies about the predominance of the iamb in our language and literature. One such study estimates that approximately 94 percent of the feet in Shakespeare's sonnets are pure iambics (meaning that Shakespeare is only varying the meter about 6 percent of the time). Since our actual speech (like ordinary prose) consists of less than 60 percent iambs, we can see that Shakespeare intentionally intensifies the regularity of his iambics (and thus the number of his accents) to give his poems power and emphasis.

The Trochee *(heártlĕss)*

Trochaic meter has an intense but falling rhythm that generally sounds peculiar to English-language speakers. The always-falling rhythm of the trochee seems so unnatural that many English poets will end their trochaic lines with a final accented syllable to satisfy their readers' craving for sonic closure. Over the centuries, the trochee has been used successfully for various short poems and for brief passages of poetic dialogue, but it's particularly effective for light verse and incantatory (often macabre) poetry. Mostly, however, the trochee is used as a substituted foot within a line of iambics (like Shakespeare's fourth foot in "To be, or not to be: that is the question"). Such substitutions vary the line, create new effects, and are always used for specific purposes. (It's important to remember that substitutions are *never* used randomly.) The masters of the English trochee are Shakespeare, William Blake, Poe, and Yeats.

The Anapest *(ĭn thĕ héart)*

Like the trochee, the anapest is generally used as a substituted foot within an iambic line. The anapest, like the iamb, is a rising foot, and our tendency to race over the two unstressed syllables to get to the accent generally gives the anapest a feeling of lightness or speed. Although most trisyllabic feet feel somewhat unnatural to speakers of the English language, the rising anapest creates a natural pleasure, and a number of famous poems have been written entirely or predominantly in an anapestic meter. The absolute master of the anapest is Poe, and in the twentieth century, James Dickey used it very effectively in some of his earlier poems.

The Dactyl *(héartlĕsslў)*

The rare dactylic foot, which creates a precipitously falling meter, seems both artificial and unnatural to English-language speakers. It's occasionally used as a substituted foot, but only a few poems have been written entirely in dactylic meter, most of them by Longfellow.

The Spondee *(héart, héart)*

The twice-accented spondee is a particularly effective foot for poetic substitution because it creates both weight and emphasis within the line. The double stress naturally slows down the line and makes it feel heavier. In truth, a true spondee is hard to find, since users of the English language, given their natural proclivity towards iambs, almost always tend to accent one of any two successively stressed syllables. Even with a repetitive foot like *heart, heart*, most readers will tend to give a bit more emphasis to one of the words. But this fact in no way diminishes the effectiveness of carefully placed spondaic substitutions.

THE POETIC LINE LENGTHS

The length of a line in English poetry is identified by the number of its feet, not by the number of its syllables. Naturally, the shorter line lengths, because they give the poet such limited space, are quite rare. As John Hollander, in his *Rhyme's Reason: A Guide to English Verse*, humorously illustrates:

If she should write
Some verse tonight
This dimeter
Would limit her.

Similarly, the longer lines are also rare in English poetry because they begin to push beyond the readers' comfort level, encourage prolixity, and create the feeling of prose. Thus, the four-foot line (tetrameter) and the five-foot line (pentameter) are the most common and effective lines in English-language poetry. The classic examples given below are generally iambic.

Monometer—the rare single-foot line

Thus I
Pass by
And die

—ROBERT HERRICK

Dimeter—the two-foot line

Hear me, O God!
A broken heart,
Is my best part

—BEN JONSON

Trimeter—the more frequent three-foot line

Go, soul, the body's guest,
Upon a trackless errand

—SIR WALTER RALEIGH

Tetrameter—the very popular four-foot line

Because I could not stop for Death

—EMILY DICKINSON

Pentameter—the five-foot line, which is the heart of English poetry

What lips my lips have kissed, and where, and why

—EDNA ST. VINCENT MILLAY

Hexameter—the six-foot line is also called the English alexandrine

> Last night, ah, yesternight, betwixt her lips and mine
>
> —ERNEST DOWSON

Heptameter—the seven-foot line

> I went into a public-'ouse to get a pint o' beer
>
> —RUDYARD KIPLING

Quite often, the heptameter line (or *fourteener*) tends to break down into tetrameter and trimeter sections; and, as a result, it's sometimes associated with the ballad stanza (see chapter six). The eight-foot octometer line similarly starts falling apart, usually into two tetrameters (see the passage from Poe's "The Raven" on page 28), and most lines of English poetry that are longer than eight feet quickly lose their sonic and structural efficiency.

HINTS FOR SCANSION

Before we do some scansion exercises, here are a few hints about how to begin scanning a line of English poetry.

1. **Always do the polysyllabic words first.** The accents in each and every English word are immutable. The four-syllable word *America*, for example, will always have an accent on its second and fourth syllables. Thus, the beginning scanner can simply check the dictionary for the accents of any English polysyllabic word.
2. **Identify the normally unaccented monosyllabic words.** In English, many of our most common and useful words are generally unstressed. These include the personal pronouns (*I*, *me*, *we*, *they*, *he*, *she*, *it*, *her*, *his*, etc.); the small conjunctions (*and*, *but*, *or*, *nor*, *yet*); forms of the verb *to be* (*is*, *are*, *was*, *were*); the articles (*a*, *an*, *the*); and the simple prepositions (*to*, *in*, *by*, *on*, *for*, *of*, etc.).
3. **Be wary of the poem's first foot.** Sometimes, for effect, poets will substitute in the first foot of their poems, so be careful.

4. **Once you establish a pattern, use it.** If the poem seems to be written in iambic tetrameter, for example, see if it continues that way. It probably will.

Let's scan the famous last line of Milton's sonnet "On His Blindness."

> They also serve who only stand and wait.

The line's only polysyllabic words (*also* and *only*) are both accented on their first syllables, and we can quickly recognize a number of words in the line that are generally unstressed (*They*, *who*, and *and*). Thus we can easily determine the line's five feet and scan the accents.

> They̆ ál | sŏ sérve | whŏ ón | lў stánd | ănd wáit.

Thus, the line is iambic pentameter. Notice that Milton is very carefully placing his stresses to emphasize all of his key words (*also*, *serve*, *only*, *stand*, and *wait*). Thus, Milton's accents and his poem's underlying rhythm reinforce the poem's meaning, which is the goal of all successful poets.

[EXERCISES]

Now try to scan the following lines.

> But, soft! what light through yonder window breaks?
>
> —WILLIAM SHAKESPEARE

> In Xanadu did Kubla Khan
> A stately pleasure-dome decree
>
> —SAMUEL TAYLOR COLERIDGE

> Double, double, toil and trouble
>
> —WILLIAM SHAKESPEARE

> Earth, receive an honoured guest;
> William Yeats is laid to rest
>
> —W.H. AUDEN

The Assyrian came down like the wolf on the fold,
And his cohorts were gleaming in purple and gold

—**LORD BYRON**

For the moon never beams without bringing me dreams
Of the beautiful Annabel Lee

—**EDGAR ALLAN POE**

Meagre and livid and screaming for misery.

—**ROBERT SOUTHEY**

Once when the snow of the year was beginning to fall

—**ROBERT FROST**

DISCUSSING THE PASSAGES

Now let's review the lines.

B˘ut, sóft! | wh˘at líght | thr˘ough yón | d˘er wín | d˘ow bréaks?

Romeo's famous line of recognition (from Shakespeare's *Romeo and Juliet*) is a perfectly regular iambic pentameter, in which each of the significant words is clearly accented. The comma after the initial word, *But*, does give it added emphasis, but it's still dominated by the following hard stress of the exclamation *soft!*

˘In Xán | ˘adú | d˘id Kúb | l˘a Khán
˘A státe | l˘y pleás | ˘ure dóme | d˘ecrée

The opening lines of Coleridge's well-known poem "Kubla Khan" are written in a perfectly regular iambic tetrameter. We can see how Coleridge uses his accents to reinforce his alliterations: *Kubla* and *Khan* and *dome* and *decree*.

Dóubl˘e, | dóubl˘e, | tóil ˘and | tróub˘le

Shakespeare brilliantly uses the oddly falling trochaic meter for the macabre tetrameter chants of *Macbeth*'s witches. Like Coleridge, he also uses his accents to stress his two alliterations.

Eárth, rĕ | céive ăn | hónoŭred | gúest;
Wílliăm | Yéats ĭs | láid tŏ | rést

The final section (part III) of Auden's renowned tribute, "In Memory of W.B. Yeats," employs an oddly effective trochaic tetrameter to draw special attention to Auden's concluding thoughts. Unlike the witches' chant from *Macbeth*, all of Auden's lines end with an extra stressed syllable, thus softening the naturally falling trochees with a rise at the end of the line. Such additional stresses (in this case, *guest* and *rest*) can be considered a truncated (cut-off or *catalectic*) foot, which would make the line trochaic tetrameter with a truncated final foot. Or the lines can also be seen more simply as trochaic trimeters with an extra final stress. In truth, it really doesn't matter what it's called, as long as we recognize the careful craftsmanship of the poet.

Thĕ Ăssýr | iăn căme dówn | lĭke thĕ wólf | ŏn thĕ fóld,
Ănd hĭs có | hŏrts wĕre gleám | ĭng ĭn púr | pĭe ănd góld

Byron's masterful "The Destruction of Sennacherib" is written in lively (thundering!) anapestic tetrameters, which seem particularly appropriate to his poem about the supernatural destruction of the invading Assyrian hordes. The second foot of the poem creates a slight problem because there are three light syllables (*-ian* and *came*) before the second accented sound (*down*). But poets will often compose by the sound—rather than by the mechanics—of the meter, and in this case Byron clearly expects us to elide the two sounds of *-ian* into one. Scanners need to expect such elisions of sound. A word like *fire*, for example, is actually composed of two distinct sounds, but most poets will use it as a single syllable.

Fŏr thĕ móon | nĕvĕr béams | wĭthŏut bríng | ĭng mĕ dréams
Ŏf thĕ béau | tĭfŭl Ánn | ăbĕl Lée

Poe's "Annabel Lee," composed in alternating tetrameter and trimeter lines that are dominated by anapests, is one of the most beautifully melodic poems ever written. Poe revels in sound, and the accents in these two lines accentuate both his internal rhyme (*beams* and *dreams*) and his extended alliteration (*beams*, *bringing*, and *beautiful*). It's also important to notice that anapestic rhythms often contain feet with diminished, or *secondary*, accents. In the second foot (*never beams*), for example, the word *never* has a natural accent on its first syllable, but within the overall anapestic rhythm of the poem, its stress is diminished so that the heaviest beat can fall on the word *beams*.

> Méagrĕ ănd | lívĭd ănd | scréamĭng fŏr | mísĕrў

This masterful dactylic tetrameter line from Southey's "The Soldier's Wife" is composed of perfectly falling dactyls in which each of the stresses forcefully accentuates the line's most significant words.

> Ónce whĕn thĕ | snów ŏf thĕ | yéar wăs bĕ | gínnĭng tŏ | fáll

Frost's oddly falling (like the snow!) dactyls in "The Runaway" immediately draw our attention to his poem, but he's clearly decided that a pure dactylic line is a bit too strange for his subject, so he adds a final, comforting stress (or truncated dactyl) at the end of his tetrameter lines.

[MORE EXERCISES]

Scan the following passages, dividing the individual feet and marking the stresses. Although the lines cited below are quite regular, notice all the places where the poets have altered their meter with substitutions.

> Quoth the Raven, "Nevermore."
> And the Raven, never flitting, still is sitting, still is sitting
> On the pallid bust of Pallas just above my chamber door;
> And his eyes have all the seeming of a demon's that is dreaming.
>
> —EDGAR ALLAN POE

> The Heads and Leaders thither haste where stood
> Their great Commander; Godlike shapes and forms

Excelling human, Princely Dignities,
And Powers that erst in Heaven sat on Thrones

—JOHN MILTON

I have gone the whole round of creation; I saw and I spoke;
I, a work of God's hand for that purpose, received in my brain
And pronounced on the rest of his handwork—returned him again
His creation's approval of censure: I spoke as I saw

—ROBERT BROWNING

Vanished the vision away, but Evangeline knelt by his bedside.
Vainly he strove to whisper her name, for the accents unuttered
Died on his lips, and their motion revealed what his tongue would
have spoken.

—HENRY WADSWORTH LONGFELLOW

DISCUSSING THE PASSAGES

Quoth the | Raven, | "Never | more."
And the | Raven, | never | flitting, | still is | sitting, | still is | sitting
On the | pallid | bust of | Pallas | just a | bove my | chamber | door;
And his | eyes have | all the | seeming | of a | demon's | that is | dreaming.

Poe's remarkable poem "The Raven" was first published in 1845 in *American Review*. The poem was immediately popular with audiences—so much so that the poet actually ended up with the nickname "the Raven." As a result, Poe gave countless public performances of his famous poem, which he read in an eerie, dark, and morose manner that greatly pleased and enchanted his audiences. In 1846, Poe published a curious essay entitled "The Philosophy of Composition" in which he discussed at length the creation of the poem.

Even today, "The Raven" is enormously popular with general readers, and much of its popularity has to do with its peculiar falling meter and the fact that the poem is a virtual tour de force of poetic sound. Poe's meter in "The Raven" is the very rare trochaic octometer, which, as pointed out earlier, often tends to break apart into two tetrameters. Clearly, Poe could have constructed his classic poem in trochaic tetrameters, but the long octometers seemed to contribute to both the oddness and the perpetual melancholy of his subject.

Three of the lines cited above from "The Raven" begin with words that are normally unstressed (*and*, *on*, and *and*), but as soon as the poem's meter is clearly established, we realize that Poe is elevating the normal sound of those particular words. Another example of a metrical *elevation* in the poem can be seen in the fourth line, where the normally light word *of* is given more weight within the overall metrical pattern: "séemiňg | óf ă | démŏn's." Such an elevation naturally maintains the meter, but it also tends to emphasize the more important previous and following words that are stressed (*seeming* and *demon's*). Poe, of course, also uses his trochaic beat to emphasize many other sound devices that he uses in the poem: the three internal rhymes in the second line (*flitting*, *sitting*, and *sitting*); the various alliterations (like *pallid* and *Pallas*); the assonance of the *e* sound in line four (*seeming*, *demon's*, and *dreaming*); etc.

> Thĕ Heáds | ăn̆d Leád | ĕrs thí | thĕr háste | whĕre stoód
> Thĕir greát | Cŏmmánd | ĕr; Gód | lĭke shápes | ăn̆d fórms
> Ĕxcéll | ĭng hú | măn, Prínce | ly̆ Díg | nĭtiés,
> Ăn̆d Pów | ĕrs thăt érst | ĭn Heáv | ĕn sát | ŏn Thrónes

This short section from book I of Milton's famous *Paradise Lost* indicates the poet's mastery of blank verse (unrhymed iambic pentameter) and his willingness to create variety in the flow of his meter. For example, Milton breaks up the third iamb in the second line with a semicolon. This puts even more emphasis on the crucial word *Godlike*, which is also heightened by its alliteration with the word *great*. In line four, Milton employs an anapestic substitution in the second foot to give more emphasis to the first stress in the line (*Powers*). In doing so, Milton also de-emphasizes the force of the line's internal rhyme (*that* and *sat*) since only *sat* receives a stress. Whereas Poe preferred to clang his internal rhymes in "The Raven," Milton intentionally mutes such sonic effects in his long religious masterpiece.

> I have gone | the whole round | of crea | tion; I saw | and I spoke;
> I, a work | of God's hand | for that pur | pose, received | in my brain
> And pronounced | on the rest | of his hand | work—returned | him again
> His crea | tion's approv | al of cen | sure: I spoke | as I saw

The pentameters of Robert Browning's "Saul" glide easily along with their distinctive anapestic beat. This pleasing meter is much appreciated by English-language readers, and it has resulted in a number of unforgettable poems.

> 'Twas the night before Christmas, when all through the house
>
> —CLEMENT CLARKE MOORE

> O, say, can you see, by the dawn's early light
>
> —FRANCIS SCOTT KEY

In his serious religious poem, Browning, like Milton in the lines quoted above, creates variety within his rhythm by disrupting several of his feet with punctuation. For example, the semicolon in the first line and the colon in the last line both disrupt the flowing anapests, and each is followed by phrases that are carefully crafted reversals of each other: *I saw and I spoke* and *I spoke as I saw*. Also, at the beginning of the second line, Browning interrupts his initial anapest with a comma to give more prominence to the word *I*, which is further enhanced by its subsequent apposition as "a work of God's hand."

> Vanished the | vision a | way, but E | vangeline | knelt by his | bedside.
> Vainly he | strove to | whisper her | name, for the | accents un | uttered
> Died on his | lips, and their | motion re | vealed what his | tongue would
>   have | spoken.

Longfellow was a bold poetic experimenter, and he's one of the few English-language poets to attempt entire poems in the peculiar and difficult dactylic meter. The oddly falling dactylic hexameters of Longfellow's long poem *Evangeline* immediately attract the reader's attention, and in the first line cited above, the poet doesn't hesitate to use his dactylic stresses to emphasize his striking alliteration (*Vanished*, *vision*, and *-vangeline*). The problem with writing a poem in dactylic meter is that the falling rhythm naturally struggles against the expectations of our fundamentally iambic (rising) language, and thus the dactyls can grow rather wearing on the reader. The unusual meter also creates problems for the writer. Notice that Longfellow, given the difficulty of composing dactylic endings, is forced to use a trochee (or truncated dactyl) to end each of his lines, and he also substitutes a trochee in the second foot of the second line.

A NOTE ABOUT METRICAL THEORY

Serious poets love to talk about metrics, which is generally a good thing, but being poets (defined by James Dickey as "natural excessives"), they can often go overboard. Thus, every few years, someone will put forth some "new" and "much more accurate" system of notation for characterizing poetic rhythm. Or somebody will suddenly "discover" that trochees are *really* the basic foot in the English language. Or others will insist that "true" scansion involves using all of the classical feet (like the amphibrach or the choriamb) to accurately render the sounds of our poetry. All of this can be rather disconcerting for aspiring poets, who should simply ignore it. As the great American poet Howard Nemerov once said:

> I have only two rules in prosody: One is, it goes ta dum ta dum ta dum ta dum ta dum, and the second is, try not to sound like that.

Although Nemerov's tone is humorous, his meaning is serious: The iamb is the basis of our language; the iambic pentameter line is the basic line in English-language poetry; and the carefully placed iambs within our poems should not prevent the language from sounding natural. An interest in metrics is crucial for the conscientious poet, but the excesses of theory are definitely not.

CHAPTER 3
THE QUATRAIN, PART I

Please scan the following short poem, find the poet's substitution, and determine the rhyme scheme. "Daniel Boone" was written by the American poet Stephen Vincent Benét, a two-time recipient of the Pulitzer Prize for poetry (1929 and 1944).

Daniel Boone

1735–1820

When Daniel Boone goes by, at night,
The phantom deer arise
And all lost, wild America
Is burning in their eyes.

CONTENT—DICTION

The most mysterious aspect of the poem's first line is the unclear meaning of the third foot, *goes by*. Fortunately, the word *phantom* in the second line helps us to realize that it's the *ghost* of Daniel Boone who's wandering around "at night." In the second line, Benét chooses *deer* to serve as his phantoms rather than any other animal associated with the American countryside. Benét wrote his poem in 1933, nine years before the release of the Disney classic *Bambi*, but his purpose is essentially the same. Deer are naturally graceful, beautiful, and sympathetic, and the word *deer* has powerful semantic connotations for all Americans. We're quite familiar with the expression *caught like a deer in the headlights*, but whenever *we* notice deer in the woods or fields, we generally stop what we're doing and watch with pleasure. Similarly, Benét uses the emotive word *burning* in the last line of his short poem. It's a word full of powerful imagery and passion.

CONTENT—MEANING

So what does the little poem mean? It seems to be saying that "lost" America rises up at the ghost of Daniel Boone and laments the destruction of the wilderness. In this way, this short historical-figure poem can also be seen as an early environmentalist poem. But is Daniel Boone an admirable figure in the poem? Surely he can be seen as the great lover of nature who moved further and further into the American frontier to be alone in the wilderness. But maybe he's actually being accused in the poem. Boone was a pioneer who opened up Kentucky for settlement as a company agent, and he later went into Missouri when his land titles were overturned. So is the historical Boone of the poem a symbol of the frontier lover or a darker agent of its eventual destruction? Given what we know about Stephen Vincent Benét, it's most likely that this little poem is intended to portray Daniel Boone as a positive figure, but the question illustrates the potential depths of even such a small poem.

SOUND AND STRUCTURE

Benét's poem is a quatrain (a four-line stanza) written in alternating lines of iambic tetrameter and trimeter. Its rhyme scheme is *abcb*, meaning that the second and fourth lines end with a rhyme (*arise* and *eyes*). Such a quatrain is traditionally called *common measure* because it was so popular in Christian hymns. It's also a favorite stanza of Emily Dickinson, and it has the same basic pattern as the ballad stanza (see chapter six). Common measure is also related to *hymnal measure*, which has the same 4-3-4-3 iambic beat, but rhymes *abab*. A well-known example of hymnal measure is John Newton's "Amazing Grace."

> Amazing grace! How sweet the sound,
> That saved a wretch like me!
> I once was lost, but now am found,
> Was blind, but now I see.

When no one is listening, please sing "Daniel Boone" to the tune of "Amazing Grace"!

> When Dán | iel Bóone | goes bý, | at níght,
> The phán | tom déer | aríse
> And áll | lost, wíld | Amér | icá
> Is búrn | ing ín | their éyes.

Please notice that the key word of the first line, the mysterious *by*, is emphasized in three ways: it's accented (elevated by the meter); it's alliterated with the word *Boone*; and it's set off by a comma. This is what skillful poets do to give sonic emphasis to the meaning of their poems. Another elevation occurs in the final line of the poem on the normally unstressed word *in*. This, of course, maintains the meter, yet despite its elevation, the word *in* still remains less significant in both sound and meaning to the crucial words *burning* and *eyes*. Finally, although Benét's iambic meter is highly regular, it could be argued that the second foot in the third line (*lost, wild*) is a spondee. The comma surely lifts up the word *lost*, which, like *wild*, is a key concept in the poem.

ASSIGNMENT I

Write a poem based on Benét's "Daniel Boone."

1. Pick a historical figure of interest—or a figure from myth or literature. Try to pick a figure who is well-known, yet not too well-known. This will make it easier to say something new and interesting about your subject in the limited space of the quatrain. For now, also avoid figures from pop culture (since they're so transitory) and limit yourself to figures from before 1900.
2. Use the same form and rhyme scheme as Benét—common measure.

3. Use exact (solid) rhymes—not near-rhymes, off-rhymes, almost-rhymes, etc.
4. Use one metrical substitution in the poem to heighten a key word.
5. Try to use punctuation or a musical device like alliteration or assonance to highlight a key word.
6. For now, avoid attacks or humor. Write a serious poem that displays some admiration for your subject.
7. Put a title on the poem. It's the modern convention to title poems, and even those poets who find it hard to do must get used to it.

All these restrictions are to help develop fundamental skills. Benét's poem looks very simple on the surface, but it's not easy to say something significant in the short space of a common measure quatrain while also employing the various sonic skills of the poet-craftsman.

A NOTE ABOUT STRUGGLING WITH THE CRAFT

This might be a good time to say a word about the difficulties of developing one's poetic craft. As Anthony Hecht reminded us in chapter one, all serious art takes hard work and apprenticeship. We can all recall our musical friends relentlessly practicing their scales, or our artist friends sitting in some museum meticulously copying a picture by one of the masters, or, in a different realm, our athlete friends endlessly training for their given endeavors. As we know, in this life, nothing of real value comes easily. But having admitted that fact, there should also be pleasure in our efforts. As William Cowper wrote in the 1700s:

> There is a pleasure in poetic pains
> Which only poets know.

The contemporary Nobelist Derek Walcott is even more emphatic:

> I try to explain to students that the difficulty *is* the joy, and that if you don't find the difficulty an elation, then there's no point in trying to write poetry—go and write something else, or do something else. But you can't separate the two.

The key is to be patient and keep working. If you love poetry, then the pain and the frustrations will soon be part of the joy. Don't be discouraged about learning craft and the meter. Meter is something that everyone can learn. In over twenty years of teaching meter, I've never found a single undergraduate who couldn't learn it within a semester, if not within a few weeks. Yes, it's definitely true that some people take to the rhythm of meter much quicker than others, but that's true of everything in life. Some kids hop on a bike and take off, but most children have to learn their craft more slowly. Eventually, they're all doing it without even thinking about what they're doing. The same thing will happen with meter and the craft of poetry.

A NOTE ABOUT CAPITALIZATION AND INDENTATION

In the past it was the convention to capitalize the first letter in the first word of every line of poetry (as Benét does in "Daniel Boone"). It was also a common practice to set off lines that rhymed with consistent indentations (which Benét does not do in his quatrain poem). Thus if a poem rhymed *abcabc*, the *a* lines would usually be flush to the margin, the *b* lines would be indented, and the *c* lines would be indented further. In modern poetry, however, these conventions are no longer typical, although some poets still use them. I would suggest, however, not capitalizing the first word of each line unless it's required by the context (such as beginning a new sentence, or using a proper noun, etc.). Contemporary poetry seems more contemporary without such capitalizations. I would also suggest restraint in the use of indentations. Modern readers are used to their poetry starting flush to the margin, and they can be alienated by either excessive or random indentation.

[STUDENT QUATRAINS]

Unfortunately, I'm unable to comment on the various poems that the reader will be writing in response to the exercises in this book. But I would like to take a look at two poems written by my former students in response to the first writing assignment. The "Daniel Boone" assignment is always one of the most difficult because writing metrically is new to almost all of my students, and the challenge of actually saying something in four short lines is truly daunting.

The following two poems were written by talented undergraduates who had never attempted a metrical poem before. "Cleo" is by Amanda Sykes, and the author of "To Zelda" is Lauren Hroblak.

Cleo

The vengeance of a Queen's vain heart
Brings whispers in the walls;
She clasps an asp, strong poison tongue,
And Cleopatra falls.

COMMENTS

The iambic meter of the poem is nicely done, and the rhymes are solid. Although there's no substituted foot in the poem, the metrical elevation of the word *of* in the first line emphasizes the impact of the powerful word *vengeance*. The meter also supports the alliterations in line one (*vengeance* and *vain*) and line two (*whispers* and *walls*) and the internal rhyme near the beginning of line three (*clasps* and *asp*). In terms of meaning, *vengeance* is the key to the poem, but it could use more clarity and specificity.

Poetically, the second line is the best, being nicely evocative, and the end of line three, *strong poison tongue*, is the weakest melodically.

Finally, the quatrain's title undercuts the seriousness of the poem with the abbreviated name, "Cleo." It would be best to simply title the poem "Cleopatra."

To Zelda

A dazzled country danced with you
In your brilliance and your grace,
And crashed, crumbling at your feet
When shadows crossed your face.

COMMENTS

Although Zelda Fitzgerald is a post-1900 figure, she's a person of great natural interest and thus an appropriate subject. The poem's nicely flowing iambics are interrupted by three metrical substitutions. The first is the anapestic foot at the beginning of line two, which successfully heightens the word *brilliance*. In line three, there are two substitutions: a trochee (*crumbling*), and a subsequent anapest (*at your feet*). As a result of these prosodic alterations, line three is composed of three different metrical feet (an iamb, a trochee, and an anapest), which is too much variation for such a short line in such a short poem. On the other hand, the author is clearly attempting to use these substitutions to enhance the meaning of the poem. This is especially true with the word *crumbling*, where the falling meter of the trochee reinforces the falling apart of Zelda's mental condition, and where the harshness of Zelda's fall is accentuated by the harshly alliterated accents on the letter *c*. Thus the young poet is attempting to use the meter effectively, even if there's too much substitution within such a short poem.

Poetically, the poem begins with a rather striking first line that clearly reinforces the author's perspective (a direct address to Zelda, as indicated in the title) and clarifies the poem's specific subject: how Zelda's behavior and lifestyle fascinated the entire country in the roaring twenties. Similarly, the poem's final description of Zelda's psychological deterioration, "When shadows crossed your face," is also nicely done. But the poem's claim that the country "crashed" when Zelda fell apart is not very believable (since the general public usually finds its celebrities rather disposable and replaceable). Also, if the word *crash* is a reference to the stock market disaster of 1929, then its relationship to Zelda's decline is only coincidental and thus not fully satisfying. Nevertheless, the poem is an admirable attempt to say something about its subject within the terribly short space of a common measure quatrain—just twenty-eight syllables!

A NOTE ABOUT ALLUSIONS

One important question that new poets will invariably ask relates to the use of allusions, whether they be historical, mythological, religious, artistic, or literary. This is a difficult and debatable issue, especially in the wake of some of the early twentieth-century poems of Pound and Eliot, which included many unexplained and sometimes obscure references. Obviously, poets can do whatever they wish, but I would point out that poetry is a matter of communication, and new poets should definitely strive for clarity. In my own opinion, it's perfectly acceptable to assume that your readers are reasonably well-educated individuals. Thus, it would be appropriate to make references to Job, Charlemagne, Merlin, Botticelli, and Ishmael, for example. It also seems reasonable to assume that, even if readers are not familiar with such references, they won't be put off or insulted by them; and, if the poem inspires them enough, they'll be willing to look them up. On the other hand, if the references are too obscure (and unexplained within the course of the poem), then the reader will often feel irritated, and the communication between the poet and the reader will quickly break down.

CHAPTER 4
BLANK VERSE, PART I

Blank verse (unrhymed iambic pentameter) is the dominant metrical form in English poetry. Paul Fussell, Jr., in his excellent book *Poetic Meter and Poetic Form*, claims that "about three-quarters of all English poetry is in blank verse." This might seem an exaggerated statement until we remind ourselves of the form's glorious history in the English language. Initially used in 1554 by Henry Howard, the Earl of Surrey, for his translation of book IV (the Dido section) of Virgil's *Aeneid*, blank verse became the prosodic basis for an incomparable series of major literary achievements. These famous works include: almost all of the great Elizabethan dramas, including Marlowe, Jonson, and the masterpieces of Shakespeare (*Romeo and Juliet*, *Hamlet*, *Macbeth*, *The Tempest*, etc.); Milton's *Paradise Lost* and most of *Samson Agonistes*; Wordsworth's *The Prelude* and "Tintern Abbey"; Shelley's *The Cenci*; Keat's "Hyperion"; Samuel Johnson's *Irene*; Tennyson's "Ulysses" and his *Idylls of the King*; Robert Browning's *The Ring and the Book*; Yeats's "The Second Coming"; Frost's "Birches" and "The Death of the Hired Man"; much of Wallace Stevens and Hart Crane; and many more. It's interesting to note that short passages of blank verse have even been isolated within the prose writings of such distinguished authors as Lincoln, Dickens, and Melville.

STRENGTHS AND DANGERS

Since blank verse has no preset stanza pattern or end rhyme, the form gives the poet a remarkable freedom. In this sense, it's easier to compose, and once a writer gets the hang of writing blank verse, a certain comfortable facility can easily develop. But as we'll learn in this book, whenever formal elements are sacrificed, certain difficulties will soon arise. Thus, the freedom of blank verse often leads to both prolixity (wordiness) and diffuseness (lack of focus). It becomes rather easy—even quite natural—to ramble on in blank verse, because both the musical tightness of end rhymes and the structural compression of preset stanzas are missing. Thus, despite the fact that blank verse seems easier to write on a superficial level, it's often said that it's one of the most difficult forms to truly master.

Nevertheless, its advantages—particularly its marvelous versatility—are obvious. Blank verse can handle any subject and achieve all kinds of various effects—from the most exalted language (like what Ben Jonson calls the "mighty line" of Marlowe) to the most natural and even colloquial language of Robert Frost. Also, since blank verse can closely approximate regular speech, it's a natural for drama (especially for dramatic monologues), as the Elizabethans clearly understood.

In the twentieth century, T.S. Eliot attempted, with some success, to revive the verse drama, and one of his comments about the process is particularly revealing.

> I have found, in trying to write dramatic verse, that however different a metre from blank verse I was working with, whenever my attention has relaxed, or I have gone sleepy or stupid, I will wake up to find that I have been writing bad Shakespearean blank verse.

A talented poet like T.S. Eliot, when he did concentrate, was very capable of writing quality blank verse, and maybe his experience will remind us all that we should "listen" to the language. Surely the language was telling Eliot something: that blank verse is a natural for dramatic expression.

WEBSTERIAN BLANK VERSE

Websterian blank verse is a derogatory term for loose (overly substituted) blank verse that has become sloppy, ineffectual, and prose-like. The term comes from the weaker passages in the work of the seventeenth-century dramatist John Webster, the author of *The Duchess of Malfi*. Webster was a talented playwright who often allowed too much variation in his dramatic poetry, thus undermining the natural strength of the blank verse line. As Shapiro and Beum point out in *A Prosody Handbook*, Milton was extremely conscious of the dangers of such excessive variation, and as a result, "Milton's blank verse is the strictest in English." Shapiro and Beum identify the following seven restrictive characteristics of Milton's blank verse.

1. insistence on ten and only ten syllables to the line
2. trochaic, spondaic, and pyrrhic [a rare foot of two unstressed syllables] substitutions only
3. reluctance to allow more than one substitution to a line
4. even greater reluctance to allow the final (fifth) foot to be anything but an iamb
5. a high percentage of run-on lines
6. few feminine endings
7. freedom in the position of the caesura

Thus, Milton, in writing his masterpiece, intentionally set a number of significant restrictions on himself in an effort to keep the poetry tight and enhance the power of the form. As Shapiro and Beum conclude, "Milton's tightly controlled verse rarely becomes monotonous, however, despite its self-imposed austerity. If his blank verse were looser, *Paradise Lost* would probably not be read at all."

A NOTE ABOUT SELF-RESTRICTIONS

We live in an era when the words *experimentation* and *freedom* are the catchwords of the day, but even political freedom must be tempered by laws, and even experimentation (most of which is hardly new) has no real meaning unless it's related to previously established rules or guidelines. The truth is, all artistic achievement is related to the self-restrictions of the artist. Does the painter choose to work in oils or watercolors? Does the composer write an aria or a sonata? Does the poet write a sonnet or a limerick? Even such fundamental choices immediately limit the artist's possibilities, but this is natural and good and typically human. We need restrictions: stoplights, for example. And we need boundaries: to establish property limits, for example. Very few people would pay to see a basketball game if the rims were only five feet off the ground—or a baseball game if the paths of the diamond were reduced to twenty feet. Forms and their restrictions do create limitations, but they also can give us unprecedented power. As Pulitzer recipient Richard Wilbur points out, the mythological genie is powerful *because* he's contained in the bottle. Poets, of course, have the right to do whatever they wish to do, but they should be aware, like Milton, that artistic self-restrictions can unleash power and create unexpected beauty.

SAMPLE BLANK VERSE POEMS

As we will do throughout the rest of this book, we will now look at a number of sample poems (or passages) written in the form under discussion, followed by a few comments about each one. Beginning in the next chapter, I will also include a number of contemporary poems written in the appropriate form. The passage that follows is from Marlowe's *Dr. Faustus*, act 5, scene 1.

> Was this the face that launched a thousand ships,
> And burned the topless towers of Ilium[1]?—
> Sweet Helen, make me immortal with a kiss! —
> Her lips suck forth my soul: see where it flees! —
> Come, Helen, come, give me my soul again.
> Here will I dwell, for heaven is in these lips,
> And all is dross that is not Helena.
> I will be Paris, and for love of thee,
> Instead of Troy, shall Wittenberg be sacked,
> And I will combat with weak Menelaus,
> And wear thy colours on my plumèd crest;

[1] Troy

> Yes, I will wound Achilles in the heel,
> And then return to Helen for a kiss.
> Oh, thou art fairer than the evening air
> Clad in the beauty of a thousand stars;
> Brighter art thou than flaming Jupiter
> When he appeared to hapless Semele;
> More lovely than the monarch of the sky
> In wanton Arethusa's azured arms;
> And none but thou shalt be my paramour!

COMMENTS

Dr. Faustus, having been granted certain earthly satisfactions in exchange for his immortal soul, reveals his shallowness of character by having his demon, Mephistopheles, conjure up the figure of Helen of Troy, whom Faustus believes to be the most beautiful woman in history. Despite his superficiality (and possibly because of it), Faustus's powerful response to the sight of Helen and her breathtaking beauty is a blank verse masterpiece. His opening line of recognition is one of the most famous lines in literature, and the entire passage is full of powerful, elevated diction (*immortal*, *heaven*, *wanton*, *azured*, and *paramour*) and melodic sound (*More lovely than the monarch of the sky*). Notice that proper nouns are particularly effective in poetry, and Marlowe's assumption that his audience should recognize Paris, Achilles, Jupiter, Semele, and Arethusa is both fair and acceptable.

The next passage is from Shakespeare's *The Merchant of Venice*, act 4, scene 1.

> The quality of mercy is not strained,
> It droppeth as the gentle rain from heaven
> Upon the place beneath: it is twice blessed;
> It blesseth him that gives and him that takes:
> 'Tis mightiest in the mightiest; it becomes
> The thronèd monarch better than his crown;
> His sceptre shows the force of temporal power,

The attribute to awe and majesty,
Wherein doth sit the dread and fear of kings;
But mercy is above this sceptred sway,
It is enthronèd in the hearts of kings;
It is an attribute to God himself,
And earthly power doth then show likest God's
When mercy seasons justice. Therefore, Jew,
Though justice be thy plea, consider this,
That in the course of justice none of us
Should see salvation: we do pray for mercy,
And that same prayer doth teach us all to render
The deeds of mercy.

COMMENTS

Portia's beautiful reflection on the essence of the virtue of mercy takes place in act 4, scene 1, when she tries to soften the heart of Shylock, who is still demanding his vengeful "pound of flesh" from Antonio. Whereas Faustus is sensuously overwhelmed and gushing, Portia is calm, and thoughtful, and intelligent. These two different yet equally brilliant passages clearly illustrate the remarkable versatility of blank verse.

Let's look at another passage from Shakespeare, this one from *Macbeth*, act 5, scene 5.

Tomorrow, and tomorrow, and tomorrow,
Creeps in this petty pace from day to day
To the last syllable of recorded time,
And all our yesterdays have lighted fools
The way to dusty death. Out, out, brief candle!
Life's but a walking shadow, a poor player
That struts and frets his hour upon the stage
And then is heard no more; it is a tale
Told by an idiot, full of sound and fury,
Signifying nothing.

COMMENTS

This famous soliloquy by Macbeth takes place near the end of the play. The hardened Macbeth has just learned of the death of Lady Macbeth, and his response is one of the most affecting expressions of defeat, despair, and nihilism in our language—or any language. The famous opening line is a perfect example of the endless metrical mastery of Shakespeare, since its three-part structure, which contains three instances of the same three-syllable word, is powerfully enhanced by the underlying beat of the iambic pentameter: "Tŏ-mór | rŏw ańd | tŏ- mór | row ańd | tŏ- mór- rŏw." Shakespeare's two, very slight elevations of the weak word *and* naturally enhance the power of the other three stresses in the line, which all fall on the accented second syllable of the key word *tomorrow*.

The next poem was written by Alfred, Lord Tennyson.

Ulysses

It little profits that an idle king,
By this still hearth, among these barren crags,
Matched with an aged wife, I mete[1] and dole
Unequal laws unto a savage race,
That hoard, and sleep, and feed, and know not me.
I cannot rest from travel; I will drink
Life to the lees. All times I have enjoyed
Greatly, have suffered greatly, both with those
That loved me, and alone; on shore, and when
Through scudding drifts the rainy Hyades
Vexed the dim sea. I am become a name;
For always roaming with a hungry heart
Much have I seen and known—cities of men
And manners, climates, councils, governments,
Myself not least, but honoured of them all—
And drunk delight of battle with my peers,
Far on the ringing plains of windy Troy.

[1] measure

I am a part of all that I have met;
Yet all experience is an arch wherethrough
Gleams that untraveled world whose margin fades
Forever and forever when I move.
How dull it is to pause, to make an end,
To rust unburnished, not to shine in use!
As though to breathe were life! Life piled on life
Were all too little, and of one to me
Little remains; but every hour is saved
From that eternal silence, something more,
A bringer of new things; and vile it were
For some three suns to store and hoard myself,
And this grey spirit yearning in desire
To follow knowledge like a sinking star,
Beyond the utmost bound of human thought.
This is my son, mine own Telemachus,
To whom I leave the scepter and the isle—
Well-loved of me, discerning to fulfill
This labour, by slow prudence to make mild
A rugged people, and through soft degrees
Subdue them to the useful and the good.
Most blameless is he, centered in the sphere
Of common duties, decent not to fail
In offices of tenderness, and pay
Meet adoration to my household gods,
When I am gone. He works his work, I mine.
There lies the port; the vessel puffs her sail;
There gloom the dark, broad seas. My mariners,
Souls that have toiled, and wrought, and thought with me—
That ever with a frolic welcome took
The thunder and the sunshine, and opposed
Free hearts, free foreheads—you and I are old;
Old age hath yet his honour and his toil.

Death closes all; but something ere the end,
Some work of noble note, may yet be done,
Not unbecoming men that strove with gods.
The lights begin to twinkle from the rocks;
The long day wanes; the slow moon climbs; the deep
Moans round with many voices. Come, my friends,
'Tis not too late to seek a newer world.
Push off, and sitting well in order smite
The sounding furrows; for my purpose holds
To sail beyond the sunset, and the baths
Of all the western stars, until I die.
It may be that the gulfs will wash us down;
It may be we shall touch the Happy Isles,
And see the great Achilles, whom we knew.
Though much is taken, much abides; and though
We are not now that strength which in old days
Moved earth and heaven, that which we are, we are—
One equal temper of heroic hearts,
Made weak by time and fate, but strong in will
To strive, to seek, to find, and not to yield.

COMMENTS

This great dramatic monologue was written by Tennyson in 1833, not long after the tragic death of his best friend, Arthur Hallam. Hallam's death plunged Tennyson into depression, and this poem, like his opus *In Memoriam*, is an effort to deal with his despondency and inertia. An obvious inspiration for the action of the poem is Dante's description of the last voyage of Ulysses (Odysseus) in canto 26 of *The Inferno*. In Dante, the actions of the aged king are seen as a final vanity and self-absorption, but for Tennyson, the boldly venturing Ulysses is portrayed in the great heroic mode, showing courage in the face of the impossible. The poem was clearly a wake-up call for Tennyson himself, and for any of his readers who might also be feeling depressed and unmotivated. The poem's final challenge to be strong in will—"To strive, to seek, to find, and not to yield"—is a perfect example of the extraordinary power of the iambic pentameter line in the hands of a master.

The next poem, Yeats's "The Second Coming," is one of the most famous short poems of the twentieth century.

The Second Coming

Turning and turning in the widening gyre
The falcon cannot hear the falconer;
Things fall apart; the centre cannot hold;
Mere anarchy is loosed upon the world,
The blood-dimmed tide is loosed, and everywhere
The ceremony of innocence is drowned;
The best lack all conviction, while the worst
Are full of passionate intensity.

Surely some revelation is at hand;
Surely the Second Coming is at hand.
The Second Coming! Hardly are those words out
When a vast image out of *Spiritus Mundi*
Troubles my sight: somewhere in sands of the desert
A shape with lion body and the head of a man,
A gaze blank and pitiless as the sun,
Is moving its slow thighs, while all about it
Reel shadows of the indignant desert birds.
The darkness drops again; but now I know
That twenty centuries of stony sleep
Were vexed to nightmare by a rocking cradle,
And what rough beast, its hour come round at last,
Slouches toward Bethlehem to be born?

COMMENTS

The sound, apocalyptic imagery, and evocativeness of this poem are unforgettable, and many of its lines are often quoted.

> The best lack all conviction, while the worst
> Are full of passionate intensity.
>
> And what rough beast, its hour come round at last,
> Slouches towards Bethlehem to be born?

It is useful to remember that Yeats was a mystic who believed that he'd communicated with the dead, specifically with a figure named Leo Africanus. As a result of those communications, Yeats came to believe that human history was a series of two-thousand-year cycles, each of which initiated with a history-altering event (like the birth of Jesus Christ). This notion of cyclical history, which Yeats discussed at length in his prose work, *A Vision* (1925), was certainly not new, since the historian Oswald Spengler (and others) had previously discussed the possibility. But Yeats, writing his poem in the midst of the hyper-violent twentieth century, created powerful and shocking imagery for his poetic vision of a fading Christian era on the verge of evolving into something alien and sinister.

The falcon and the gyre (the bird's funnel-shaped path of flight) are common symbols in Yeats's writings. The path of the falcon's upward flight, with its ever widening circles, symbolizes the inevitable dissolution of the moribund two-thousand-year cycle, as everything whirls out of control and "Things fall apart." Obviously, readers who are unfamiliar with Yeats's historical and mystical notions will not comprehend all the particulars of his vision in "The Second Coming." But the poem still communicates, perfectly clearly, the poet's apocalyptic vision of a present "anarchy" that faces the imminent arrival of some extremely dangerous "beast."

A NOTE ABOUT AMBIGUITY

As mentioned earlier, new poets should strive for clarity in their poetry, but ambiguity can sometimes be used as a powerful poetic device. Although there are no hard-and-fast rules, I would always refer back to the readers and their natural preferences. Since we write poetry to communicate, we'll be most successful in our efforts when we please our readers. It's perfectly clear that poetry readers (like almost all human beings) appreciate melodic sound, striking images, interesting sentences, and thoughtful ideas. They also like surprises, mysteries, and evocative moods. Thus, most readers will be willing to sacrifice a bit of clarity if they feel that the resultant ambiguity is particularly effective. On the other hand, they will be immediately turned off by any ambiguity that seems easy, lazy, or pretentious. This is certainly not the case with Yeats's "The Second Coming," where the vagaries of the poem are part of the mystery of what's to come—which is naturally intriguing and thought-provoking.

Now let's look at a longer, narrative poem by Robert Frost.

The Death of the Hired Man

Mary sat musing on the lamp-flame at the table
Waiting for Warren. When she heard his step,
She ran on tip-toe down the darkened passage
To meet him in the doorway with the news
And put him on his guard. "Silas is back."
She pushed him outward with her through the door
And shut it after her. "Be kind," she said.
She took the market things from Warren's arms
And set them on the porch, then drew him down
To sit beside her on the wooden steps.

"When was I ever anything but kind to him?
But I'll not have the fellow back," he said.
"I told him so last haying, didn't I?
If he left then, I said, that ended it.
What good is he? Who else will harbour him
At his age for the little he can do?
What help he is there's no depending on.
Off he goes always when I need him most.
He thinks he ought to earn a little pay,
Enough at least to buy tobacco with,

So he won't have to beg and be beholden.
'All right,' I say, 'I can't afford to pay
Any fixed wages, though I wish I could.'
'Someone else can.' 'Then someone else will have to.'
I shouldn't mind his bettering himself
If that was what it was. You can be certain,
When he begins like that, there's someone at him
Trying to coax him off with pocket-money—
In haying time, when any help is scarce.
In winter he comes back to us. I'm done."

"Sh! not so loud: he'll hear you," Mary said.

"I want him to: he'll have to soon or late."

"He's worn out. He's asleep beside the stove.
When I came up from Rowe's I found him here,
Huddled against the barn door fast asleep,
A miserable sight, and frightening, too—
You needn't smile—I didn't recognize him—
I wasn't looking for him—and he's changed.
Wait till you see."

"Where did you say he'd been?"

"He didn't say. I dragged him to the house.
And gave him tea and tried to make him smoke.
I tried to make him talk about his travels.
Nothing would do: he just kept nodding off."

"What did he say? Did he say anything?"

"But little."

"Anything? Mary, confess
He said he'd come to ditch the meadow for me."

"Warren!"

"But did he? I just want to know."

"Of course he did. What would you have him say?
Surely you wouldn't grudge the poor old man
Some humble way to save his self-respect.
He added, if you really care to know,
He meant to clear the upper pasture, too.
That sounds like something you have heard before?
Warren, I wish you could have heard the way
He jumbled everything. I stopped to look
Two or three times—he made me feel so queer—
To see if he was talking in his sleep.
He ran on Harold Wilson—you remember—
The boy you had haying four years since.
He's finished school, and teaching in his college.
Silas declares you'll have to get him back.
He says they two will make a team for work:
Between them they will lay this farm as smooth!
The way he mixed that in with other things.
He thinks young Wilson a likely lad, though daft
On education—you know how they fought
All through July under the blazing sun,
Silas up on the cart to build the load,
Harold along beside to pitch it on."

"Yes, I took care to keep well out of earshot."

"Well, those days trouble Silas like a dream.
You wouldn't think they would. How some things linger!
Harold's young college-boy's assurance piqued him.
After so many years he still keeps finding
Good arguments he sees he might have used.
I sympathize. I know just how it feels
To think of the right thing to say too late.
Harold's associated in his mind with Latin.

He asked me what I thought of Harold's saying
He studied Latin, like the violin,
Because he liked it—that an argument!
He said he couldn't make the boy believe
He could find water with a hazel prong—
Which showed how much good school had ever done him.
He wanted to go over that. But most of all
He thinks if he could have another chance
To teach him how to build a load of hay—"

"I know, that's Silas' one accomplishment.
He bundles every forkful in its place,
And tags and numbers it for future reference,
So he can find and easily dislodge it
In the unloading. Silas does that well.
He takes it out in bunches like big birds' nests.
You never see him standing on the hay
He's trying to lift, straining to lift himself."

"He thinks if he could teach him that, he'd be
Some good perhaps to someone in the world.
He hates to see a boy the fool of books.
Poor Silas, so concerned for other folk,
And nothing to look backward to with pride,
And nothing to look forward to with hope,
So now and never any different."

Part of a moon was falling down the west,
Dragging the whole sky with it to the hills.
Its light poured softly in her lap. She saw it
And spread her apron to it. She put out her hand
Among the harplike morning-glory strings,
Taut with the dew from garden bed to eaves,
As if she played unheard some tenderness

That wrought on him beside her in the night.
"Warren," she said, "he has come home to die:
You needn't be afraid he'll leave you this time."

"Home," he mocked gently.

"Yes, what else but home?
It all depends by what you mean by home.
Of course he's nothing to us, any more
Than was the hound that came a stranger to us
Out of the woods, worn out upon the trail."

"Home is the place where, when you have to go there,
They have to take you in."

"I should have called it
Something you somehow haven't to deserve."

Warren leaned out and took a step or two,
Picked up a little stick, and brought it back
And broke it in his hand and tossed it by.
"Silas has better claim on us, you think,
Than on his brother? Thirteen little miles
As the road winds would bring him to his door.
Silas has walked that far no doubt today.
Why doesn't he go there? His brother's rich,
A somebody—director in the bank."

"He never told us that."

"We know it though."

"I think his brother ought to help, of course.
I'll see to that if there is need. He ought of right
To take him in, and might be willing to—
He may be better than appearances.
But have some pity on Silas. Do you think

If he'd had any pride in claiming kin
Or anything he looked for from his brother,
He'd keep so still about him all this time?"

"I wonder what's between them."

"I can tell you.
Silas is what he is—we wouldn't mind him—
But just the kind that kinsfolk can't abide.
He never did a thing so very bad.
He don't know why he isn't quite as good
As anybody. Worthless though he is,
He won't be made ashamed to please his brother."

"*I* can't think Si ever hurt anyone."

"No, but he hurt my heart the way he lay
And rolled his old head on that sharp-edged chair-back.
He wouldn't let me put him on the lounge.
You must go in and see what you can do.
I made the bed up for him there tonight.
You'll be surprised at him—how much he's broken.
His working days are done; I'm sure of it."

"I'd not be in a hurry to say that."

"I haven't been. Go, look, see for yourself.
But, Warren, please remember how it is:
He's come to help you ditch the meadow.
He has a plan. You mustn't laugh at him.
He may not speak of it, and then he may.
I'll sit and see if that small sailing cloud
Will hit or miss the moon."

It hit the moon.
Then there were three there, making a dim row,
The moon, the little silver cloud, and she.

Warren returned—too soon, it seemed to her—
Slipped to her side, caught up her hand and waited.

"Warren?" she questioned.

"Dead," was all he answered.

COMMENTS

Frost's masterful narrative poem "The Death of the Hired Man" is one of the most famous poems of its length (not too short, and not too long) of the twentieth century. Unlike Yeats's "The Second Coming," with its exalted diction (*ceremony*, *revelation*, *Spiritus Mundi*, etc.), Frost's poem is a marvel of ordinary language and expression heightened by the blank verse beat. In the first few lines, we encounter such ordinary objects and expressions as *the table*, *tip-toe*, *Silas is back*, *Be kind*, *market things*, and *the wooden steps*. Frost is so accomplished at writing in a normal and colloquial manner that we can sometimes lose sight of his metrical mastery.

Let's take a look at line five, for example. Mary is waiting for Warren to return from the store, and when she hears him arrive, she rushes through the house to the front porch to tell him the news:

And put him on his guard. "Silas is back."

The light metrical elevation of the word *on* naturally highlights the more significant words, *put* and *guard*, before the heavy caesura of the first period. Then Frost substitutes a trochee, *Silas* (most two-syllable names are trochees), before ending the line with a final iamb that emphasizes the word *back*, followed by the concluding and emphatic period. Yes, "Silas is back." This is the key to the entire poem, and it's spoken with an economy of language that seems perfectly appropriate. Thus, Frost is meticulously using his meter to tell his story more effectively, and this continues throughout every line of his poem.

Also, please note that because blank verse has no preset stanza length, poets can divide up their blank verse poems however they wish. Frost uses stanza breaks to help his reader follow the shifts in dialogue and also to break up his long narrative. In "The Second Coming," Yeats divided his poem into two unequal stanzas to clearly indicate and contrast the present (the state of anarchy) and the future (what's coming). Notice, also, that Yeats ends each stanza very powerfully—with his strongest and most memorable lines.

A NOTE ABOUT ENJAMBMENT

Enjambment is a French term for a run-on line—a line of poetry that has no syntactical or punctuational marker at its conclusion. Although the end of *every* line of poetry has a certain natural pause (given its uniqueness and its visual placement on the page), some lines are much more heavily end-stopped than others. Enjambment can be an especially effective device because it allows poets an opportunity to break up the potential monotony of a series of heavily end-stopped lines. On the other hand, too much enjambment can undercut the natural power of the individual lines and start to make them feel more like prose than poetry.

In "The Death of the Hired Man," Frost uses his enjambments carefully and sparingly to loosen up his long narrative. For example, near the end of the poem, he has Mary saying of Silas:

> He don't know why he isn't quite as good
> As anybody. Worthless though he is,
> He won't be made ashamed to please his brother.

The enjambment at the end of the first line gives a natural feeling to Mary's speech, and it also gives more attention to the enjambed phrase *As anybody*. Then, fifteen lines later, Mary tells Warren to check on Silas, explaining:

> I'll sit and see if that small sailing cloud
> Will hit or miss the moon.

This run-on line, which connects the subject *cloud* with its verbs (*hit* and *miss*) and its object (*moon*), not only gives visual action to the poem, but it also creates the symbolism of Silas's imminent death.

As effective as these enjambments are, it's important to notice that Frost tends to surround his run-on lines with numerous lines that are heavily end-stopped.

ASSIGNMENT 2

Write a poem consisting of twenty lines of blank verse, with the folowing restraints.

1. Keep your meter very regular—with no more than ten substitutions. This will help you get the feel of the iambic pentameter line, and it will encourage you to make only necessary and productive substitutions. Remember that all substitutions *must* serve a specific poetic purpose. Random substitutions diminish the craft.
2. Use no more than three enjambments in the twenty lines. This will help you appreciate the integrity of the blank verse line.
3. Allow for no more than two feminine endings. This will force you to control the endings of your lines. As with metrical substitutions, feminine endings should always be used with a justifiable purpose in mind.
4. Don't waste time worrying about subject matter. If something doesn't strike you right away, write a response to Macbeth, or write your own passage about mercy (or another virtue), or compose a narrative about Ulysses, or describe Yeats's "rough beast," or write about the death of Mary or Warren, etc. I suggest that you try a dramatic monologue. You might pick an interesting figure from history, legend, or literature, and let that figure speak. As previously discussed, blank verse is a natural for dramatic monologues.

A NOTE ABOUT GETTING THE RHYTHM

When you start writing, it's perfectly acceptable to draft your poem in prose lines and then, by adjusting the words and phrases, transform your lines into iambic pentameter. I would suggest, however, that before you actually begin writing, you pick a favorite line of blank verse and repeat it over and over (out loud)—maybe twenty or thirty times—to force the rhythm into your head. When I was younger, as a limbering up exercise, I would repeatedly rattle off Romeo's famous line before actually composing: "But, soft! what light through yonder window breaks?"

A feel for iambic pentameter, the key line in English poetry, is crucial to our overall development as poets. One way to develop this feel is to continually read—out loud—classic blank verse poems. Years ago, when I was teaching myself metrics, I would tape, in my own voice, a passage from *Paradise Lost* (in my Bronx/New Jersey accent!), then play the passage over and over while driving in the car, especially late at night, especially on long trips to California and back. Then I would shut off the tape and talk to myself in blank verse. Whether we like to admit it or not, everyone likes to talk to himself, and I was able, rather quickly, to say whatever I wanted to say in blank verse.

If it seems odd that aspiring poets should be able, in essence, to recite poetry on the spot, it shouldn't. As Baldassare Castiglione pointed out in *The Courtier* (1528), being able to create and recite poetry for one's beloved—at any given moment—was as much a mark of the Renaissance courtier as the skills of riding, hunting, and combat. Edmond Rostand, in his famous play *Cyrano de Bergerac*, uses Cyrano's uncanny ability to recite brilliant love poetry extemporaneously as a key to the narrative. Again, what seems terribly difficult (like riding a bike, to a four-year-old) is not really that difficult with time, practice, and determination.

WORKSHOPPING & EVALUATION

Unfortunately, a book of this kind cannot actually "workshop" the readers' poems. If at all possible, readers should try to find someone they trust to read their work and give an honest response. Almost all writers have special readers whom they show their work to, but beginning writers can especially benefit from participating in a small workshop to discuss their creative writings. Such workshops are often available at local colleges, but they can also be created by any group of people interested in improving their work.

A NOTE ABOUT CRITICISM

All aspiring writers need to listen to criticism. New poets who believe they are writing sacred, perfect, and publishable texts are, of course, kidding themselves. We should all be open to criticism; and, in time, you'll be easily able to discern for yourself which advice is useful and which is not. Being defensive is a foolish waste of time. On the other hand, criticism should be offered in a pleasant and constructive manner, and maybe the notion of offering suggestions is more useful than that of giving criticism.

Ideally, a poetry workshop should consist of three to twelve people who meet at a regular time and place (maybe once a week or once a month). Typically, a poem should first be read out loud by someone other than the author (maybe even read twice), and then the discussion should begin. It's generally best if the author remains silent during the discussion, taking notes. Those commenting on the poem should always begin by citing something that's effective in the poem (something the author has done successfully) before making suggestions for improvement. Such discussions should also be time-limited (maybe ten or fifteen minutes); otherwise, they can go on endlessly and become counterproductive.

TEN THINGS TO CONSIDER IN EVALUATING A POEM

1. **Is it interesting?** Is it memorable? This is where the fundamental worth of the poem begins; and, as Pulitzer winner W.D. Snodgrass once pointed out: "If my poems aren't interesting, then why should anyone want to read them?"
2. **Is the poem melodic?** Is the meter correct and appropriate? Do the substitutions and enjambments and feminine endings enhance the poem?

3. **Does the poem say anything?** Does it have some depth? Does it express something unique or thought-provoking? Does it communicate its intentions clearly, or is it damaged by unwarranted ambiguity?
4. **Is the poem's point of view appropriate?** Sometimes a poem can be instantly improved by using another point of view—either by changing to the perspective of another character or by simply shifting to a different grammatical person. Effective poems have been written from every point of view: *I*, *we*, *he*, *she*, *they*, and even *you*. In recent times, in the wake of so much confessional poetry, many newer poets assume that the first person is always the most appropriate perspective, but in many cases the third person *he* or *she* can create an effective distance that gives unexpected power to the poem's observations.
5. **Does the poem have specificity?** Ezra Pound rightly warned, "Go in fear of abstractions." This is not to say that poets shouldn't write about love and courage and faith, but that they should do so with a specificity of image and language; otherwise, the reader will quickly get bored with all the generalization. The old adage of *show, don't tell* is a very helpful guideline. Don't let your poems go on and on about love in the abstract; rather, have them signify that love with specifics: a memory, an incident, an object, a spoken remark, etc.
6. **Does the poem have power or beauty or both?** These two concepts, sometimes foolishly disparaged in the twentieth century, are at the very heart of the poetic experience.
7. **Is the poem marred by easy clichés and old-fashioned diction?**
8. **Is the poem's syntax convoluted to conform to the meter?** Or in a rhymed poem, is the syntax twisted to accommodate the end rhyme? Readers like interesting sentence structures, but their pleasure is diminished when the natural flow of the syntax is disrupted simply to conform to either the beat or the rhyme.

9. **Is the poem's punctuation used effectively?** Punctuation is a powerful tool for the poet, but it must be used effectively.
10. **Are there any interesting words in the poem?** Readers like interesting diction, and new writers should strive to use some unusual words in their poetry—but they should also be careful not to overdo it.

Even without the benefit of a workshop, we can still ask ourselves these questions (and more) about our own poetic efforts, and then revise accordingly. Most poets are inveterate revisers, always fiddling with their words and phrases to get things just right. This is a necessary and often quite enjoyable aspect of the writing process; but sometimes, if something's just not working, it can be best to put the piece away for a while, then come back to it weeks, months, or even years later with a fresh perspective.

CHAPTER 5
BLANK VERSE, PART 2

In order to participate in the great poetic tradition, it's crucial to know the great literary works of the past. On the other hand, it's also crucial that contemporary poets never write anachronistically. No matter how much we might love the work of Chaucer or Shakespeare or Tennyson or Frost, simply imitating their modes and styles will be a fruitless endeavor. Such imitation can often be a useful exercise, but it can never produce a successful contemporary poem. Shakespeare didn't write like Chaucer; Tennyson didn't write like Shakespeare; and Frost didn't write like Tennyson. The only successful author of anachronistic poetry in the English tradition was the marvelously talented Thomas Chatterton, who forged medieval manuscripts. Eventually, he was exposed, and he committed suicide.

All serious poets write in the idiom of their time. With this in mind, it's important that we consider contemporary examples of the various forms we're examining in this book. Thus, this chapter consists entirely of poems written much more recently than the classic examples given in the previous chapter. We'll begin with three poems written by Pulitzer recipient Howard Nemerov, one of the great twentieth-century masters of blank verse.

Death and the Maiden

Once I saw a grown man fall from a tree
and die. That's years ago, I was a girl.
My father's house is sold into a home
for the feeble-minded gentlefolk who can't
any longer stand the world, but in those days

there was money to maintain the mile or so
of discipline that kept the hungry grass
parading to the lake, and once a year
bring men to prune the files of giant trees
whose order satisfied and stood for some
euclidean ancestor's dream about the truth:
elms, most of them, already dying of
their yellow blight, and blackened with witches' broom
in the highest branches—but they could die for years,
decades, so tall their silence, and tell you nothing.
Those men came in October every year,
and among the last leaves, the driven leaves,
would set their ladders for assault and swarm
like pirates into the shrouds, thrusting with hook
and long-handled bill against the withered members
of those great corporations, amputating
death away from the center. They were called
tree surgeons, on the ground they were surly-
polite and touched their caps, but in the air
they dared. I would watch one straddle a branch
on a day of rainy wind, his red shirt patched
on the elm's great fan of sky, his pruning claw
breaking the finger-bones from the high hand
which held him, and I'd dream of voyages.
My father said: "It looks more dangerous
than it really is." But if your hand offend,
I thought, cut off the hand, and if your eye
offend, pluck out the eye. I looked at him
out of my window all one afternoon,
and I think he looked back once, a young man
proud and probably lecherous, while I—
was a maiden at a window. Only he died
that day. "Unlucky boy," my father said,
who then was dying himself without a word

to anyone, the crab's claw tightening
inside the bowel that year to the next
in a dead silence. I do not know if things
that happen can be said to come to pass,
or only happen, but when I remember
my father's house, I imagine sometimes
a dry, ruined spinster at my rainy window
trying to tally on dumb fingers a world's
incredible damage—nothing can stand it!—and
watching the red shirt patched against the sky,
so far and small in the webbed hands of the elm.

COMMENTS

Nemerov's powerful blank verse poem begins in a most natural way, "Once I saw a grown man fall from a tree," which then immediately enjambs into the overall theme of the poem: "and die." The trees are dying, the young man dies from his fall, the father is dying of cancer ("the crab's claw"), and, most importantly, the narrator, as she conjures memories of a specific incident from her youth, reveals the emotional death ("damage") that has marked her subsequent life. Nemerov uses vivid images, bits of extremely effective dialogue (especially to illustrate the detached insensitivity of the father), and, occasionally, risky dictional choices to make his poem unique and memorable. The poem's description of the "tree surgeons" swarming in the branches of the trees "like pirates" is a quite logical and appealing simile, but the description of the trees as "great corporations" is much odder and more daring. It's the kind of dictional risk that will work for some readers, but not for others. Another poetic risk that Nemerov takes in the poem is his use of the exclamation mark in the third-to-last line ("nothing can stand it!"). Generally, it's best to avoid exclamation marks in modern poetry, but Nemerov often finds ways to use them effectively. In this case, the exclamatory emphasis seems perfectly appropriate given the desperation in the voice of the narrator (the "spinster"), as she reflects back on the lost possibilities of her life.

Moment

Now, starflake frozen on the windowpane
All of a winter night, the open hearth
Blazing beyond Andromeda, the sea-
Anemone and the downwind seed, O moment
Hastening, halting in a clockwise dust,
The time in all the hospitals is now,
Under the arc-lights where the sentry walks
His lonely wall it never moves from now,
The crying in the cell is also now,
And now is quiet in the tomb as now
Explodes inside the sun, and it is now
In the saddle of space, where argosies of dust
Sail outward blazing, and the mind of God,
The flash across the gap of being, thinks
In the instant absence of forever: now.

COMMENTS

In sharp contrast to the more narrative structure of "Death and the Maiden," Nemerov uses his versatile blank verse in "Moment" to try to describe the impossible: a single instant of time, a single moment. He does this by relentlessly conjuring a series of momentary images that start with the natural world, move into the human realm, and then, with gathering momentum, burst into the endlessness of space toward the "mind of God." It's an extremely bold poem, and it's boldly constructed—with its string of striking images, its effective repetition of the key word *now* (seven times!), and its curious dictional choices, like "saddle of space" and the amazing "argosies of dust."

Striders

The little striders are so light and lean
They can walk atop the water's thinnest skin,
The surface tension that seals and varnishes

The table of the shallow-running stream
Supports their insubstantial shapes just as
In sunlight the sandy or stony floor beneath
Supports the quincunx of their abstract shadows,

But with the one and mortal difference that
Like mariners also committed to the deep
They cannot swim; putting a foot down wrong
Or hammered under in a heavy rain,
Caught in a breaking weather, they will drown.

COMMENTS

Again displaying the remarkable versatility of his blank verse, Nemerov uses the predicament of the little "striders," along with devastating understatement ("they will drown"), to express the fragility of human life. As with "Death and the Maiden," Nemerov heightens his generally natural language with powerful dictional choices, such as the marvelous "insubstantial" in line five, and his subsequent description of the little bug's shadow on the floor of the stream as a "quincunx" (an arrangement of five things in a rectangle or square, with one centered in the middle). Nemerov also uses the telling simile "Like mariners" to compare the perilous situation of the striders to that of so many sailors who were, especially in the past, unable to swim.

Howard Nemerov died in 1991. The following poems were written by four poets—Wyatt Prunty, Dana Gioia, Joseph S. Salemi, and A.E. Stallings—from subsequent and thus more contemporary generations.

The Funerals

You'd think we'd have them down by now,
Dark suits and all that driving back and forth
And walking in and walking out again
With hearing yet another's lost his lines
Somewhere inside the never-plot's last turn
Where "good show" equals "dumb show" equals "end."

Instead, there's but the low sun through the door,
And the sundial floor telling what comes next,
As tile-by-tile the light grows long beneath
Us solemn few who fill the rows and watch
Our shadows climb the wall's blunt vertical,
Where later on it does no harm that when
We size the stone on which the last word's etched
We mind the light and skip the epitaph.

COMMENTS

Wyatt Prunty's excellent blank verse meditation (which initiates with an effective tetrameter) begins in a most natural and colloquial manner before it shifts into a serious reflection about not only the recent death ("another's lost his lines"), but also about the coming death of everyone in attendance, including the narrator's. In the poem's second stanza, Prunty uses the sunlight and the rising shadows to symbolize the passage of time and "what comes next." Then he ends his poem with his narrator's approving observation that, once the funeral is over, it's really the "light" (with all its various symbolisms, including hope) that matters, and not the few words ("the epitaph") that have been written about the deceased.

Cleared Away

Around the corner there may be a man
who shop by shop, block by ruined block,
still sees the neighborhood which once was here,

who, standing in the empty lot, can hear
the vacancies of brick and broken glass
suddenly come to life again, who feels

the steps materialize beneath his feet
as he ascends the shattered tenement,
which rises with him in the open air—

story by story, out of memory,
filled with the smells of dinners on the stove
and the soft laughter of the assembled dead.

COMMENTS

Dana Gioia's eerie blank verse poem, structured in three-line stanzas, is not only about loss, but also about our inability to fully remember *what* we've lost. In the poem, the narrator (who probably *can't* remember) speculates that "there may be a man" who can still remember the now-demolished neighborhood in such a way that the old neighborhood, rather surrealistically, seems to reconstruct itself around him, "story by story." At the end of the poem, we realize that it's really the lost people ("the soft laughter of the assembled dead") who matter the most, and not just the "cleared away" neighborhood. Gioia makes his poem intriguing from the opening line, and he fills it with unusual action, excellent descriptions, and interesting sounds (as in line two, for example).

Contract Murder

No one is ever quite sure how it's planned—
What's clear is that a grievance is expressed
By injured parties, who directly make
Complaints to the Commission, which in turn
Investigates, considers, and decides.
There are some instances where no one brings
Specific charges—bad blood or distrust
Hamper a business, and to clear the air
Someone proposes purgative redress.
In any case, should the Commission find
Cause for coercive measures of the sort
That silence all discussion instantly,
Nothing is done at first. Nothing at all.
Deliberations simply cease, as if
A seminar on Plato's *Dialogues*

Came to some small conclusion, and moved on
To deal with matters equally abstruse.
Then slowly, as the weeks pass into months,
Word of the sentence filters through the ranks.
Even now there may be a reprieve:
Someone speaks up defending the accused,
Or points out circumstances that require
Different procedures, or at least delay.
A friend might offer mediation, while
Others may bring up facts that the Commission
Had not known, and so at every step
The thing can be reversed. But, barring these,
Consensus and a general will are formed
About its patent, plain necessity.
What happens now is anybody's guess—
Myriad factors operate, but gears
Begin to mesh. Small signs can be observed:
The man from Philadelphia who knows
A cousin of the felon in Detroit
Slips out of town discreetly. Or perhaps
An unnamed party visits for a week,
Lives in a basement room, plays solitaire,
The telephone seems quirky in its rings—
Hands rush to silence it, and single words
Constitute conversations. Tempers fray,
There is finality in every sigh.
Soon afterwards, the focus of this stir
Turns an ignition key in his parked car,
Or walks along an unfrequented street,
Or lifts his head before an open window,
Or stops to advise a tall, accosting stranger.
The scene is immaterial, the means
Standard, though pains are taken that they be

Sudden, unlooked for, and unstoppable.
At the Commission, dinner is subdued—
A few quick whispers tie up the loose ends.
And the police, who do not for an instant
Suppose they can unravel what occurred,
Stretch yellow tape to form a small enclosure,
Since that is standardized routine as well.

COMMENTS

Joseph S. Salemi's "Contract Murder" deals with our inability to fully comprehend what's really going on in our lives, and this underlying desperation is symbolized in the poem by the unknowable processes of a contract murder. It's clear that the assassination is proposed to the "Commission," then there's a hiatus for discussion, eventually a "consensus" is formed, and then it happens—although the exact mechanics of the process are "anybody's guess." Salemi loads his poem with excellent and telling details like "The man from Philadelphia," the stranger playing "solitaire," the ringing telephone, and the terse phone conversations. When the murder actually occurs, the poem offers a number of possible methods, each connected by the conjunction *or*. But in the end, even the police, just like us, are baffled by the inexplicability of what's happened, and they simply go about their routine, stretching their "yellow tape" around the murder scene.

Hades Welcomes His Bride

Come now, child, adjust your eyes, for sight
Is here a lesser sense. Here you must learn
Directions through your fingertips and feet
And map them in your mind. I think some shapes
Will gradually appear. The pale things twisting
Overhead are mostly roots, although some worms
Arrive here clinging to their dead. Turn here.
Ah. And in this hall will sit our thrones,

And here you shall be queen, my dear, the queen
Of all men ever to be born. No smile?
Well, some solemnity befits a queen.
These thrones I have commissioned to be made
Are unlike any you imagined; they glow
Of deep-black diamonds and lead, subtler
And in better taste than gold, as will suit
Your timid beauty and pale throat. Come now,
Down these winding stairs, the air more still
And dry and easier to breathe. Here is a room
For your diversions. Here I've set a loom
And silk unraveled from the finest shrouds
And dyed the richest, rarest shades of black.
Such pictures you shall weave! Such tapestries!
For you I chose those three thin shadows there,
And they shall be your friends and loyal maids,
And do not fear from them such gossiping
As servants usually are wont. They have
Not mouth nor eyes and cannot thus speak ill
Of you. Come, come. This is the greatest room;
I had it specially made after great thought
So you would feel at home. I had the ceiling
Painted to recall some evening sky—
But without the garish stars and lurid moon.
What? That stark shape crouching in the corner?
Sweet, that is to be our bed. Our bed.
Ah! Your hand is trembling! I fear
There is, as yet, too much pulse in it.

COMMENTS

A.E. Stallings studied classics at the University of Georgia and Oxford University; and, in a number of her poems, she finds new and striking ways to re-employ the ancient Greek myths. Sometimes, as in this poem, she does so by giving voice to a classical figure and allowing us to hear the figure speak in his own unique and individual manner. In allowing such mythological characters to speak, Stallings is careful not to radically alter the fundamentals of the myth, which would be counterproductive, and she forces us to focus on the individual aspects of the god's personality, his dark environment, and the potential terrors awaiting Persephone, his abducted bride. Notice the poem's telling descriptions of the two thrones, the eyeless and mouthless servants, the matrimonial bed, and Hades' awareness of the horrified reaction of young Persephone: "Ah! Your hand is trembling! I fear / There is, as yet, too much pulse in it."

ASSIGNMENT 3

Write a blank verse poem of sixteen to twenty-four lines on a subject of your choice.

1. In order to keep the meter regular, limit yourself to twelve substitutions and eight enjambments for sixteen lines (and keep these proportional to any additional lines).
2. Keep the meter tight, but be aware of all the ways you can create variety within the line.
3. Be wary of abstractions and generalizations. Again, it's best to *show* something, rather than just say it to your readers. Nemerov's poem "Moment" gives us a unique sense of the difficult and abstract notion of an instant in time by showing us numerous specifics.
4. Be wary of old-fashioned diction. In Stallings's "Hades Welcomes his Bride," the poet's subject matter allows her to take certain dictional liberties since Hades is speaking. His use of such expressions as "my dear," "Come, come," and "Ah!" are all perfectly appropriate, and they're never overdone.
5. Avoid the pop culture (see page 76).

A NOTE ABOUT FINDING IDEAS FOR POETRY

Where do poets get their ideas? This is a common and very reasonable question often asked by younger poets. Naturally, most practicing poets find the germs of their poems in the world around them: a story, an interesting object, an interesting word, an anecdote, an overheard comment, something in a piece of literature, a work of art, a personal experience, an item in the newspaper, or even a certain sound or melody. Sometimes aspiring poets find it helpful to keep journals in which they write down their various ideas and their thoughts about those particular ideas, which will, hopefully, serve as a spur to eventual composition. Other poets simply keep a list of the many things that intrigue them. Such a list might include things like: *a tree surgeon falls to his death*, *an instant of time*, *bugs that glide on the surface of the water*, *attending a funeral*, *a rematerializing neighborhood*, *a contract murder*, or *How would Hades welcome Persephone?* I have no idea, of course, how the seven sample poems in this chapter *actually* came about, but the germs of those poems certainly came from somewhere in the poet's remembered experience.

I would highly recommend that all poets keep a list of intriguing poetic ideas. Since such ideas can come to us at any time (and anywhere), it's always wise to carry a pencil or pen—and to keep one close to one's bedside! Some poets, in the act of composition, let their ideas develop naturally, while others think a great deal about their ideas before they actually begin writing. (Some poets even compose entire poems in their head before they ever lift up a pencil or pen.) But the good news is that either method can work, and aspiring poets will eventually discover the method that works best for them.

Finally, I would also like to suggest that incidents are an especially good place for a poem to begin and germinate. Incidents allow us, as authors, to describe the event with reflection. They also naturally tend towards action, specificity, and sometimes dialogue, all of which readers instinctively appreciate (if they're not overdone), since these things generally arouse our interest.

A NOTE ABOUT POP CULTURE

The pop culture, though often intriguing (and often quite significant in our personal lives), is naturally ephemeral. Very few of us would know who sang the top song on the 1935 "Hit Parade" (Allan Jones, singing "Alone") or who won the Oscar that year for best actor (Victor McLaglen). So if a poem from that decade had casually referred to either Jones or McLaglen, the reference would not only date the poem, it would also, eventually, have to be footnoted. W.H. Auden once used the word *Garbo* in one of his poems, and when his work was translated into Chinese he was shocked to learn that the word had no meaning to a billion Chinese and, as a consequence, it needed to be footnoted. Sometimes such references can be explained within the poem itself, without disrupting the meaning. For example, if a poem describes a person listening to the "soulful songs of Otis Redding," the readers will probably get the idea that Redding was a soul singer of some kind. Nevertheless, even such an explained reference could also date the poem—which might, or might not, be useful. In the end, we need to use our own judgment, but I suggest that new poets be especially wary of the ever-fading pop culture. As Mick Jagger (lead singer of the The Rolling Stones) once wrote, "Who wants yesterday's papers?"

A NOTE ABOUT AUDIENCE

Sometimes young poets will announce, rather self-importantly, "I only write for myself." Well, it's certainly fine and reasonable to try and please oneself, but if we don't write for others (and thus communicate), we're undermining the fundamental poetic objective. So *who* is our audience? Writing for friends and family can also be disastrous, especially if they praise (or abhor) everything we write. And writing for our poetic contemporaries can be equally limiting and dangerous. I suggest to my students that they write their poems with an unborn descendant in mind, that they write for some great-great-great-granddaughter whom they'll never see, but to whom they have this marvelous opportunity to communicate—to leave behind something memorable and inspiring. T.S. Eliot once suggested poets write about "the permanent things," and that's very sound advice.

CHAPTER 6
THE QUATRAIN, PART 2

In the twentieth century, lyric poetry—verse that expresses the personal thoughts of the author—has dominated English-language poetry. This has produced some exceptional poetry, but it has also tended to oversubjectify ("*me*-ize") our recent poetry and induce us to forget that poetry can do many other things as well—like tell a story. Actually, story-poetry is where Western literature begins, with the great epics of Homer. This is also true of Eastern poetry, with the Sumerian/Babylonian *Epic of Gilgamesh*, the Indian *Mahabharata*, and other foundational Eastern works. Thus poetry was *created* to tell stories! Yet, in more recent times, despite the long and popular history of the ballad, we've tended to forget that even *shorter* poems can serve this noble and traditional function.

The *ballad* is a short, superficially simple narrative poem, usually written in quatrains, the most popular English stanza. The typical ballad stanza is essentially the same as common measure: alternating tetrameter and trimeter lines that rhyme *abcb*. There are, of course, many variants used for the ballad, including stanzas of longer length (especially five-line stanzas known as *cinquains*). One popular variant on the typical ballad quatrain is the *long ballad*, in which all four lines are tetrameters.

So if the standard ballad stanza and common measure are essentially the same, then what distinguishes the two and creates the distinctive rhythm of the well-crafted ballad? Actually, it's rather simple: the addition of an anapest or two (or more) in each stanza, which gives the rhythm, and thus the narrative, more speed and pace. This seemingly small metrical alteration, as we shall see, makes a tremendous difference.

FOLK BALLADS

The early folk ballads arose from the common folk of society, and the specific authors of the poems are unknown (attributed to Anonymous). These folk ballads were very popular story-poems that were often sung, and they thrived in the 1400s, 1500s, and 1600s, especially in Scotland, England, and Ireland. Since the poems were passed down from generation to generation, the ballads would naturally be improved (or, at least, altered) over the years, and there are usually many variants of the more popular poems. At the beginning of the nineteenth century, interest in the ballad was revived by the Romantics, and various collectors, including Robert Burns and Sir Walter Scott, began to write down the poems and their variants.

When the English, Scots, and Irish came to North America, they naturally brought their folk ballads with them, and sometimes the poems were reconfigured to fit their new environments, whether it was Appalachia, the Canadian Maritimes, or the American West. The famous cowboy ballad "The Streets of Laredo," for example, is believed by many scholars to be an adaptation of an old English broadside ballad entitled "The Unfortunate Rake," about a young soldier dying of syphilis. Eventually, the poem was shifted to the American Wild West, where a young cowboy, who is dying of a bullet wound, requests, oddly enough, "So beat the drum slowly and play the fife lowly"—an incongruous remnant of the original military version. The eventual popularity of American country music, initiated in 1927 by Victor Record's recordings of the Carter Family and Jimmie Rodgers, ensured that the ballad would continue to be written and sung in more modern times, whether it be Johnny Horton's "The Ballad of New Orleans," Marty Robbins's "El Paso" (or his version of "The Streets of Laredo"), or Porter Wagoner's "The Carroll County Accident."

THE TWELVE TRAITS OF THE FOLK BALLAD

1. **Tells a story**. Usually the narrative will revolve around a single incident (or possibly two), and like all good stories, ballads are most effective when they offer some kind of mystery or surprise.

2. **Often romantic**. Ballads have medieval roots, and they're full of passion, often involving lost, thwarted, or unrequited love.
3. **Objective tone**. This is a crucial element of the ballad. Ballad narratives are always told in an impersonal, objective, and generally understated tone that gives great power and memorability to the poem.
4. **Little character development**. All stories have characters, but in the ballad, the characters are never fully developed or analyzed. They simply do what they do, without reflection.
5. **The moral is implied**. Although all ballads have a moral point, their purpose is never explicitly stated.
6. **Extreme compression in the story telling**. Any good ballad could serve as the basis of an epic or novel, but the ballad is marked by its brevity—and by its ability to tell its story quickly and efficiently.
7. **Highly dramatic, often violent**. As already mentioned, passions run high in the traditional ballad, and the key action is always vivid, powerful, dramatic (even over the top), and often bloody. Sometimes the supernatural also plays a role of some kind.
8. **Abrupt beginnings and scene shifts**. Epics usually begin *in medias res* ("in the middle of things"), and so do ballads. Since there's no time to develop the backstory (or the characters' personalities), ballads usually begin abruptly (often with action), and if the scene shifts within the narrative, it also does so abruptly.
9. **Simple and colloquial language**. Ballads were extremely popular with the common people, and they always employ language and expressions that are appropriate for their audience.
10. **Dialogue**. Ballads often use dialogue to tell the story and move it along. Often the ballad's brief lines of dialogue are so well-constructed that the traditional *he said* or *she said* is not necessary and is often omitted.
11. **Repetition**. Ballads are famous for their repeated words, lines, and stanzas (refrains).

12. **Anapests.** The key to the rhythmic feel of the ballad is the careful placement of a few (but not too many!) anapestic substitutions into the iambic flow.

LITERARY AND MODERN BALLADS

In the wake of the Romantic revival, many well-known poets began to compose *literary ballads*. These ballads maintained the traditional traits of the anonymous folk ballads, but they were more self-consciously crafted. Coleridge's famous "Rime of the Ancient Mariner," which is mostly written in the ballad stanza, is a perfect example. Coleridge's long story-poem begins:

It is an ancient Mariner,
And he stoppeth one of three.
"By thy long gray beard and glittering eye,
Now wherefore stopp'st thou me?"

Other literary ballads were written by Keats, Scott, Longfellow, Kipling, and Oscar Wilde. In the twentieth century, only a few poets have written what we call the *modern ballad*, but Yeats, Auden, Charles Causley, and several other poets have kept the tradition alive. Modern ballads are literary ballads that were written after 1900, and they usually have a more contemporary setting.

[SAMPLE BALLADS]

We'll begin with two well-known folk ballads.

The Demon Lover (The Carpenter's Wife)

"O where have you been, my long, long love,
This long seven years and mair[1]?"
"O I'm come to seek my former vows
Ye granted me before."

[1] more

"O hold your tongue of your former vows,
For they will breed sad strife;
O hold your tongue of your former vows,
For I am become a wife."

He turned him right and round about,
And the tear blinded his ee[2]:
"I wad never hae trodden on Irish ground,
If it had not been for thee.

"I might have had a king's daughter,
Far, far beyond the sea:
I might have had a king's daughter,
Had it not been for love o thee."

"If ye might have had a king's daughter,
Yer sel ye had to blame:
Ye might have taken the king's daughter,
For ye kend[3] that I was nane[4].

"If I was to leave my husband dear,
And my two babes also,
O what have you to take me to,
If with you I should go?"

"I have seven ships upon the sea—
The eighth brought me to land—
With four-and-twenty bold mariners,
And music on every hand."

She has taken up her tow[5] little babes,
Kiss'd them baith cheek and chin:
"O fair ye weel, my ain two babes,
For I'll never see you again."

[2] eye [3] knew [4] not one [5] two

She set her foot upon the ship.
  No mariners could she behold:
But the sails ware o the taffetie[6]
  And the masts o the beaten gold.

They had not sailed a league, a league,
  A league but barely three,
When dismal grew his countenance,
  And drumlie[7] grew his ee.

They had not sailed a league, a league,
  A league but barely three,
Until she espied his cloven foot,
  And she wept right bitterlie.

"O hold your tongue of your weeping," says he.
  "Of your weeping now let me be;
I will show you how the lilies grow
  On the banks of Italy."

"O what hills are yon, yon pleasant hills,
  That the sun shines sweetly in?"
"O yon are the hills of heaven," he said,
  "Where you will never win."

"O whaten mountain is yon," she said,
  "All so dreary wi frost and snow?"
"O yon is the mountain of hell," he cried,
  "Where you and I will go."

He strack[8] the tap-mast wi his hand,
  The fore-mast wi his knee,
And he brake that gallant ship in twain,
  And sank her in the sea.

[6] a fine, glossy silk [7] gloomy [8] struck

COMMENTS

This classic story-poem exhibits all the traits of the typical folk ballad. It begins abruptly; it uses dialogue (often without *he said* or *she said*); it's highly dramatic and violent; it's about illicit romance; etc. It also includes the effective repetition of words (like *long* and *league*); the repetition of lines (like the ballad's first line and *They had not sailed a league, a league*); and appropriate colloquialisms (like *O hold your tongue*).

Most significant, of course, is the ballad's underlying rhythm, and its careful inclusion of well-placed anapests. Let's look at the first stanza.

> "Ŏ whére | hăve yŏu béen, | mȳ lóng, | lŏng lóve,
>   Thĭs lóng | sēvĕn yéars | ănd máir?"
> "Ŏ I'm cóme | tŏ séek | mȳ fór | mĕr vóws
>   Yĕ gránt | ĕd mé | bĕfóre."

Each of the first three lines includes an anapestic substitution that dramatically alters the regular iambic rhythm and gives the poem its anticipated ballad feel.

Much of the power of this particular ballad derives from its compression, time shifts, and objective tone. Notice, for example, the abrupt shift after the fifth stanza. The carpenter's wife has just told her lover that he's missed his chance; but then, suddenly and unexpectedly, she asks what he has to offer, "If I was to leave my husband." Then, when her demon lover promises her riches and excitement (the "fast" life), we're shocked to observe her kissing her children good-bye, without a moment's reflection, and saying callously and almost matter-of-factly, "For I'll never see you again." Eventually, the ballad will end with an even more powerful understatement of fact, "And sank her in the sea."

The Bailiff's Daughter of Islington

There was a youth, and a well-beloved youth,
  And he was a squire's son:
He loved the bailiff's[1] daughter dear,

[1]sheriff's

That lived in Islington.

Yet she was coy, and would not believe
That he did love her so,
No nor at any time would she
Any countenance to him show.

But when his friends did understand
His fond and foolish mind,
They sent him up to fair London,
An apprentice for to bind.

And when he had been seven long years,
And never his love could see,—
"Many a tear have I shed for her sake,
When she little thought of me."

Then all the maids of Islington
Went forth to sport and play,
All but the bailiff's daughter dear;
She secretly stole away.

She pulled off her gown of green,
And put on ragged attire,
And to fair London she would go,
Her true love to enquire.

And as she went along the high road,
The weather being hot and dry,
She sat her down upon a green bank,
And her true love came riding by.

She started up, with a colour so red,
Catching hold of his bridle-rein;
"One penny, one penny, kind sir," she said,
"Will ease me of much pain."

"Before I give you one penny, sweet-heart,
Pray tell me where you were born."
"At Islington, kind sir," said she,

"Where I have had many a scorn."

"I prythee, sweet-heart, then tell to me,
O tell me, whether you know
The bailiff's daughter of Islington."
"She is dead, sir, long ago."

"If she be dead, then take my horse,
My saddle and bridle also;
For I will into some far country,
Where no man shall me know."

"O stay, O stay, thou goodly youth,
She standeth by the side;
She is here alive, she is not dead,
And ready to be thy bride."

"O farewell grief, and welcome joy,
Ten thousand times therefore;
For now I have found mine own true love,
Whom I thought I should never see more."

COMMENTS

This excellent love ballad highlights the boldness and cleverness of the bailiff's daughter, who, realizing that she's been too "coy" in her dealings with her true love, abruptly (after "seven long years"!) heads off to London to find him. The absurd coincidence that she actually meets him on the way (and that he no longer recognizes her) is acceptable within the folk ballad tradition, as are her lover's impulsive (and almost ridiculous) preparations for suicide and his over-the-top expression of joy when she finally reveals herself, "O farewell grief, and welcome joy." We can see that this classic ballad, like "The Demon Lover," employs various anapestic substitutions to give the rhythm its distinctive flavor, and the poem concludes with a rush of anapests.

Whŏm Ĭ thóught | Ĭ shŏuld név | ĕr sĕe móre.

The following samples are literary ballads, and the first was written by Keats.

La Belle Dame Sans Merci

O what can ail thee, knight-at-arms,
  Alone and palely loitering?
The sedge[1] has withered from the lake,
  And no birds sing.

O what can ail thee, knight-at-arms,
  So haggard and so woe-begone?
The squirrel's granary is full,
  And the harvest's done.

I see a lily on thy brow
  With anguish moist and fever dew,
And on thy cheek a fading rose
  Fast withereth too.

I met a lady in the meads[2],
  Full beautiful—a faery's child;
Her hair was long, her foot was light,
  And her eyes were wild.

I made a garland for her head,
  And bracelets too, and fragrant zone;
She looked at me as she did love,
  And made sweet moan.

I set her on my pacing steed,
  And nothing else saw all day long,
For sidelong would she bend, and sing
  A faery's song.

She found me roots of relish sweet,
  And honey wild, and manna dew,
And sure in language strange she said—

[1]grassy plants [2]meadow

"I love thee true."

She took me to her elfin grot[3],
And there she wept and sighed full sore,
And there I shut her wild wild eyes
With kisses four.

And there she lullèd me asleep,
And there I dreamed—ah! woe betide[4]!
The latest dream I ever dreamed
On the cold hill side.

I saw pale kings and princes too,
Pale warriors, death-pale were they all;
They cried—"La Belle Dame sans Merci
Hath thee in thrall!"

I saw their starved lips in the gloam[5],
With horrid warning gapèd wide,
And I awoke and found me here,
On the cold hill's side.

And this is why I sojourn here,
Alone and palely loitering,
Though the sedge is withered from the lake
And no birds sing.

COMMENTS

The figure of the femme fatale, "La Belle Dame Sans Merci" (the beautiful woman without mercy), is given a supernatural twist in Keats's famous and carefully crafted ballad of 1819. Maybe it's the eerie nature of his subject that compelled Keats to slightly alter the traditional ballad stanza by truncating each of his final lines from a trimeter to a dimeter ("And no birds sing," etc.). As we've seen, even the smallest metrical changes have substantial effects, and Keats's truncations leave every stanza (even the poem itself) feeling somehow incomplete, which contributes to the creepy feeling. Right

[3]elves' grotto [4]befell me [5]twilight

from the poem's first line ("O what can ail thee, knight-at-arms"), it's perfectly clear that something's not right, and the missing foot accentuates that feeling.

The Ballad of Father Gilligan

The old priest Peter Gilligan
  Was weary night and day,
For half his flock were in their beds,
  Or under green sods lay.

Once while he nodded on a chair,
  At the moth-hour of eve,
Another poor man sent for him,
  And he began to grieve.

"I have no rest, nor joy, nor peace,
  For people die and die";
And after cried he, "God forgive!
  My body spake, not I!"

And then, half-lying on the chair,
  He knelt, prayed, fell asleep;
And the moth-hour went from the fields,
  And stars began to peep.

They slowly into millions grew,
  And leaves shook in the wind;
And God covered the world with shade,
  And whispered to mankind.

Upon the time of sparrow chirp
  When the moths came once more,
The old priest Peter Gilligan
  Stood upright on the floor.

"*Mavrone, mavrone!*[1] The man has died,
  While I slept on the chair";
He roused his horse out of its sleep,
  And rode with little care.

He rode now as he never rode,
By rocky lane and fen[2];
The sick man's wife opened the door:
"Father! You come again!"

"And is the poor man dead?" he cried.
"He died an hour ago."
The old priest Peter Gilligan
In grief swayed to and fro.

"When you were gone he turned and died,
As merry as a bird."
The old priest Peter Gilligan
He knelt him at that word.

"He Who hath made the night of stars
For souls who tire and bleed,
Sent one of His great angels down
To help me in my need.

"He Who is wrapped in purple robes,
With planets in His care,
Had pity on the least of things
Asleep upon a chair."

COMMENTS

Yeats's beautiful ballad about the exhausted priest who falls asleep when he's needed at a parishioner's deathbed is given a clever twist when Father Gilligan discovers that, in his absence, an angel (appearing in the priest's own shape) had comforted the dying man. Yeats is one of the most melodic poets in the history of English literature, and this poem illustrates his mastery of sound and rhythm. We can also see that Yeats's more modern ballad occasionally moves away from the typical tightness of the folk ballad as Yeats indulges in several passages of lyric description. The entire fifth stanza, for example, is a lovely—but atypical—

[1]Alas! [2]marsh

poetic description of the falling nighttime. This stanza also employs the use of a sight rhyme (*wind* and *mankind*), which would not be appropriate in a folk ballad because it would disappoint the sound expectations of its traditional audience.

Ballad of Birmingham

(On the bombing of a church in Birmingham, Alabama, 1963)

"Mother dear, may I go downtown
Instead of out to play,
And march the streets of Birmingham
In a Freedom March today?"

"No, baby, no, you may not go,
For the dogs are fierce and wild,
And clubs and hoses, guns and jails
Aren't good for a little child."

"But, mother, I won't be alone.
Other children will go with me,
And march the streets of Birmingham
To make our country free."

"No, baby, no, you may not go,
For I fear those guns will fire.
But you may go to church instead
And sing in the children's choir."

She has combed and brushed her night-dark hair,
And bathed rose petal sweet,
And drawn white gloves on her small brown hands,
And white shoes on her feet.

The mother smiled to know her child
Was in the sacred place,
But that smile was the last smile
To come upon her face.

For when she heard the explosion,
Her eyes grew wet and wild.
She raced through the streets of Birmingham
Calling for her child.

She clawed through bits of glass and brick,
Then lifted out a shoe.
"O, here's the shoe my baby wore,
But, baby, where are you?"

COMMENTS

This powerful narrative poem by Dudley Randall is the most famous ballad of the twentieth century, and it reveals the ballad's remarkable ability to deal with contemporary issues—in this particular case, a true and tragic incident in 1963, when four children were murdered by racists during the civil rights activities in the American South. Even though Randall gives away much of his subsequent narrative in his parenthetical epigraph, the ballad's powerful rhythm, engaging narrative, and telling details keep the reader on edge until the tragic and anticipated end. The poet's use of irony (the "safety" of the church), symbolism (the shoes), and marvelous colloquialism ("No, baby, no, you may not go") are all reinforced by his melodic lines and masterful use of rhythm. Like Yeats, Randall devotes an entire stanza to a lyrical interlude ("She has combed and brushed her night-dark hair"), but in this poem, the poetic pause clearly serves to heighten the reader's tension and enhance the narrative.

Although Randall's poem is highly regular, notice its odd but crucial line in the sixth stanza: *But that smile was the last smile*. Given its position in the stanza, this line should be a tetrameter, but it's extremely difficult to scan, and it intentionally throws off the meter—and everything else in the poem. This disruption foreshadows the coming chaos (the "explosion") that will alter the mother's life and prevent her from ever smiling again. It's an excellent example of masterful poetic craftsmanship.

The Ballad of Charles Starkweather

To the tune of "Henry Lee"
or "Once I Knew a Pretty Girl"

He was just a young Nebraska boy.
His hair was fiery red.
His father gave him a gun for a toy—
"What's your hurry?" Charlie said.

He shot eleven men for play
And left them there for dead,
And when they tried to crawl away,
"What's your hurry?" Charlie said.

His girlfriend watched him burn them down,
She watched them while they bled.
"Oh, Charlie, give them another round."
"What's your hurry?" Charlie said.

He shot her father while he ate,
Her mother in her bed.
Caril cried out, "Let's celebrate!"
"What's your hurry?" Charlie said.

Young Jensen was sitting in his Ford
With the girl he was soon to wed.
Charlie stepped up on the running-board—
"What's your hurry?" Charlie said.

"Don't shoot, don't shoot!" young Jensen cried,
His voice was full of dread.
He tried to get out on the other side—
"What's your hurry?" Charlie said.

They stole a car and headed west,
Into Wyoming they sped.
"Oh, Charlie, won't we ever rest?"
"What's your hurry?" Charlie said.

The twelfth man had a gun of his own.
He aimed at Charlie's head.
"I'll give you two seconds to drop your gun!"
"What's your hurry?" Charlie said.

They brought young Charlie into court
To pay for the blood he shed.
The jury said, "Your time is short."
"What's your hurry?" Charlie said.

The hot-rods drove up in a crowd
While he was being fed.
They turned their radios up loud.
"What's your hurry?" Charlie said.

They came for him at 12:04
And quickly shaved his head.
They hustled him down to the death-house door—
"What's your hurry?" Charlie said.

He sat in the chair, they strapped him in;
The weight in his chest was like lead.
The warden signaled to begin—
"What's your hurry?" Charlie said.

His girl lay in her prison cell,
Alone on her narrow bed.
"Oh, Charlie, I wish I was down with you in hell!"
"What's your hurry?" Charlie said.

COMMENTS

In 1958, the country was horrified by the murder spree of Charles Starkweather and his girlfriend, Caril Fugate, as they drove west from Nebraska, killing innocent people as they went. Unfortunately, Starkweather intrigued a number of the younger generation's discontented youth, and this intrigue was enhanced by Starkweather's supposed resemblance to James Dean. This peculiar fascination explains the tenth stanza of the ballad, where the local kids drive up to the jail where Starkweather is confined and blast rock-and-roll music from their car radios. The cold-bloodedness of Starkweather's crimes inspired several Hollywood movies (including Terrence Malick's *Badlands*); the well-known acoustic song "Nebraska" (written by Bruce Springsteen); and this eerie ballad written by Donald Justice and his former student Robert Mezey.

The effectiveness of this particular ballad lies in its impersonal descriptions of the violence (and Charlie's apparent disinterest), and in the writers' ability to satisfy their readers' expectation that each new stanza will successfully set up the ballad's refrain line, *"What's your hurry?" Charlie said*. Such a demanding self-restriction by the authors forces them to create new and interesting setups for each repetition of the refrain line, and, of course, each of those setups *must* rhyme with the word *said*. Thus the poem requires thirteen rhymes for the key sound (*said*), and only two (*bed* and *head*) are repeated. Thus the poem, both in its narrative and its rhymes, lives up to our expectations in every stanza, and the poem maintains its normal ballad rhythm until its penultimate line, "'Oh, Charlie, I wish I was down with you in hell!'" Given that the line should naturally be tetrameter, its solid five beats throw off the poem's relentless rhythm just before the final refrain. This is clearly an intentional alteration of the meter, but the effectiveness of this disruption of the rhythm, especially so close to the end of this masterfully crafted poem, is debatable.

ASSIGNMENT 4

Write a ballad, either in the folk, literary, or more modern vein.

1. Use the familiar ballad stanza, with its 4-3-4-3 iambic beat.
2. Incorporate two or three anapests into each stanza. But limit yourself to no more than three in each stanza, so you can de-

velop a better control of the rhythm. On the other hand, be sure to use at least two in every stanza to create the ballad feel.

3. Use the standard rhyme scheme (*abcb*), and use solid rhymes.
4. Write at least eight stanzas, not counting repeated refrains. A ballad story always takes some time to tell.
5. Keep all of the traditional characteristics of the folk ballad in mind, and try to incorporate them all.
6. Current events are fine, but avoid the pop culture. Of course, not all historical occurrences will have enough story in them to be appropriate for a ballad, so don't be afraid to make up your own story.
7. Avoid humor. There are many successful humorous ballads, but for this assignment, write a serious story-poem. Sometimes humor can create a sense of sloppiness in new writers (a feeling that the humor allows them to get away with breaking certain normal requirements). So we'll save humor, which must be very carefully crafted, for upcoming assignments.
8. Above all, tell an interesting story! People love intriguing stories. Keep your readers interested with action, twists, and surprises.

A NOTE ABOUT RHYMING

There can be no doubt that human beings appreciate rhyming sounds, and English poets, when not using blank verse, have consistently used this fact to enhance their work. In the early twentieth century, some poets, like Yeats and Wilfred Owen, began to experiment with off-rhymes to achieve certain effects: either to mute the sound of the rhyme or to disappoint the reader's expectation for some logical or semantic reason (like creating sonic disorder to imitate thematic disorder). At the present time, even in the midst of the current Formalist revival, many formalist poets feel that they need to "hide" their rhymes, and they seem quite pleased if someone says, "What a nice poem—and I didn't even realize it was rhymed!" For such poets, it seems a kind of sophistication to minimize the natural effects of their rhymes by using slant-rhymes, off-rhymes, near-rhymes, almost-rhymes, and hey-I'm-not-really-a-rhyme rhymes. In my own opinion, the only reason to use rhyme in a poem is to give your readers pleasure, and if they can't hear the rhyme, then they'll derive no pleasure from it. Also, despite the debatable notion that it's more sophisticated to use near-rhymes, one can't help thinking when reading such poems that maybe, just maybe, the writer simply couldn't do it properly!

Thus, for the purposes of the assignments in this book, I encourage you to use only solid rhymes in your poems, even avoiding plural rhymes (like *look* and *books*). Even if you disagree with my comments above, the best way to learn how to rhyme is to master solid rhymes; then, if you wish, you can experiment with off-rhymes. I should conclude by mentioning that, on certain occasions, slant-rhyme can work very effectively (see, for example, Richard Wilbur's poem on page 134 in chapter nine), particularly when the unmet expectation of the rhyme truly enhances the meaning or the tone of the poem.

CHAPTER 7 | THE COUPLET

The couplet consists of two rhyming lines, generally of the same length. Although some poems contain uneven couplets (rhymed lines of unequal length), most English-language couplets consist of either two tetrameters or two pentameters. The couplet (we sometimes forget) has had a long and distinguished history in the annals of English poetry. If *The Canterbury Tales* is the seminal work of modern English literature, then the couplet was right there at the beginning—in the famous "General Prologue" to Chaucer's great work.

From Chaucer to Richard Wilbur, the couplet has had numerous practitioners, especially in the eighteenth century, and a short and incomplete listing would include: Marlowe, Shakespeare, Milton, John Donne, Andrew Marvell, Dryden, Pope, Coleridge, Keats, Robert Browning, Dickinson, Yeats, Frost, Hilaire Belloc, Sir John Betjeman, and Wendy Cope.

Here are some familiar English couplets.

> Whan that Aprill with his shoures soote[1]
> The droghte[2] of March hath perced to the roote,
> And bathed every veyne in swich licour
> Of which vertu[3] engendred is the flour[4]
>
> —GEOFFREY CHAUCER

> Double, double, toil and trouble;
> Fire burn and cauldron bubble.
>
> —WILLIAM SHAKESPEARE

[1] sweet showers [2] dryness [3] power [4] flower

Know then thyself, presume not God to scan,
The proper study of Mankind is Man.

—ALEXANDER POPE

Listen, my children, and you shall hear,
of the midnight ride of Paul Revere

—HENRY WADSWORTH LONGFELLOW

That's my last Duchess painted on the wall,
Looking as if she were alive, I call
That piece a wonder, now: Fra Pandolf's hands
Worked busily a day, and there she stands.

—ROBERT BROWNING

And therefore I have sailed the seas and come
To the holy city of Byzantium.

—WILLIAM BUTLER YEATS

In the room the women come and go
Talking of Michelangelo.

—T.S. ELIOT

Even this brief sampling reveals the remarkable (and surprising) versatility of the couplet. Throughout English literary history, couplets have been used for narrative poetry (like Pope's translation of *The Iliad*); lyric poetry (see Marlowe on page 100); philosophical verse (especially by Dryden and Pope); and satirical verse (the Augustans, Belloc, Roy Campbell, and others). The fact that the Shakespearean sonnet ends with a couplet has also created many memorable English couplets, and the same is true of the concluding couplet of the eight-line ottava rima stanza, the Yeats quote cited above.

As a result of its perfect symmetry and powerful rhyme, the couplet is naturally heightened and intensified. Its tight structure creates emphasis and remarkable individuality. As a consequence, couplets have a natural aphoristic quality, and they're especially useful for epigrams, maxims, and adages. As mentioned above, the couplet's extreme compression and bold rhyme make it particularly appropriate for wit and satire. Sometimes poets will also use the two-part structure of the couplet for antithesis by contrasting each of the two lines, or by contrasting one couplet against its subsequent couplet. All of these inherent attributes and tendencies reinforce the couplet's natural mnemonic quality. In truth, it's hard to forget good couplets. They stick in our memory, and they're a pleasure to recite out loud.

OPEN AND CLOSED COUPLETS

The difficulty with writing couplets is that they take considerable poetic skill to master. One of the potential dangers of composing in couplets is that they can sometimes get monotonous for the reader—starting to feel like individual bricks stacked on top of each other. This is especially true of the closed couplet, in which the first line is a syntactical unit and the second line is heavily end-stopped after the rhyme. Some talented poets, like Robert Browning, have tried to remedy this problem by including occasional open couplets in their poems for variety. In an open couplet, neither line is necessarily a complete expression or syntactical unit, and such couplets often involve some kind of enjambment within or between couplets. In the example above from Browning's famous dramatic monologue "My Last Duchess," the poet's first couplet enjambs into his second, and the first line of the second couplet carries over into the next line. This is very hard to do, and it's most effective in couplet poems written as conversational dramatic monologues.

HEROIC COUPLETS

The traditional pentameter closed couplet is also known as the heroic couplet, and the term is most frequently associated with the eighteenth century and the English Neoclassical period (although Dryden was also a master of the couplet during the previous Restoration period). The era of Swift, Pope, and Johnson was dominated by the couplet, which was considered to be the absolute poetic height of reason, elegance, and civilized sophistication. Pope boldly referred to all previous poetry as "that former savagery," and he and several of his contemporaries wrote profound and masterful works using the heroic couplet. The *short couplet* (consisting of two tetrameters) was often preferred by the witty Jonathan Swift for its tight and hard-hitting effects. While the heroic couplet's two extra syllables allow for additional adjectives or adverbs, which can give the lines intellectual subtlety, the tighter tetrameter couplet is much leaner (and potentially meaner) and perfectly suited to satire, humor, and sarcasm.

[SAMPLE COUPLETS]

Despite its "natural" tendencies, the short tetrameter couplet, in the right hands, still has a remarkable ability to carry the lyric.

The Passionate Shepherd to His Love

Come live with me and be my love,
And we will all the pleasures prove,
That valleys, groves, hills and fields,
Woods or steepy mountains yields.

And we will sit upon the rocks,
Seeing the shepherds feed their flocks
By shallow rivers, to whose falls
Melodious birds sing madrigals.

And I will make thee beds of roses,
And a thousand fragrant posies,
A cap of flowers and a kirtle[1]
Embroidered all with leaves of myrtle;

A gown made of the finest wool,
Which from our pretty lambs we pull;

[1] gown

Fair-linèd slippers for the cold,
With buckles of the purest gold;

A belt of straw and ivy buds,
With coral clasps and amber studs;
And if these pleasures may thee move,
Come live with me and be my love.

The shepherd swains[2] shall dance and sing
For thy delight each May morning;
If these delights thy mind may move,
Then live with me and be my love.

COMMENTS

The narrator of Marlowe's famous pastoral invites his lover to "Come live with me and be my love." The language and the gentle rhythm of the poem's iambic tetrameters are perfectly lovely, but a few of the poem's rhymes are less pleasing to our modern ears. Some Elizabethan scholars believe that Marlowe's sight rhymes, like those beginning the poem (*love* and *prove*) and those ending the poem (*move* and *love*), are actually true rhymes because the Elizabethans pronounced the word *love* like *loove*. This is certainly debatable, but Marlowe's rhyming off the accent is not. For example, in the last stanza, the word *sing* rhymes with the unaccented second syllable (*-ing*) of the word *morning*. Such a rhyme naturally diminishes the impact of the rhyme, and, although it was acceptable to Marlowe's audience, it's generally unsatisfying for modern readers.

The next sample is an excerpt from Dryden's "Mac Flecknoe."

All human things are subject to decay,
And when Fate summons, monarchs must obey,
This Flecknoe found, who, like Augustus, young
Was call'd to empire, and had govern'd long:
In prose and verse, was own'd, without dispute,

[2] country lovers

Through all the realms of *Nonsense*, absolute.
This aged prince, now flourishing in peace,
And blest with issue of a large increase,
Worn out with business, did at length debate
To settle the succession of the State;
And, pond'ring which of all his sons was fit
To reign, and wage immortal war with wit,
Cried: "'Tis resolv'd; for Nature pleads, that he
Should only rule, who most resembles me.
Sh— alone my perfect image bears,
Mature in dullness from his tender years:
Sh— alone of all my sons is he
Who stands confirm'd in full stupidity,
The rest to some faint meaning make pretense,
But Sh— never deviates into sense.
Some beams of wit on other souls may fall,
Strike through, and make a lucid interval;
But Sh—'s genuine night admits no ray,
His rising fogs prevail upon the day.
Besides, his goodly fabric fills the eye,
And seems design'd for thoughtless majesty:
Thoughtless as monarch oaks that shade the plain,
And, spread in solemn state, supinely reign.

COMMENTS

The couplet, despite its surprising versatility, seems to especially enjoy (in its heart of hearts) poking fun at things, and Dryden effectively uses the couplet's natural tendency in his celebrated "Mac Flecknoe." The poem is a brutal satire about the rise of the untalented poet Thomas Shadwell to take the place of the reigning literary lion of "dullness," Richard Flecknoe.

The next passage comes from Alexander Pope's remarkable poem "An Essay on Criticism."

True ease in writing comes from art, not chance,
As those move easiest who have learned to dance.
'Tis not enough no harshness gives offense,
The sound must seem an echo to the sense:
Soft is the strain when Zephyr gently blows,
And the smooth stream in smoother numbers flows:
But when loud surges lash the sounding shore,
The hoarse, rough verse should like the torrent roar:
When Ajax strives some rock's vast weight to throw,
The line too labors, and the words move slow;
Not so, when swift Camilla scours the plain,
Flies o'er the unbending corn, and skims along the main.
Hear how Timotheus' varied lays surprise,
And bid alternate passions fall and rise!

COMMENTS

This famous section of Pope's "An Essay on Criticism" illustrates the poet's mastery of the heroic couplet as well as the form's uncanny ability to carry the most sophisticated and intellectual content. As was typical with Pope, these are extremely tight closed couplets, in which every line ends with some kind of punctuation and all of the rhymes are solid—yet the passage still flows perfectly naturally. It would take an entire book to properly analyze this short and masterful passage, but we should definitely take notice that Pope, in constructing these lines, is actively illustrating his point that the meaning of a poem should be reinforced by the sound (which is also a theme of this book!): "The sound must seem an echo to the sense." So Pope gives us several examples in his poetic passage, and we'll take a quick look at three.

In the third couplet, Pope employs various soft vowels and six sibilant alliterations (on the sound of the letters *s* and *z*) to give a light and delicate feel to his lines about the wind (*Zephyr*). Later, he uses slow monosyllables and numerous words beginning or ending with the letter *t* (which must be carefully enunciated) to give the ponderous sense of mighty Ajax struggling to hoist up his huge rock. Then, to give the sense of the swiftness of Camilla (whom Virgil claimed was so fast-of-foot that she could run across a field of corn without bending the stalks!), Pope employs both polysyllabic words (*Camilla* and *unbending*) and an anapestic substitution (*the unbend-*) to speed up his couplet and allow his sound to echo his sense.

Since some of the previous selections have illustrated the couplet's ability to carry both the lyric and more intellectual verse, the rest of the samples in this chapter will focus on various twentieth-century uses of the form for wit, light verse, and satire.

Lord Lucky

Lord Lucky, by a curious fluke,
Became a most important duke.
From living in a vile Hotel
A long way east of Camberwell
He rose, in less than half an hour,
To riches, dignity and power.
It happened in the following way: —
The Real Duke went out one day
To shoot with several people, one
Of whom had never used a gun.
This gentleman (a Mr. Meyer
Of Rabley Abbey, Rutlandshire),
As he was scrambling through the brake,
Discharged his weapon by mistake,
And plugged about an ounce of lead
Piff-bang into his Grace's Head—
Who naturally fell down dead.
His Heir, Lord Ugly, roared, "You Brute!
Take that to teach you how to shoot!"
Whereat he volleyed, left and right;
But being somewhat short of sight,
His right-hand Barrel only got

The second heir, Lord Poddleplot;
The while the left-hand charge (or choke)
Accounted for another bloke,
Who stood with an astounded air
Bewildered by the whole affair
—And was the third remaining heir.
After the Execution (which
Is something rare among the Rich)
Lord Lucky, while of course he needed
Some help to prove his claim, succeeded.
—But after his succession, though
All this was over years ago,
He only once indulged the whim
Of asking Meyer to lunch with him.

COMMENTS

Hilaire Belloc was a twentieth-century master of the tetrameter couplet. On occasion, Belloc would heighten his effects by adding an extra rhymed line to one of his couplets (thus creating a triplet). For example, when the first Duke is shot, Belloc exaggerates the dark humor of the situation by injecting a triplet into the poem.

And plugged about an ounce of lead
Piff-bang into his Grace's Head—
Who naturally fell down dead.

Later in the poem, Belloc further satirizes the British aristocracy with another triplet, ending with the rhymes *air*, *affair*, and *heir*.

Here's another short-couplet poem from Belloc.

The Example

John Henderson, an unbeliever,
Had lately lost his Joie de Vivre
From reading far too many books.

He went about with gloomy looks;
Despair inhabited his breast
And made the man a perfect pest.
Not so his sister, Mary Lunn,
She had a whacking lot of fun!
Though unbelieving as a beast
She didn't worry in the least.
But drank as hard as she was able
And sang and danced upon the table;
And when she met her brother Jack
She used to smack him on the back
So smartly as to make him jump,
And cry, "What-ho! You've got the hump!"
A phrase which, more than any other,
Was gall and wormwood to her brother;
For, having an agnostic mind,
He was exceedingly refined.
The Christians, a declining band,
Would point with monitory hand
To Henderson his desperation,
To Mary Lunn her dissipation,
And often mutter, "Mark my words!
Something will happen to those birds!"
Which came to pass: for Mary Lunn
Died suddenly, at ninety-one,
Of Psittacosis[1], not before
Becoming an appalling bore.
While Henderson, I'm glad to state,
Though naturally celibate,
Married an intellectual wife
Who made him lead the Higher life
And wouldn't give him any wine;

[1] Parrot's Fever

Whereby he fell in a decline,
And, at the time of writing this,
Is suffering from paralysis,
The which, we hear with no surprise,
Will shortly end in his demise.

Moral
The moral is (it is indeed!)
You mustn't monkey with the Creed.

COMMENTS

The intellectually sophisticated John Henderson and his wild sister Mary Lunn both end up badly: the sister becoming "an appalling bore," and her brother declining without his wine. So there *really* is a moral to the poem, even though Belloc can't resist playing with that notion as well. Once again, his tight tetrameter couplets are impeccable.

A much younger contemporary of Belloc was the talented South African poet Roy Campbell, who frequently used the couplet to vent his frustrations. When the British public exposed its unabashed sentimentality by its enthusiastic response to J.C. Squire's poem "To a Bull-dog," Campbell was disgusted. In the poem, Squire laments the death of his friend Willy (Major William Smith) to Mamie, the dead man's bull-dog.

We shan't see Willy any more, Mamie,
He won't be coming any more:
He came back once and again and again,
But he won't get leave any more.

According to Campbell's biographer, Peter Alexander, the poet hated dogs as much as he hated sentimentality. This is Campbell's response in "The Georgiad":

Jack Squire though his own tear-drops sploshes
In his great, flat, trochaical galoshes . . .
Now as he would exalt to deathless Fame

His vanished Lycidas, "Willie" by name,
And to the dead man's pet his grief expresses,
Outslobbering the bulldog he caresses . . .
The patient monster as he listens drops
A sympathetic trickle from his chops,
And both together mix the mutual moan,
Squire for the dead, and Fido for a bone.

When Campbell and his wife Mary lived in London, they sometimes associated with the Bloomsbury Group, although Campbell detested their pretentiousness and most of their *au courant* notions, especially the sexual freedom that was vigorously espoused and practiced by Vita and Harold Nicolson. In the following excerpt from "The Georgiad," Campbell compares their casual sexual encounters to the random matings of dogs.

The garden lawn provides a sort of Lido
For basking "Billykins" and sprawling "Fido,"
The garden path—a sort of Rotten Row
Where oft a merry pick-a-back they go;
While "Snap" and "Spot" their playful whiskers twitch
The lustful "Towser" quits his lawful bitch,
The bashful "Mamie," famed in Georgian lay,
Who straight is covered by the faithful "Tray,"
And so the amorous springtime glides away.

Devoid of Campbell's bitterness, but equally effective is the black humor in the following couplet poem written by the distinguished contemporary poet X.J. Kennedy.

At the Last Rites for Two Hotrodders

Sheeted in steel, embedded face to face,
They idle now in feelingless embrace,
The only ones at last who had the nerve
To meet head-on, not chicken out and swerve.

Inseparable, in one closed car they roll
Down the stoned aisle and on out to a hole,
Wheeled by the losers: six of fledging beard,
Black-jacket and glum, who also steered
Toward absolute success with total pride,
But, inches from it, felt, and turned aside.

Another master of the contemporary couplet is the English poet Wendy Cope. One of her excellent short poems is a response to Belloc's famous couplet poem entitled "Fatigue."

Fatigue

I'm tired of Love: I'm still more tired of Rhyme.
But Money gives me pleasure all the time.

Here's Cope's response.

Variation on Belloc's "Fatigue"

I hardly ever tire of love or rhyme—
That's why I'm poor and have a rotten time.

Here are three more couplet poems written by Cope. Notice that in the first couplet of the first poem, Cope's clever and rather ridiculous rhyme of *talk a lot* and *Eliot* forces us to sound out the poet's name incorrectly, which, in the humorous context of the poem, enhances our pleasure.

Poem Composed in Santa Barbara

The poets talk. They talk a lot.
They talk of T.S. Eliot.
One is anti. One is pro.
How hard they think! How much they know!
They're happy. A cicada sings.
We women talk of other things.

The South Bank Poetry Library, London

This is a pleasant library. I'd enjoy every minute
But for the danger of meeting other poets in it.

Two Cures for Love

1 Don't see him. Don't phone or write a letter.
2 The easy way: get to know him better.

A NOTE ABOUT THE FIGURES OF SPEECH

Pope and the Augustans, those masters of the heroic couplet, were also renowned for their high eloquence, their classical allusions, and their sophisticated use of tropes. These literary tropes (meaning "turns of phrase") are also known as the figures of speech. The figures are poetic devices used by poets and other writers to enhance their work. Although fuller definitions can be found in numerous poetry handbooks, it might be a good time to quickly review the more popular figures. In doing so, I'll cite one example from the countless examples contained in the many poems included in this book.

apostrophe: a direct address to someone absent (possibly deceased), something abstract (like envy), or something not human (such as the wind). (See Yeats's "O chestnut-tree" on page 194 in chapter thirteen.)

conceit: an extended metaphor. (See Marlowe's comparison of Faustus and Paris on page 43 in chapter four.)

hyperbole: an exaggeration, often an outlandish one. (See Dryden's comparison of Richard Flecknoe to Augustus Caesar in this chapter.)

images: sharp descriptions that create a visual picture in the mind of the reader. (See Yeats's description of the Sphinx-like beast on page 49 in chapter four.)

irony: an intentional discrepancy between what's being said and what's actually meant. There are many types of literary irony. (See page 117 in chapter eight for Shelley's Ozymandias, who boasts, "Look on my works, ye Mighty, and despair!")

metonymy: a reference to something (or someone) which employs a word or phrase related to the referent. For example, referring to *the crown* for a king. (See Milton's use of *light* for *vision* on page 116 in chapter eight.)

metaphor: a comparison between two things which are generally not associated with each other. (See Shakespeare comparing death to an "undiscovered country" on page 17 in chapter one.)

onomatopoeia: a word or phrase that seems to imitate its meaning. For example, *thud*, or *crack*, or *hiss*. (See Poe's raven "tapping, tapping" on page 161 in chapter eleven.)

oxymoron: a combination of words that seems contradictory. (See Pope's "shallow draughts intoxicate" on page 177 in chapter twelve.)

personification: treating a concept as if it were a person. (See Milton's personification of patience on page 117 in chapter eight.)

pun: a play on words, usually for humorous purposes. There are many kinds of puns. (See Jan D. Hodge's pun on the word *parts* on page 188 in chapter twelve.)

rhetorical question: a question that doesn't expect a reply. (See Shelley's "If Winter comes, can Spring be far behind?" on page 132 in chapter nine.)

simile: a metaphor using the words *like* or *as*. (See Keats's "like some watcher of the skies" and "like stout Cortez" on page 118 in chapter eight.)

synecdoche: using a part to represent the whole. (See Shakespeare's use of *rhyme* for his entire poem on page 115 in chapter eight.)

These are only a few of the many tropes that poets use to enhance their work. It's important to recognize them in our reading (and study) of the great poetic tradition so that, eventually, they might start to appear naturally in our own work. Nevertheless, the tropes can also be dangerous, especially if they seem forced or (even worse) silly. This can be particularly true with similes, since so many young poets seem to believe that this useful trope is actually the essence of poetic expression, and that it's necessary to fill their poems with *like* and *as* comparisons that are often quite strained. On the other hand, it's better to attempt such tropes and fail (as with unusual diction) than to never work at developing a facility for the various figures.

ASSIGNMENT 5

Write a satirical poem of at least sixteen lines in tetrameter couplets.

1. Attack someone. Pick a well-known figure (even one from the pop culture) who gets under your skin. Then use the inherent powers of the couplet to poke fun at the person and entertain your readers. In my workshop classes, I always eliminate politicians because they seem to be such easy targets. Also, be sure to pick a single person, not a group or a concept, as this will allow for more specificity.
2. Use the hard-hitting short couplet, trying to control your tetrameters the way Belloc does. Keep the iambs tight, and try to limit yourself to only one substitution within every four lines.
3. Use only closed couplets and solid rhymes.
4. Try to incorporate some unique rhymes. In satirical and humorous poetry, readers greatly appreciate the occasional peculiar rhyme, even one that makes them roll their eyes.
5. Be careful not to syntactically force your rhymes. Sometimes syntactical inversions made to hit the rhyme can be effectively humorous, but they're also difficult to pull off, so avoid them for this particular assignment.
6. Have fun!

CHAPTER 8 | THE SONNET

The sonnet, from the Italian *sonetto* ("little song"), is one of the most popular and exacting of all poetic forms, and it's the most popular fixed form in English-language poetry. Usually lyric in manner, the little sonnet has contributed countless and unforgettable works of art to the history of Western civilization. In the various European languages, extraordinary sonnets have been written by Dante, Petrarch, Camões, Pierre de Ronsard, Joachim du Bellay, Goethe, Pushkin, Charles Baudelaire, Stéphane Mallarmé, Rainer Maria Rilke, and Borges. Similarly, a listing of the English-language masters of the sonnet reads like a virtual who's who of English and American literature: Shakespeare, Donne, Milton, Wordsworth, Shelley, Keats, Elizabeth Browning, Edwin Arlington Robinson, Frost, Millay, Nemerov, and many others.

The sonnet is a rather short poem, being only fourteen lines of iambic pentameter. Thus, the challenge is to say something significant and memorable in such a limited space (approximately 140 syllables). Pound once claimed that "six lines can make you immortal," and this is certainly true if we extend the number of lines to fourteen. Wordsworth, in his classic sonnet "Nuns Fret Not at Their Convent's Narrow Room," discusses the seemingly contradictory fact that confinement can actually create not only power but freedom.

Nuns Fret Not at Their Convent's Narrow Room

Nuns fret not at their convent's narrow room;
And hermits are contented with their cells;
And students with their pensive citadels;
Maids at the wheel, the weaver at his loom,

> Sit blithe and happy; bees that soar for bloom,
> High as the highest Peak of Furness-fells,
> Will murmur by the hour in foxglove bells:
> In truth the prison, into which we doom
> Ourselves, no prison is: and hence for me,
> In sundry moods, 'twas pastime to be bound
> Within the Sonnet's scanty plot of ground;
> Pleased if some Souls (for such there needs must be)
> Who have felt the weight of too much liberty,
> Should find brief solace there, as I have found.

Thus, the isolated nun praying in her small cell does not feel inhibited at all. Instead, she's able to more effectively concentrate on higher things and be content. Similarly, the sonnet itself is never a "prison" for the serious poet, but rather the perfect place of "solace" where writers can pursue the sublime.

THE ORIGINS OF THE SONNET

The first sonnet was created in the medieval Sicilian court of Frederick II, the Holy Roman Emperor, in the thirteenth century. It was later used by Dante, but it truly came into its own with Petrarch and the Renaissance. Later, as the Renaissance spread west and north, so did the sonnet, moving into Spain, Portugal, France, and finally England. The first English sonnets were composed by Sir Thomas Wyatt, and the English form of the sonnet was created by his friend Henry Howard, the Earl of Surrey. Eventually, the sonnet was taken up by Edmund Spenser, Shakespeare, Donne, and Milton. After the Augustan age of the heroic couplet, Wordsworth and the Romantics revived the sonnet, and it has been written by serious poets ever since. (See appendix II for more information about the history of the sonnet.)

THE ITALIAN (PETRARCHAN) SONNET

Although there are numerous variations on the sonnet form, there are two fundamental formats: the Italian sonnet and the English sonnet.

The Italian sonnet employs a two-part structure consisting of an octave and a sestet. The octave always rhymes *abbaabba*, whereas the sestet can rhyme in a variety of ways, most commonly *cdecde* or *cdcdcd*. Given its two-part structure, the Italian sonnet is generally seen as a *response* format, in which a theme (or issue, or query, or problem, or argument) is raised in the octave, and a response (or solution, or reflection, or conclusion) is offered in the sestet. Since its rhyme scheme demands at least four rhymes on two different sounds, it would be reasonable to assume that Italian sonnets would be very difficult to compose in English, but this difficulty has not discouraged countless English-language poets from writing masterful Italian sonnets.

THE ENGLISH (SHAKESPEAREAN) SONNET

The English sonnet consists of three quatrains rhyming *abab*, *cdcd*, and *efef*, followed by a concluding couplet, *gg*. The advantages of the English sonnet are obvious: a less demanding rhyme scheme, the potential power of the final couplet, and more structural options (since the lines of the English sonnet can be divided in numerous ways: 4-4-4-2, 12-2, 8-6, 4-4-6, etc.). The concluding couplet is especially attractive to many poets because its natural compression, emphasis, and epigrammatic nature allow it—when used effectively—to end the sonnet firmly and memorably.

Originally, of course, the sonnet was exclusively a love poem, but the Portuguese poet Camões (and later, Milton in England) expanded the form's thematic parameters, and now there seems to be no subject that the little sonnet can't tackle.

[SAMPLE SONNETS]

Let's begin with Shakespeare.

Not Marble, Nor the Gilded Monuments

Not marble, nor the gilded monuments
Of princes, shall outlive this powerful rhyme;

But you shall shine more bright in these contents
Than unswept stone besmear'd with sluttish time.
When wasteful war shall statues overturn,
And broils root out the work of masonry,
Nor Mars his sword nor war's quick fire shall burn
The living record of your memory.

'Gainst death and all-oblivious enmity
Shall you pace forth; your praise shall still find room
Even in the eyes of all posterity
That wears this world out to the ending doom.
So, till the judgment that yourself arise,
You live in this, and dwell in lovers' eyes.

COMMENTS

Shakespeare audaciously exalts the power of his sonnet ("this powerful rhyme"), which he claims will outlast all other human tributes and monuments, to praise his beloved until the end of time (the final "judgment"). Given the beauty and the popularity of this little poem, Shakespeare's lovely *sonetto* just might succeed in doing exactly what it says it will do!

As we continue through the many sample poems in this book, it will be impossible, of course, to stop at every line to observe the careful and skilled use of meter employed by the various poets. Hopefully, the reader will closely observe what all of these poetic masters are doing. Shakespeare, for example, in his unforgettable opening two lines, uses alliteration, punctuation, a metrical elevation (*nor*), and a final anapestic substitution (*-erful rhyme*) to enhance his key words with the powerful stresses of his iambic pentameter.

On His Blindness

When I consider how my light is spent
Ere half my days in this dark world and wide,
And that one talent which is death to hide
Lodged with me useless, though my soul more bent

To serve therewith my Maker, and present
My true account, lest he returning chide,
"Doth God exact day-labour, light denied?"
I fondly ask. But Patience, to prevent
That murmur, soon replies, "God doth not need
Either man's work or his own gifts. Who best
Bear his mild yoke, they serve him best. His state
Is kingly: thousands at his bidding speed,
And post o'er land and ocean without rest;
They also serve who only stand and wait."

COMMENTS

Milton's famous Italian sonnet about his blindness deals with a crucial question that assailed the poet's Puritan conscience: How can I satisfy "my Maker" if I'm unable to work as I did before? In raising this problem, Milton alludes to the famous Parable of the Talents (Matt. 24:14–30) in which the wary servant who foolishly buried his master's gold piece (talent) is reprimanded when the master returns because he didn't increase its value like the other two servants. Thus, God gives everyone special "talents" in life, and we are required to use them effectively. But Milton's concern about his inability to properly use his talents (because he is blind) is answered in the sonnet by the personified figure of Patience, who points out that God doesn't need his talents, and that Milton's eagerness to act is sufficient, since "They also serve who only stand and wait."

In this poem, and in some of his other Italian sonnets, Milton intentionally breaks down the traditional distinction between the octave and the sestet by enjambing the eighth line into the ninth. But he does this enjambment so smoothly that his blurring of the normal two-part structure is barely noticeable to most readers.

Ozymandias

I met a traveler from an antique land
Who said: Two vast and trunkless legs of stone

Stand in the desert. Near them, on the sand,
Half sunk, a shattered visage lies, whose frown,
And wrinkled lip, and sneer of cold command,
Tell that its sculptor well those passions read
Which yet survive, stamped on these lifeless things,
The hand that mocked them and the heart that fed;
And on the pedestal these words appear:
"My name is Ozymandias, king of kings:
Look on my works, ye Mighty, and despair!"
Nothing beside remains. Round the decay
Of that colossal wreck, boundless and bare
The lone and level sands stretch far away.

COMMENTS

Shelley's ingenious sonnet with its odd rhyme scheme was written in 1817, two years after Waterloo, and it clearly refers to Napoleon. Notice how its excellent final line seems to mimic the meaning and thus "stretch" away—due to Shelley's long vowel sounds and his mostly monosyllabic words.

On First Looking Into Chapman's Homer

Much have I travelled in the realms of gold,
And many goodly states and kingdoms seen;
Round many western islands have I been
Which bards in fealty to Apollo hold.
Oft of one wide expanse had I been told
That deep-browned Homer ruled as his demesne;
Yet did I never breathe its pure serene
Till I heard Chapman speak out loud and bold:
Then felt I like some watcher of the skies
When a new planet swims into his ken;
Or like stout Cortez when with eagle eyes
He stared at the Pacific—and all his men
Looked at each other with a wild surmise—
Silent, upon a peak in Darien.

COMMENTS

Late one autumn evening in 1816, Keats and his good friend Charles Cowden-Clarke were entranced by their first encounter with the Homeric translations of George Chapman, which had been published two hundred years earlier. Apparently, Keats was unable to sleep later that night, since the next morning at ten o'clock, Cowden-Clark found this immortal Italian sonnet waiting at his door. Within the sonnet, after its careful and enthusiastic setup in the octave, Keats uses two striking similes to express his powerful feelings of discovery: the astronomer who discovers a new heavenly body and the explorer who discovers a vast new ocean. (The fact that it was actually Balboa who discovered the Pacific Ocean in 1513, and not Cortez, has never undermined the success and the popularity of Keats's poem!)

How Do I Love Thee?

How do I love thee? Let me count the ways.
I love thee to the depth and breadth and height
My soul can reach, when feeling out of sight
For the ends of Being and ideal Grace.
I love thee to the level of everyday's
Most quiet need, by sun and candle-light.
I love thee freely, as men strive for Right;
I love thee purely, as they turn from Praise.
I love thee with the passion put to use
In my old griefs, and with my childhood's faith.
I love thee with a love I seemed to lose
With my lost saints—I love thee with the breath,
Smiles, tears, of all my life!—and, if God choose,
I shall but love thee better after death.

COMMENTS

Certainly Robert Browning was a very fortunate man to be loved in such a powerful way! Elizabeth Browning's justly famous love sonnet is a rather risky "list" poem that's full of repetition, especially the words *I love thee* (which she uses eight times, with a ninth variant in the final line). But the poet finds ways to make her relentless structure work effectively, especially her careful use of specifics, her engaging and enthusiastic tone, and her careful rhythm.

Leda and the Swan

A sudden blow: the great wings beating still
Above the staggering girl, her thighs caressed
By the dark webs, her nape caught in his bill,
He holds her helpless breast upon his breast.

How can those terrified vague fingers push
The feathered glory from her loosening thighs?
And how can body, laid in that white rush
But feel the strange heart beating where it lies?

A shudder in the loins engenders there
The broken wall, the burning roof and tower
And Agamemnon dead.
Being so caught up,
So mastered by the brute blood of the air,
Did she put on his knowledge with his power
Before the indifferent beak could let her drop?

COMMENTS

Although Yeats didn't write many sonnets, the great success of this poem about the seduction of Leda (mother of Helen and Clytemnestra), certainly makes us wish he'd written more. The violence and the horror of the rape is immediately signaled in the sonnet's first two iambs ("A sudden blow"), and it continues throughout the poem. Nevertheless, the sonnet also wonders if, during her perverse violation by Zeus, the beautiful Leda, a mere mortal, somehow fathomed some aspect of the god's divinity ("put on his knowledge").

Within his Italian sonnet, Yeats chooses to divide his octave into two distinct stanzas and to modify the normal rhyme scheme to *abab*, *cdcd*. Yeats was known to have had an extraordinary natural talent for both rhythm and rhyme. Eventually, he began to believe that his rhyming was a bit too facile, so he started using off-rhymes and sight-rhymes in his work (like *up* and *drop* or *push* and *rush*).

What Lips My Lips Have Kissed, and Where, and Why

What lips my lips have kissed, and where, and why,
I have forgotten, and what arms have lain
Under my head till morning; but the rain
Is full of ghosts tonight, that tap and sigh
Upon the glass and listen for reply,
And in my heart there stirs a quiet pain
For unremembered lads that not again
Will turn to me at midnight with a cry.
Thus in the winter stands the lonely tree,
Nor knows what birds have vanished one by one,
Yet knows its boughs more silent than before:
I cannot say what loves have come and gone,
I only know that summer sang in me
A little while, that in me sings no more.

COMMENTS

In this powerful Italian sonnet, Edna St. Vincent Millay, an American Pulitzer recipient (1923), portrays a tragic woman who's living alone after a lifetime of forgotten lovers—who now haunt her like "ghosts." The fact that her "summer" is still vaguely remembered, although it "sings no more," makes the poem especially poignant. Throughout the sonnet, Millay individualizes her rather common theme (lost love) with her careful language and her natural expression. Right from the poem's title (and its opening line), Millay intrigues us with a syntactically curious (yet natural-sounding) string of ten monosyllabic words. This kind of direct, simple, and evocative language continues throughout the poem, which ends effectively with seven more monosyllabic words.

Yet Do I Marvel

I doubt not God is good, well-meaning, kind.
And did He stoop to quibble could tell why
The little buried mole continues blind,
Why flesh that mirrors Him must someday die,
Make plain the reason tortured Tantalus
Is baited by the fickle fruit, declare
If merely brute caprice dooms Sisyphus
To struggle up a never-ending stair.
Inscrutable His ways are, and immune
To catechism by a mind too strewn
With petty cares to slightly understand
What awful brain compels His awful hand.
Yet do I marvel at this curious thing:
To make a poet black, and bid him sing!

COMMENTS

Like the Biblical Job, Countee Cullen, one of the foremost poets of the Harlem Renaissance, wonders why God allows suffering in the world, and he uses (rather curiously) the mythological figures of Sisyphus and Tantalus as examples. Tantalus was a son of Zeus who was punished for giving ambrosia and nectar to human beings. As a consequence, Tantalus was placed chin-deep in water with branches of fruit hanging over his head, just out of reach (thus the word *tantalize*). Also like Job, Cullen clearly accepts the fact that he can never comprehend the answer to his question, since his small human mind could never apprehend God's "awful brain" (where the word *awful* is being used in the Biblical sense of "awesome" or "awe-inspiring"). Then Cullen ends his sonnet with gratitude, reflecting with wonder on the fact that God has given him poetic talents and "bid him sing!"

"Yet Do I Marvel" is an oddly constructed sonnet that begins with two English sonnet quatrains and concludes with three couplets. Fortunately, Cullen carefully constructs his poem so that his first two couplets do not diminish or detract from the rising power of his final couplet.

Two Girls

I saw again in a dream the other night
Something I saw in daylight years ago,
A path in the rainy woods, a shaft of light,
And two girls walking together through shadow,
Through dazzle, till I lost them on their way
In gloom embowering beyond the glade.
The bright oblivion that belongs to day
Covered their steps, nothing of them remained,
Until the darkness brought them forth again
To the rainy glitter and the silver light,
The ancient leaves that had not fallen then.
Two girls, going forever out of sight,
Talking of lovers, maybe, and of love:
Not that blind life they'd be the mothers of.

COMMENTS

Howard Nemerov's excellent Shakespearean sonnet deals with the fact that young people can never conceive (or even imagine) the lives that they will eventually create for themselves. The poem ends with a marvelous couplet, effectively using the word *of* to rhyme with the rhyme-poor word *love*.

At the Center

The pianist is playing Debussy
Beside the lobby cappuccino bar—
Soft smiles and pastels everywhere. You see,

The point's not to remind you where you are
Or *how* you are; the point is not to dwell
On thoughts like these. Look at this normal crowd,
Such as you'd find in any good hotel.
But why does no one say its name out loud?

Later you pass through elevator doors;
Rising to higher levels, you recall
Rumors you've heard of rumors from these floors—
How some guests never leave, how they display
A preference for short hair, or none at all,
How no one asks how long you plan to stay.

COMMENTS

This eerie sonnet by the contemporary poet R.S. Gwynn skillfully uses memorable specifics ("the pianist," "Debussy," "cappuccino bar," etc.) to describe the unidentified but ominous "Center." Then right before the break, in the eighth line, the mysterious narrator asks, "But why does no one say its name out loud?" The reason, of course, is clearly revealed in the poem's sestet: This is a cancer center where some of the patients will "never leave" and where "no one asks how long you plan to stay."

The Psychic

Yes, the police have called me many times,
And generally they've taken my advice.
I keep a scrapbook of uncommon crimes
I've helped with, when the vision was precise
Enough to lead the searchers to the scene—
Most murders, as it happens, are within
Three miles of home and in the day's routine,
Stopped by a stranger (or the next of kin).

Hand me a scarf the victim wore around
Her neck—or else her glasses, or a ring.

I'll see a place: and there the body's found.
Finding the killer? That's a different thing.
Bodies are easy; their passivity
Gives them away. Guilt is too quick for me.

COMMENTS

Gail White, another contemporary author of ingenious sonnets, uses this carefully crafted English sonnet to carry a short dramatic monologue. The conversational voice of the psychic is engaging, direct, and revealing—finally reflecting on her psychic inability to perceive the guilt of the killer (and possibly her own guilts as well).

The Road

He sometimes felt that he had missed his life
By being far too busy looking for it.
Searching the distance, he often turned to find
That he had passed some milestone unaware,
And someone else was walking next to him,
First friends, then lovers, now children and a wife.
They were good company—generous, kind,
But equally bewildered to be there.

He noticed then that no one chose the way—
All seemed to drift by some collective will.
The path grew easier with each passing day,
Since it was worn and mostly sloped downhill.
The road ahead seemed hazy in the gloom.
Where was it he had meant to go, and with whom?

COMMENTS

Gioia's reflection about a man's path in life begins with a rather flat yet highly effective statement about the man's sense that he's "missed his life." Then the poem actually shows the man as he (metaphorically) walks down his life's path ("The Road"). The sonnet's rather unusual rhyme scheme still concludes with a powerful couplet, which reveals that not only is the path ahead "hazy," but that the man's original intentions have now been forgotten: "Where was it he had meant to go, and with whom?"

A NOTE ABOUT DIFFICULT THEMES

New poets are naturally attracted to difficult themes—love, death, religion, patriotism and war, and social issues (like the environment, etc.). This is perfectly natural, since these are subjects of momentous importance in all our lives, but for that very reason, they're potentially dangerous topics for poetry. The reason is two-fold: (1) so much has already been written about these subjects in the past, and (2) there can be a tendency in writing such poems to get rather preachy.

Regarding the first problem, the solution is clear: Poets must find new and unique ways to deal with these subjects. Often this can be achieved by combining an interesting starting point with specific images and details. For example, the Gwynn sonnet cited above is clearly about death, but it's not full of grand pronouncements that we've all heard before. On the contrary, it's set at a cancer center which doesn't, at first, seem like a cancer center at all, and the poem is full of very specific details and "rumors" that make us think about human mortality—and maybe even about our own mortality.

Regarding the second problem, there's nothing more doomed to failure than those countless well-intentioned poems that tell us how important peace is, or how wonderful the rainforests are, or how terrible racism is, etc. Such poems often sound rather self-righteous (and childish), and sophisticated modern poets wisely deal with such subjects through specificity and understatement. One of the best poems about racism in the twentieth century is Dudley Randall's "Ballad of Birmingham," which we read in chapter six. Randall's poem speaks for itself; it doesn't have to preach. In fact, it's far more effective in its intentions because it *refuses* to fall into any of the obvious clichés about the evils of racism. Thus, poets can certainly have strong opinions about difficult subjects, but they need to find new and intriguing ways to make them work poetically. Donne, Milton, and Gerard Manley Hopkins (to name a few) wrote powerful poems about their Christian faith that are still memorable today because they found new and interesting ways to avoid clichéd and simple-minded thinking.

ASSIGNMENT 6

Write a sonnet, using either the Italian or English format. Although there are many variants of the sonnet form, it's preferable that new writers learn to use the two classic formats that have served poets so well for over six hundred years.

1. Use only pentameters and solid rhymes.
2. Avoid the pop culture.
3. Avoid old-fashioned diction.
4. Avoid convoluted syntax that's manipulated to hit the rhymes.

CHAPTER 9 | THE TERCET

A tercet is a poetic stanza consisting of three lines, usually with rhyme. A poem consisting of such stanzas is called a *tercet poem*. The three-line structure is certainly peculiar, lacking the natural symmetry of the couplet or the quatrain. Some prosodists feel that the form is inherently unsettling to the reader, but that does not seem to be the case in practice. On the other hand, there's no denying the oddness of the tercet (which immediately attracts our attention visually), and this peculiarity can definitely be used to the poet's advantage.

A triplet is a tercet that consists of three lines that end with the same rhyme sound, thus *aaa*. A triplet poem continues the same pattern: *aaa*, *bbb*, *ccc*, etc. Sometimes the terms *triplet* and *tercet* are used interchangeably, but for the purposes of this book, the term *triplet* will be used to indicate the rather rare *aaa* tercet. Obviously, the rhymes in a triplet are extremely conspicuous, and the dominance of its final rhyme-sounds tends to give each triplet stanza a uniqueness and individuality that sharply contrasts with the other stanzas in the poem. Thus, triplets draw a lot of attention to themselves.

Also, given the demands of the rhymes, triplet poems are difficult to write successfully; thus, they're quite rare in English—and usually quite short. As we've seen with Belloc's "Lord Lucky" (on page 104 in chapter seven), sometimes triplets are inserted into couplet poems for emphasis and expansion. In the seventeenth century, Dryden was especially fond of incorporating occasional triplets into his heroic couplets for development and intensification. Nevertheless, in the long history of English-language verse, there are only a few famous triplet poems. Here's one by Robert Herrick.

Upon Julia's Clothes

Whenas in silks my Julia goes,
Then, then, methinks, how sweetly flows
The liquefaction of her clothes.

Next, when I cast mine eyes, and see
That brave vibration, each way free,
O, how that glittering taketh me!

COMMENTS

The sensuality of Herrick's poem seems to be enhanced by his smooth iambic tetrameter and his triplet (thus excessively sensuous) rhymes. Also, in such a short poem, the poet's dictional choices are given much more weight, as we can see with Herrick's unforgettable usage of the words *liquefaction* and *vibration*.

Similarly memorable is Tennyson's very different triplet poem, "The Eagle."

The Eagle

He clasps the crag with crooked hands;
Close to the sun in lonely lands,
Ringed with the azure world, he stands.

The wrinkled sea beneath him crawls;
He watches from his mountain walls,
And like a thunderbolt he falls.

COMMENTS

Notice that Tennyson, a master of poetic sound, is not at all ashamed to alliterate the letter *c* three times in his first tetrameter line, and then to emphasize a fourth *c* with the trochaic substitution (*Close to*) that begins his subsequent line. Notice also, at the end of the first triplet, that the poet uses the comma to set off, rather majestically, the last iamb (*he stands*)—thus also isolating the regal bird itself. With the exception of the rather exotic word *azure*, the diction of the poem is both simple and effective, yet at the heart of the poem's last line, Tennyson employs his only trisyllabic word (*thunderbolt*) to speed up the line and accentuate the sense of the eagle's downward flight.

[TERZA RIMA]

Terza rima poems consist of interlocking tercets that rhyme *aba*, *bcb*, *cdc*, etc. Thus, except for the first rhyme, the poem demands three rhymes for all its subsequent rhyme sounds. These interlocking rhymes tend to pull the listener's attention forward in a continuous flow. Sometimes the drive of a terza rima poem can seem endless, and often poets will conclude such poems with a couplet that rhymes with the central rhyme of the preceding stanza, thus creating three rhymes for that particular sound. Given this natural tendency to glide forward, terza rima is especially well-suited for narration and description.

The most famous terza rima poem, of course, is Dante's *Commedia* (*The Divine Comedy*). Unfortunately, the three rhyme sounds of Dante's tercets naturally create difficulties for English translators, who will often modify the rhyme scheme (typically using *aba*, *cdc*, *efe*, etc.). Laurence Binyon, however, managed to compose a true English terza rima for his masterful translation of the *Commedia*, which was published in 1947. Here are the classic opening lines of canto III of *The Inferno*, in which Dante and Virgil (Dante's guide and master) approach the gates of Hell and read the sign (the first three tercets) posted above the gates.

> Through me the way is to the City of Woe:
>   Through me the way into the Eternal Pain;
>   Through me the way among the lost below.
> Righteousness did my maker on high constrain[1].
>   Me did Divine Authority uprear[2];
>   Me Supreme Wisdom and Primal Love sustain.

[1]compel [2]uphold

BEFORE I WAS, NO THINGS CREATED WERE
SAVE THE ETERNAL, AND I ETERNAL ABIDE.
RELINQUISH ALL HOPE, YE WHO ENTER HERE.
THESE WORDS, OF A DIM COLOUR, I ESPIED
WRITTEN ABOVE THE LINTEL OF A DOOR.
WHEREAT: "MASTER, THE SENSE IS HARD," I CRIED.
AND HE, AS ONE EXPERIENCED IN THAT LORE:
"HERE ALL MISGIVING MUST THY MIND REJECT.
HERE COWARDICE MUST DIE AND BE NO MORE.
WE ARE COME TO THE PLACE I TOLD THEE TO EXPECT,
WHERE THOU SHOULDST SEE THE PEOPLE WHOM PAIN STINGS
AND WHO HAVE LOST THE GOOD OF THE INTELLECT."
HIS HAND ON MINE, TO UPHOLD MY FALTERINGS,
WITH LOOKS OF CHEER THAT BADE ME COMFORT KEEP,
HE LED ME ON INTO THE SECRET THINGS.
HERE LAMENTATION, GROANS, AND WAILINGS DEEP
REVERBERATED THROUGH THE STARLESS AIR,
SO THAT IT MADE ME AT THE BEGINNING WEEP.
UNCOUTH TONGUES, HORRIBLE SHRIEKINGS OF DESPAIR,
SHRILL AND FAINT VOICES, CRIES OF PAIN AND RAGE,
AND, WITH IT ALL, SMITING OF HANDS, WERE THERE,
MAKING A TUMULT, NOTHING COULD ASSUAGE,
TO SWIRL IN THE AIR THAT KNOWS NO DAY OR NIGHT,
LIKE SAND WITHIN THE WHIRLWIND'S EDDYING CAGE.

COMMENTS

Dante took the symbology of numbers very seriously, especially the number three, which relates to the theological doctrine of the Holy Trinity. Thus, his masterpiece is composed in three-line terza rimas, and it's divided into three major parts (*Inferno*, *Purgatorio*, and *Paradiso*). Throughout the various cantos of the *Commedia*, Dante constantly uses other three-part structures, and we can clearly see an example in the second tercet above, where three crucial attributes are cited for God: authority, wisdom, and love.

The ninth line of canto III is one of the most famous lines in world literature, "Relinquish all hope, Ye who enter here," and the shrieking that the poet hears within the gates of Hell begins to prepare the reader for the coming horrors of the damned. For Dante, of course, the underlying cause of all these miseries is sin, which he considered to be a failure of the intellect. Like Aristotle, who believed that man was, foremost, an intelligent creature, Dante believed that vice was an abdication of our reasoning faculties and thus a betrayal of God. This crucial overall theme of the *Commedia* surfaces again in the last line of the sixth tercet, when Virgil explains to Dante that those in hell "have lost the good of the intellect." Thus, Binyon, in his carefully crafted translation, not only gives us the descriptions and the theological content of Dante's original, but he approximates the melodic feel of its ever-flowing terza rima.

In the English language, the most well-known terza rima poem is Shelley's "Ode to the West Wind." This poem is also highly descriptive, effectively using the flowing nature of the terza rima to mimic the west wind. Shelley's seventy-line poem consists of five sections, each containing four tercets with a concluding couplet, and it ends with Shelley's famous question: "If Winter comes, can Spring be far behind?"

The following poem is a much more modern (and odder) use of terza rima; it was written by the English poet James Elroy Flecker.

In Hospital

Would I might lie like this, without the pain,
  For seven years—as one with snowy hair,
Who in the high tower dreams his dying reign—

  Lie here and watch the walls—how grey and bare,
The metal bed-post, the uncoloured screen,
  The mat, the jug, the cupboard, and the chair;

And served by an old woman, calm and clean,
  Her misted face familiar, yet unknown,
Who comes in silence, and departs unseen,

And with no other visit, lie alone,
Nor stir, except I had my food to find
In that dull bowl Diogenes might own.

And down my window I would draw the blind,
And never look without, but, waiting, hear
A noise of rain, a whistling of the wind.

And only know that flame-foot Spring is near
By trilling birds, or by the patch of sun
Crouching behind my curtain. So, in fear,

Noon-dreams should enter, softly, one by one,
And throng about the floor, and float and play
And flicker on the screen, while minutes run—

The last majestic minutes of the day—
And with the mystic shadows, Shadow grows.
Then the grey square of wall should fade away,

And glow again, and open, and disclose
The shimmering lake in which the planets swim
And all that lake a dewdrop on a rose.

COMMENTS

Flecker, a graduate of Oxford, joined the British consular service and was posted to Beirut, where he contracted tuberculosis. He eventually died in 1915 at the age of thirty in Switzerland. In his terza rima poem, Flecker heightens our sense of his entrapment in the hospital bed with a series of mundane but very effective details ("The mat, the jug, the cupboard, and the chair," the "old woman," "the blind" on the window, etc.). The narrator's illness has essentially trapped him within his mind, where he feels like the ancient Greek cynic Diogenes, who lived in an earthenware tub. But his illness, and maybe the drugs, have left his perception of the world around him rather uncertain, and the poem ends with a fantastic and quite surreal image of the entire universe as "a dewdrop on a rose."

Here's a much more contemporary use of terza rima by Richard Wilbur.

Parable

I read how Quixote in his random ride
Came to a crossing once, and lest he lose
The purity of chance, would not decide

Whither to fare, but wished his horse to choose.
For glory lay wherever he might turn.
His head was light with pride, his horse's shoes

Were heavy, and he headed for the barn.

COMMENTS

As Flecker did in the previous poem, Wilbur heightens the flow of his terza rima with various enjambments, both within the tercets and between them. The last enjambment is particularly effective because we're forced to wait until the last line of the poem (which is also its own stanza) to learn that the horse's shoes "Were heavy," thus setting up the ironic ending of the poem, which powerfully skewers the terrible vanity of Don Quixote and his self-important notions about "glory" and the "purity of chance." As mentioned earlier, terza rima poems often end with a couplet that rhymes with the middle line of the previous tercet. This gives a natural closure to the form's forward movement, but Wilbur ends his poem with a single-line stanza, giving the poem a rather flat ending. This is further reinforced by his intentional off-rhyme in the final word of the poem (*barn*). Both of these poetic devices combine to bring the poem to a thudding end, which is perfectly appropriate in this "parable," which, following Cervantes, successfully deflates the pretensions of Don Quixote.

[OTHER TERCET FORMS]

Over the centuries, English poets have used other tercet rhyme schemes beside the triplet and terza rima. Here's a rather extraordinary tercet poem written by Oscar Wilde that rhymes *aab*, *ccb*, *dde*, *ffe*, etc., interlocking the final lines of each pair of tercets.

The Harlot's House

We caught the tread of dancing feet,
We loitered down the moonlit street,
And stopped beneath the harlot's house.

Inside, above the din and fray,
We heard the loud musicians play
The "Treues Liebes Herz" of Strauss.

Like strange mechanical grotesques,
Making fantastic arabesques,
The shadows raced across the blind.

We watched the ghostly dancers spin
To sound of horn and violin,
Like black leaves wheeling in the wind.

Like wire-pulled automatons,
Slim silhouetted skeletons
Went sliding through the slow quadrille.

They took each other by the hand,
And danced a stately saraband;
Their laughter echoed thin and shrill.

Sometimes a clockwork puppet pressed
A phantom lover to her breast,
Sometimes they seemed to try to sing.

Sometimes a horrible marionette
Came out, and smoked its cigarette
Upon the steps like a live thing.

Then, turning to my love, I said,
"The dead are dancing with the dead,
The dust is whirling with the dust."

But she—she heard the violin,
And left my side and entered in:
Love passed into the house of lust.

Then suddenly the tune went false,
The dancers wearied of the waltz,
The shadows ceased to wheel and whirl.

And down the long and silent street,
The dawn, with silver-sandalled feet,
Crept like a frightened girl.

COMMENTS

This terrifying poem is made even more so by the beautiful and lulling melody of Wilde's iambic tetrameters and his creepy dictional choices (*grotesques*, *automatons*, *marionette*, etc.). When things go shockingly wrong near the end of the poem (stanza ten), Wilde uses a telling dash in the tercet's first line, "But she—she heard the violin." Later, he brings his tercet poem to a rather hopeless and horrific conclusion by truncating the last line to an unsettling trimeter. Wilde also introduces his final line with a powerful trochaic substitution (*Crept like*)—since even the personified dawn is "frightened" by what has happened.

In the twentieth-century, the distinguished American poet May Sarton used a more common variant of the tercet (rhyming *aba*, *cdc*, *efe*, etc.) in the following poem.

Dutch Interior

Pieter de Hooch (1629–1682)

I recognize the quiet and the charm,
This safe enclosed room where a woman sews
And life is tempered, orderly, and calm.

Through the Dutch door, half-open, sunlight streams
And throws a pale square down on the red tiles.
The cosy black dog suns himself and dreams.

Even the bed is sheltered, it encloses,
A cupboard to keep people safe from harm,
Where copper glows with the warm flush of roses.

The atmosphere is all domestic, human,
Chaos subdued by the sheer power of need.
This is a room where I have lived as woman,

Lived too what the Dutch painter does not tell—
The wild skies overhead, dissolving, breaking,
And how that broken light is never still,

And how the roar of waves is always near,
What bitter tumult, treacherous and cold,
Attacks the solemn charm year after year!

It must be felt as peace won and maintained
Against those terrible antagonists—
How many from this quiet room have drowned?

How many left to go, drunk on the wind,
And take their ships into heartbreaking seas;
How many whom no woman's peace could bind?

Bent to her sewing, she looks drenched in calm.
Raw grief is disciplined to the fine thread.
But in her heart this woman is the storm;

Alive, deep in herself, holds wind and rain,
Remaking chaos into an intimate order
Where sometimes light flows through a windowpane.

COMMENTS

In observing a Vermeer-like interior painted by the Dutch master Pieter de Hooch, the narrator not only sees through the serene, gently lit domestic scene of the picture, but she actually enters into the poem at the end of the fourth stanza: "This is a room where I have lived as woman." In doing so, the narrator is then able to describe what's going on *beneath* the surface of the picture, describing what Pieter de Hooch "does not tell": the "chaos" and the "bitter tumult." Eventually, the narrator reveals that the Dutch woman, who appears so calm, is not only the center of the storm, but she *is* the storm. Notice how Sarton uses her iambic meter and a powerful elevation to create this effect in the last line of the penultimate tercet.

> Bŭt ín | hĕr heárt | thĭs wóm | ăn ís | thĕ stórm;

The metrical elevation of the word *is* gives great power to the line and to the meaning of the poem. Similarly, Sarton's placement of the word *sometimes* in the poem's final line gives increased emphasis to her overall point that de Hooch's serenity is only a "sometimes" thing. The word *sometimes* is given special attention by the natural strength of its second syllable (*-times*), which, in this case, is reinforced by the immediate assonance of the subsequent word, *light*, followed by three monosyllabic words. It's certainly true that the second syllable of the word *sometimes* still doesn't create a true spondee in the second foot of the line (*-times light*), but the poet has employed skillful ways to give this crucial word unusual strength at the end of her poem.

In more recent times, a number of American poets have tended to write blank (unrhymed) tercets, and this includes the talented Rachel Hadas. But in the following poem, she chooses instead to use a variant rhyme scheme for her tercets (*abb*, *cdd*, *eff*, etc.).

Super Nivem

> Asperges me hyssopo, et super nivem dealbador.
>
> —*Psalm LI*

> My scars are slow in healing, dark
> thin crowns of wounds where none should be,
> marring what wraps me, marring me.
>
> I am not sad at anything,
> not stung, but scars remember more
> and make me veteran of a war

I fought forgetting. Stenciled on
wide unresisting planes of skin,
they trace my alphabet of sin,

the language undeciphered still.
But clotted letters I can read.
They mark the parts of me that bleed.

COMMENTS

The title and the epigraph for this powerful tercet poem come from the Fifty-First Psalm, also known as the Fourth Penitential Psalm, which David wrote after a visit from the prophet Nathan regarding the king's adultery with Bathsheba. The epigraph, part of David's direct plea to God for forgiveness, is usually translated, "Thou shalt sprinkle me with hyssop, and I shall be made white as snow." In Hadas's tight tetrameter tercets, the narrator explains that she has not been fully cleansed of "the alphabet of sin," which has left behind scars which "are slow in healing."

In writing this unforgettable poem (which can be compared to Millay's sonnet on page 121 in chapter eight), Hadas clearly illustrates how solidly rhymed tercets can carry the most contemporary language as well as present-day (and timeless) concerns.

A NOTE ABOUT TRANSLATION

Since we've mentioned translation in this chapter, this might be a good time to say a word about the noble art of translation. In my opinion, translating (or even just attempting to translate) from another language is an invaluable exercise that will invariably teach its practitioners a tremendous amount about how poetry, language, and poetic restraints actually work. Most of the readers of this book, somewhere in their past, will have had some kind of training in a foreign or ancient language. Others will have grown up in a household hearing another language, while others will actually be multilingual. Whatever the case, I highly recommend the instructive and pleasurable (and frustrating) activity of translating. Even if your linguistic skills are weak, you can still benefit from the experience.

I would suggest, for example, that you find a short poem that you especially like. Maybe a sonnet from Baudelaire. Then go over the original word by word, and, if they're available, read other translations. Naturally, the more one knows about the poet (and the poem) the better, so some background research would be very helpful. Similarly invaluable would be discussing the poem with a friend or colleague who's fluent in the language—and also asking that person to recite the sonnet in French (maybe taping the recitation for later listenings). Finally, it's time to put away the research and the other translations, and attempt to capture the poet's meanings, form, expressions, and sound—as much as possible—in your English version. Such ambitions are, of course, inherently impossible to fulfill—no translation can ever *fully* capture the original—but the process of translation teaches us a great deal about language, poetry, and the composition of poetry.

Also, translations are absolutely necessary, being the source of most of our cultural knowledge. For example, the most widely read book in the history of the world, the Bible, is almost always read in translation. Without translation, most of us would never have encountered Homer or Dostoyevsky (etc.), and we would be greatly diminished as a people and a culture.

Obviously, a whole book could be written about the practice and the various theories of translating. But if you are so inclined, try it. Don't be intimidated. After all, *every* translation is, in effect, doomed to failure!

ASSIGNMENT 7

Write a tercet poem—either a triplet poem, a terza rima poem, or a poem using one of the three variant rhyme schemes we looked at (Wilde, Sarton, or Hadas).

1. Use either tetrameter or pentameter lines.
2. Use only solid rhymes.
3. Avoid the pop culture.

CHAPTER 10 | THE FRENCH FORMS

France and England, given their geographical proximity, have had a long history of interaction—politically, religiously, artistically, and even linguistically. The French language (as discussed in chapter one) was a primary source in the development of the English language. Thus, it's hardly surprising that English poets, over time, would attempt to adapt some of the French poetic forms for English usage. The problem is that the process has been a rather haphazard one, and many of the original French forms had a flexibility or fluidity of form that made them difficult to pin down. Another problem for the English poets is that many of the original French forms turn on only two rhymes, which, of course, is a much greater challenge in English—sometimes leading to English variations. So even today, one can find contradictory definitions of certain French forms in various literary reference books. In this chapter, we'll focus on three of the most fixed and popular French forms to have been adopted by the English.

Nevertheless, before we begin, it might be appropriate to say something about the "natural" tendencies and capabilities of these adapted French forms. R.F. Brewer, in his very useful *Orthometry: The Art of Versification and the Technicalities of Poetry*, essentially dismissed the French forms as "poetic trifles." He did so because the natural excess of repeated rhyme sounds and repeated lines seemed to doom the French forms to an inevitable cleverness, if not frivolousness, in English usage—thus making them incapable of carrying thematic weight. When Brewer wrote his book in the early twentieth century, most of the best-known English poems in the various French forms were translations from French originals by Francophiles like Algernon Charles Swinburne, along with a few promising English originals by the Neo-Parnassians—particularly Austin Dobson —and the *fin-de-siècle* Decadents—most notably Ernest Dowson. Both Dobson and Dowson had started to use the French forms in ways that carried them beyond the common dismissal of "poetic trifles," but it was not until the twentieth century that English-language poets ingeniously found ways to give unexpected power and weight to the French poetic forms.

[THE VILLANELLE]

The villanelle is the most popular, adaptable, and successful of the various French forms. In France, the villanelle was originally a pastoral, but its early English usage was extremely limited and often rather silly, relying almost entirely on the form's natural musicality. Many of the early villanelles would try to be cute or clever, often discussing the form itself—as in, "The villanelle is a dainty thing," etc. At the end of the 1800s, Oscar Wilde, Ernest Dowson, and other poets began to take the form more seriously, and even though their villanelles often seem rather stiff and clichéd to modern readers, they opened up new possibilities—which were, nevertheless, slow to develop.

The villanelle consists of five tercets and a concluding quatrain. The poem's nineteen lines turn on only two rhymes, and two of the poem's lines are subsequently repeated three more times. The rhyme scheme is as follows: *aba*, *aba*, *aba*, *aba*, *aba*, *abaa.* As for the repetitions, the first line is repeated at the end of the second and fourth tercets, and the third line is repeated at the end of the third and fifth tercets—then the first and third lines are repeated one last time to complete the poem (in the final quatrain's last two lines). Although this seems rather complicated, it's really not; and, as is true with all the French forms, it's easiest just to learn the format by looking at the sample poems. But before we do so, it should be pointed out that a villanelle can never be successful unless it's crafted on two basic building blocks: (1) two rhyme sounds that will offer a variety of interesting rhyming possibilities, and (2) two refrain lines with the ability to stay fresh throughout the poem, before coming together effectively in the last two lines.

Let's begin just before the twentieth century with an early villanelle by the great American poet Edwin Arlington Robinson.

The House on the Hill

They are all gone away,
  The House is shut and still,
There is nothing more to say.

Through broken walls and gray
  The winds blow bleak and shrill:
They are all gone away.

Nor is there one to-day
  To speak them good or ill:
There is nothing more to say.

Why is it then we stray
  Around the sunken sill?
They are all gone away,

And our poor fancy-play
  For them is wasted skill:
There is nothing more to say.

There is ruin and decay
  In the House on the Hill:
They are all gone away,
There is nothing more to say.

COMMENTS

This well-known villanelle is a masterpiece of mood, and Robinson's ability to smoothly incorporate all that rhyme into his melodic trimeters is truly amazing. In the fourth stanza, the narrative voice wonders why the undefined "we" are so attracted by this eerie and deserted old house.

The poem, of course, never tells us specifically, but it fully captivates us with its melody and its incantatory repetitions to create an unforgettable sense of atmosphere.

In 1940, with World War II under way, W.H. Auden wrote the following villanelle.

If I Could Tell You

Time will say nothing but I told you so.
Time only knows the price we have to pay:
If I could tell you I would let you know.

If we should weep when clowns put on their show,
If we should stumble when musicians play,
Time will say nothing but I told you so.

There are no fortunes to be told, although,
Because I love you more than I can say,
If I could tell you I would let you know.

The winds must come from somewhere when they blow,
There must be reasons why the leaves decay;
Time will say nothing but I told you so.

Perhaps the roses really want to grow,
The vision seriously intends to stay;
If I could tell you I would let you know.

Suppose the lions all get up and go,
And all the brooks and soldiers run away;
Will Time say nothing but I told you so?
If I could tell you I would let you know.

COMMENTS

Auden, one of the great metrical masters of the twentieth century, uses his little villanelle to comment on both the war and the inexplicability of the human condition. In the poem, the narrator would definitely like to explain things (the "reasons") to his lover, but he can't. And even if things go awry, as they do in the final quatrain, "Time" will still, most likely, continue to reveal "nothing." As is common with many modern and contemporary authors of villanelles, Auden, for effect and variety, subtly alters one of his refrain lines, turning the poem's opening declarative into an interrogative when it's repeated in the last stanza.

Twelve years later, the Welsh poet Dylan Thomas wrote the following poem, surely the most famous and influential villanelle ever written.

Do Not Go Gentle Into That Good Night

Do not go gentle into that good night,
Old age should burn and rave at close of day;
Rage, rage against the dying of the light.

Though wise men at their end know dark is right,
Because their words had forked no lightning they
Do not go gentle into that good night.

Good men, the last wave by, crying how bright
Their frail deeds might have danced in a green bay,
Rage, rage against the dying of the light.

Wild men who caught and sang the sun in flight,
And learn, too late, they grieved it on its way,
Do not go gentle into that good night.

Grave men, near death, who see with blinding sight
Blind eyes could blaze like meteors and be gay,
Rage, rage against the dying of the light.

And you, my father, there on the sad height,
Curse, bless, me now with your fierce tears, I pray.
Do not go gentle into that good night.
Rage, rage against the dying of the light.

COMMENTS

Thomas's villanelle emphatically illustrates the potential power of the "dainty" villanelle, and it inspired many other poets to try to achieve similar effects. The poem, written by the poet for his dying father (who never saw or heard the poem), is given immediate strength and vigor by its authoritative voice, which begins (and ends) the poem with a powerful command. Within his villanelle, Thomas uses the four central tercets to comment on the reactions of different types of men ("wise," "Good," "Wild," and "Grave") to the inevitability of death. His dignified and often exalted language ("blaze like meteors") combines perfectly with his skillful use of the poem's pentameters, which give him just enough room to discuss his subject seriously. This villanelle set the bar for all subsequent villanelles.

The following poem, from *The Fall of the Magicians*, was written by the American poet Weldon Kees.

1

The crack is moving down the wall.
Defective plaster isn't all the cause.
We must remain until the roof falls in.

It's mildly cheering to recall
That every building has its little flaws.
The crack is moving down the wall.

Here in the kitchen, drinking gin,
We can accept the damndest laws.
We must remain until the roof falls in.

And though there's no one here at all,
One searches every room because
The crack is moving down the wall.

Repairs? But how can one begin?
The lease has warnings buried in each clause.
We must remain until the roof falls in.

These nights one hears a creaking in the hall,
The sort of thing that gives one pause.
The crack is moving down the wall.
We must remain until the roof falls in.

COMMENTS

This poem was the first of a series entitled "Five Villanelles," which explains its numerical title. Kees's creepy examination of our tenuous situation in life skillfully modulates between pentameters and tetrameters to create one of the most memorable of all villanelles. His clever use of *falls in* as the final foot of his repeated third line (which also ends the poem) is particularly effective because the meter tries to elevate the word *in* over the more dominant word *falls*.

Weldon Kees was a rather "hip" artist (into jazz, modern art, radical politics, and film), but he had deep bouts of depression, and he apparently told some of his friends that he had suicidal urges, while telling others that he planned to vanish, take up a new identity, and disappear into Mexico. On July 18, 1955, his car was found near the entrance to the Golden Gate Bridge, and despite reports of Weldon Kees sightings in remote regions of South America, he is generally believed to have leaped to his death. Although such information is certainly not crucial to an appreciation of Kees's villanelle, for those who know even these basic facts about the poet's life, the poem takes on even more ominous possibilities.

The next villanelle was written by the distinguished American poet Elizabeth Bishop, who spent much of her adult life living in Brazil.

One Art

The art of losing isn't hard to master;
so many things seem filled with the intent
to be lost that their loss is no disaster.

Lose something every day. Accept the fluster
of lost door keys, the hour badly spent.
The art of losing isn't hard to master.

Then practice losing farther, losing faster:
places, and names, and where it was you meant
to travel. None of these will bring disaster.

I lost my mother's watch. And look! my last, or
next-to-last, of three loved houses went.
The art of losing isn't hard to master.

I lost two cities, lovely ones. And, vaster,
some realms I owned, two rivers, a continent.
I miss them, but it wasn't a disaster.

—Even losing you (the joking voice, a gesture
I love) I shan't have lied. It's evident
the art of losing's not too hard to master
though it may look like (*Write* it!) like disaster.

COMMENTS

In her well-known villanelle about the "art" of losing things, Bishop increases the stakes as the poem progresses, from losing one's keys to losing a continent and finally to losing a loved one. Bishop enhances the effectiveness of her poem with clever rhymes (*with the intent* and *continent*, and *disaster* and *my last, or*), and she skillfully gives emotional power to her ending quatrain by altering her final refrain lines. Especially effective in that final stanza are her two parentheticals; the italicized self-address; and her substitution of *not too hard* in the next-to-last line for the original words *isn't hard*—since, now, the unstressed *too* is given more weight by its unexpected substitution into the familiar refrain.

At the present time in the United States, in the midst of the contemporary Formalist revival, many skillful poets, like Jared Carter, have been writing excellent villanelles. Another one of those poets is the talented author and translator Charles Martin.

Death Will Do Nothing

Death will do nothing to advance your claim

For everything you didn't get to do:
Life and its circumstances are the same,

And when they add the scores up for the game,
You'll get no extra points for being you:
Death will do nothing to advance your claim

Nor should it please that someone is to blame
For the false conviction or the bad review:
Life and its circumstances are the same.

You watched and waited: orders never came.
Among the unknowns, you are known as "Who?"
Death will do nothing to advance your claim.

Your cell door won't spring open? That's a shame,
It really is, my dear. And yet it's true;
Life and its circumstances are the same,

And no one is tending the eternal flame.
A needless lesson, for you always knew
Death will do nothing to advance your claim:
Life and its circumstances are the same.

COMMENTS

Despite the poet's intentional black humor and his effective personification of death, the villanelle still carries an ominous tone that makes the poem hard to forget.

THE RONDEAU

The rondeau is another French form that turns on only two rhyme sounds and includes multiple repetition. Reflecting the form's original flexibility in the French tradition, the English version of the rondeau has had numerous variant forms. The early English rondeaux were usually thirteen lines, but the form gradually evolved into a fifteen-line poem arranged in three stanzas, with the last two stanzas concluding with a short refrain line that repeats the beginning of the poem's first line. Given that the rondeau's three stanzas can be either quatrains, cinquains, or sestets (in various orders!), one possible rhyme scheme for a modern rondeau is *aabb*, *aaabc*, *aabbac*, where the two *c* rhymes occur at the end of the truncated refrain lines (see Henley below). Another possibility is *aabba*, *aabc*, *aabbac* (see Dunbar below).

Here's a popular rondeau written by the British poet W.E. Henley (1849–1903).

In Rotten Row

In Rotten Row a cigarette
I sat and smoked, with no regret
For all the tumult that had been.
The distances were still and green,

And streaked with shadows cool and wet
Two sweethearts on a bench were set,
Two birds among the boughs were met;
So love and song were heard and seen
In Rotten Row.

A horse or two there was to fret
The soundless sand; but work and debt,
Fair flowers and falling leaves between,
While clocks are chiming clear and keen.
A man may very well forget
In Rotten Row.

COMMENTS

Obviously, when writing a rondeau (as with the villanelle), it's crucial to have a striking refrain line. Henley's "In Rotten Row" was particularly memorable in its day, referring to a wide riding track that runs along the south side of London's Hyde Park.

The following rondeau was written by the American poet Paul Laurence Dunbar (1872–1906).

We Wear The Mask

We wear the mask that grins and lies,
It hides our cheeks and shades our eyes—
This debt we pay to human guile;
With torn and bleeding hearts we smile,
And mouth with myriad subtleties.

Why should the world be over-wise,
In counting all our tears and sighs?
Nay, let them only see us, while
    We wear the mask.

We smile, but, O great Christ, our cries
To thee from tortured souls arise.
We sing, but oh the clay is vile
Beneath our feet, and long the mile;
But let the world dream otherwise,
    We wear the mask.

COMMENTS

Dunbar, the son of Kentucky slaves, spent most of his life in his native Dayton, Ohio. As the poet and critic John Drury has pointed out, this well-known poem about the "mask" worn by an oppressed people is perfectly suited to the formal "mask" of the intricate rondeau.

[THE TRIOLET]

This short medieval relative of the rondel (see page 154), with all its rhyme and repetition, seems a most unlikely candidate for meaningful poems in the English language, yet the little triolet has, more and more, revealed surprising capabilities. The triolet is an eight-line, single-stanza poem that rhymes *abaaabab*, where the first line is repeated in the fourth and seventh lines, and the second line reappears to conclude the poem. Some poets, like Thomas Hardy, Barbara Howes, and, more recently, Dana Gioia, have written longer poems consisting of triolet stanzas, but most poets have chosen to tackle the demanding little triolet as a single-stanza poem.

Here's an early example from the British poet Austin Dobson.

Urceus Exit

I intended an Ode,
   And it turned out a Sonnet,
It began *à la mode*,
I intended an Ode;
But Rose crossed the road
   In her latest new bonnet.
I intended an Ode,
   And it turned out a Sonnet.

COMMENTS

The poem's title is an abbreviated reference to a celebrated line from Horace's *Ars Poetica*: "Instituti; currente rota cur urceus exit?" which can be translated: "A vase is begun; but why, as the wheel goes round, does it turn out to be a pitcher?" Dobson, in his little triolet, plays off the ancient truism that, in the process of creating art, an intention (like creating an ode) might lead to something entirely different (like creating a sonnet). Of course, in this particular case the reason is perfectly clear: Rose has walked across the street wearing her new bonnet! In carefully crafting his little triolet, Dobson reinforces the form's natural sonic exuberance (rhyme and repetition) with his jaunty anapestic dimeters to construct a delightful light verse poem. But his contemporary, the English Poet Laureate Robert Bridges, employs the more substantial iambic tetrameter line to push the form a little bit harder.

When First We Met

When first we met, we did not guess

That love would prove so hard a master;
Of more than common friendliness
When first we met we did not guess.
Who could foretell the sore distress,
The inevitable disaster,
When first we met?—We did not guess
That Love would prove so hard a master.

COMMENTS

Bridges skillfully adjusts his refrain in the seventh line to make its first half an interrogative, and, in the previous line, he uses the quick polysyllabic words *inevitable disaster* to accelerate his mostly monosyllabic poem and to echo the sense of the rapidity and inevitability of the romantic "disaster."

The following poem, written by the contemporary American poet Joshua Mehigan, is one of the most effective triolets ever written.

Last Chance at Reconciliation

He's certain where he's headed it's too late.
West Broadway glitters in a mist of rain
that cones of light alone elucidate.
He's certain. Where he's headed, it's too late
to stop for flowers, dry off, or get things straight:
a story, his misshapen hat, his brain.
He's certain where he's headed. It's too late.
West Broadway glitters in a mist of rain.

COMMENTS

This masterful little poem shows what the triolet (once poorly regarded as a "poetic trifle") can actually do. Mehigan's pentameters give him just enough room to create unexpected depth in his poem, which he does by effectively using his title (with its key word, *Reconciliation*); creating a tangible atmosphere (*glitters*, *mist*, and *cones of light*); incorporating action; listing pertinent specifics (*flowers*, *story*, *hat*, and *brain*); and effectively adjusting his refrain in the fourth and seventh lines.

[OTHER FRENCH FORMS]

As mentioned earlier, there are many variations and/or "cousins" of the basic rondeau, including the roundel, the roundelay (rondelet), the rondeau redoublé, the rondeau prime, and the various rondels. A much different French form is the sestina, a seven-stanza, thirty-nine-line poem, which consists of six sestets and a final tercet. But the lines of the French sestina do not conclude with rhymes, but rather with the repetition of certain key words. Thus, each line in each sestet ends with one of the six key words (in various orders), and the final tercet employs all six of the key words (three at the end of the lines, and three within the lines). Although several interesting sestinas and sestina variations have been written by poets like Ezra Pound and Donald Justice, the form has not proven itself especially adaptable to English. It lacks true rhyme, its six key words can get tiresome, and its length encourages padding and prolixity. In contemporary times, the poor sestina has often been used as a free-verse workshop poem with disastrous results. As Donald Justice explained a few years ago:

> How the sestina ever became a workshop form is beyond me. One reason, I suppose, is that it's awfully easy to write if you don't take it seriously. Originally, there was, of course, meter in the sestina, but in order to write the sestina easily you simply abandon meter, hit the end word and then stop, and then go on to the next end word. If the sestina were taken seriously as a form, it could remain a real possibility, but right now we need to declare a moratorium.

Another French form, the ballade, has had more success in English (beginning with Chaucer), but its greatest achievements have come from the many enjoyable English translations (by Swinburne, Dante Gabriel Rossetti, Richard Wilbur, and others) of the great French master of the ballade, François Villon. The ballade consists of three octave stanzas each rhymed *ababbcbc*, followed by a quatrain coda (or *envoi*) that rhymes *bcbc*. As for repetition, the final line of the first stanza is also used as the final refrain line for each of the following octaves as well as for the final quatrain. Yet, oddly enough, in his most famous ballade ("Ballade des pendus"), Villon used a ten-line stanza, rhyming *ababbccdcd*. Here's an excellent translation of Villon's celebrated ballade (maintaining the original's rhyme scheme) by the contemporary poet and translator Marion Shore.

Ballade of the Hanged

Mortal brothers who after us live on
Be not hardened when our fate is known,
But pity us our ills when we are gone,
And likewise God will pity you your own.
You see us hanging, nameless and unknown,
The flesh that we so recently did sate,
Mouldering now, devoured and decayed,
And we, the bones, are bleaching in the sun.
Let nobody despise our wretched state;
But pray that God absolve us, everyone.

And if we call you brothers, then forbear
To scorn us, even though you see us dead
Through justice. All the same you are aware
That not all men possess a level head.
Have mercy on us now our souls are fled,
And that we may be pardoned for our shame,
And gain salvation from eternal flame,
Commend us to the blessed Virgin's son.
Now we are dead, let no one speak our blame;
But pray that God absolve us, everyone.

We have been washed and cleansed by rainy skies,
And burnt and blackened by the sunlight's glare;

Magpies and crows have fed upon our eyes
And from our beards and brows plucked out our hair.
Never in repose, now here, now there,
Swaying always as the winds decree,
Our bodies hang for all the world to see,
For birds and beasts to peck and prey upon.
Then be not one of our society;
But pray that God absolve us, everyone.

Prince Jesus, you who reign in majesty,
Vouchsafe to guard us from the enemy
That his infernal kingdom we may shun.
Men, here there is no trace of mockery;
But pray that God absolve us, everyone.

COMMENTS

According to French literary tradition, it seems that Villon spent as much of his time engaged in criminal activity as he did in writing poetry. In 1462, as a previously jailed brigand and violent felon, Villon was involved in a murder and was condemned to death. While awaiting execution, he wrote this powerful ballade; but, a year later, his sentence was commuted to ten years of exile, and Villon vanished. He was never heard from again. Whatever the poet's proclivities, there's no reason to doubt the sincerity of this poem, which is skillfully rendered by Marion Shore.

ASSIGNMENT 8

Write a poem in one of the following French forms: a villanelle, a rondeau, or a triolet. (If you chose the triolet, write two!)

1. As seems appropriate to your mood, tone, and subject, use either trimeter, tetrameter, or pentameter lines.
2. Use solid rhymes.
3. Avoid the pop culture.

CHAPTER II

TROCHAIC AND ANAPESTIC VERSE

[TROCHAIC POEMS]

As discussed in chapter two, the primary function of the trochaic foot (as well as the anapestic foot) is to serve the iambic line as a metrical substitution that can give emphasis and variety to the line. Nevertheless, some poets have written whole poems, or sections of longer poems, in trochaic meter, and this chapter will highlight some distinguished examples. We'll begin with the witches in *Macbeth* (act 4, scene 1), and I would suggest that the passage be read aloud, maybe along with friends taking various roles.

[A Witches' haunt. In the middle, a boiling Cauldron.]

[Thunder. Enter the Three Witches.]

First Witch. Thrice the brinded[1] cat hath mewed.

Second Witch. Thrice and once the hedge-pig whined.

Third Witch. Harper[2] cries. 'Tis time, 'tis time.

First Witch. Round about the caldron go:
In the poisoned entrails throw.
Toad, that under cold stone
Days and nights has thirty-one
Swelter'd venom sleeping got,
Boil thou first i' the charmed pot.

[1] dark-streaked [2] a spirit

All. Double, double, toil and trouble;
Fire burn and caldron bubble.

Second Witch. Fillet of a fenny snake,
In the caldron boil and bake;
Eye of newt and toe of frog,
Wool of bat and tongue of dog,
Adder's fork and blindworm's sting,
Lizard's leg and howlet's[3] wing,
For a charm of pow'rful trouble,
Like a hell-broth boil and bubble.

All. Double, double, toil and trouble;
Fire burn and caldron bubble.

Third Witch. Scale of dragon, tooth of wolf,
Witch's mummy, maw[4] and gulf[5]
Of the ravined[6] salt-sea shark,
Root of hemlock digged i' the dark,
Liver of blaspheming Jew,
Gall of goat, and slips of yew
Slivered in the moon's eclipse,
Nose of Turk and Tartar's lips,
Finger of birth-strangled babe
Ditch-delivered by a drab[7],
Make the gruel thick and slab[8]:
Add thereto a tiger's chaudron[9],
For the ingredients of our caldron.

All. Double, double, toil and trouble;
Fire burn and caldron bubble.

Second Witch. Cool it with a baboon's blood,
Then the charm is firm and good.

[3] owlet [4] stomach [5] gullet [6] ravenous [7] harlot [8] sticky [9] entrails

[Enter Hecate.]

Hecate. O! well done! I commend your pains;
And every one shall share i' the gains:
And now about the caldron sing,
Like elves and fairies in a ring,
Enchanting all that you put in.

Music and a song: "Black Spirits," &c.

[Exeunt Hecate.]

Second Witch. By the pricking of my thumbs,
Something wicked this way comes:
Open, locks,
Whoever knocks!

[Enter Macbeth.]

Macbeth. How now, you secret, black and midnight hags!
What is it you do?

COMMENTS

In this famous dramatic passage, Shakespeare uses four metrical variations to give distinct voices to his speakers:

1. When the witches chant in unison, they use perfect trochaic tetrameters, and the natural incantatory feel of the falling trochaics is further enhanced by the couplet's rhymes.
2. When the witches speak individually, they also use rhymed trochaic tetrameters, but the last foot in every line is truncated so the line (and the rhyme) will end on an accent. As discussed in chapter two, maintaining a pure trochee in the final foot of a poetic line is very difficult, so writers generally accept the natural expectations of the language (and their readers) and end with a stress.

3. When Hecate, the goddess of the moon and the underworld, enters the witches' haunt, she speaks in a more authoritative and dignified iambic tetrameter, as fits her station.
4. Finally, when Macbeth enters the eerie scene, Shakespeare reverts back to the play's normal, unrhymed iambic pentameter (blank verse), which can closely approximate natural human speech.

Throughout English literary history, various other poets—like Thomas Campion, Tennyson, Hardy, and Millay—have all written successful poems in trochaic meter, but without question, the most famous trochaic poem is Poe's "The Raven," composed in unusual trochaic octometers. This poem, of course, should also be read aloud; and, in the tradition of Poe himself, it should be read with as much drama, mood, and creepiness as possible.

The Raven

Once upon a midnight dreary, while I pondered, weak and weary,
Over many a quaint and curious volume of forgotten lore—
While I nodded, nearly napping, suddenly there came a tapping,
As of some one gently rapping, rapping at my chamber door.
"'Tis some visiter," I muttered, "tapping at my chamber door—
Only this, and nothing more."

Ah, distinctly I remember it was in the bleak December;
And each separate dying ember wrought its ghost upon the floor.
Eagerly I wished the morrow;—vainly I had sought to borrow
From my books surcease of sorrow—sorrow for the lost Lenore—
For the rare and radiant maiden whom the angels named Lenore—
Nameless *here* for evermore.

And the silken, sad, uncertain rustling of each purple curtain
Thrilled me—filled me with fantastic terrors never felt before;
So that now, to still the beating of my heart, I stood repeating
"'Tis some visiter entreating entrance at my chamber door—
Some late visiter entreating entrance at my chamber door;—
This it is and nothing more."

Presently my soul grew stronger; hesitating then no longer,
"Sir," said I, "or Madam, truly your forgiveness I implore;
But the fact is I was napping, and so gently you came rapping,
And so faintly you came tapping, tapping at my chamber door,
That I scarce was sure I heard you"—here I opened wide the door;—
Darkness there, and nothing more.

Deep into that darkness peering, long I stood there wondering, fearing,
Doubting, dreaming dreams no mortal ever dared to dream before;
But the silence was unbroken, and the darkness gave no token,
And the only word there spoken was the whispered word, "Lenore?"
This I whispered, and an echo murmured back the word, "Lenore!"
Merely this, and nothing more.

Back into the chamber turning, all my soul within me burning,
Soon I heard again a tapping somewhat louder than before.
"Surely," said I, "surely that is something at my window lattice;
Let me see, then, what thereat is, and this mystery explore—
Let my heart be still a moment and this mystery explore;—
'Tis the wind, and nothing more!"

Open here I flung the shutter, when, with many a flirt and flutter,
In there stepped a stately Raven of the saintly days of yore;
Not the least obeisance made he; not an instant stopped or stayed he;
But, with mien of lord or lady, perched upon my chamber door—
Perched upon a bust of Pallas[1] just above my chamber door—
Perched, and sat, and nothing more.

Then this ebony bird beguiling my sad fancy into smiling,
By the grave and stern decorum of the countenance it wore,
"Though thy crest be shorn and shaven, thou," I said, "art sure no craven,
Ghastly grim and ancient Raven wandering from the Nightly shore—
Tell me what thy lordly name is on the Night's Plutonian shore!"
Quoth the Raven, "Nevermore."

[1] Athena

Much I marvelled this ungainly fowl to hear discourse so plainly,
Though its answer little meaning—little relevancy bore;
For we cannot help agreeing that no living human being
Ever yet was blessed with seeing bird above his chamber door—
Bird or beast upon the sculptured bust above his chamber door,
With such name as "Nevermore."

But the Raven, sitting lonely on the placid bust, spoke only
That one word, as if his soul in that one word he did outpour.
Nothing farther then he uttered—not a feather then he fluttered—
Till I scarcely more than muttered "Other friends have flown before—
On the morrow *he* will leave me, as my Hopes have flown before."
Then the bird said, "Nevermore."

Startled at the stillness broken by reply so aptly spoken,
"Doubtless," said I, "what it utters is its own stock and store
Caught from some unhappy master whom unmerciful Disaster
Followed fast and followed faster till his songs one burden bore—
Till the dirges of his Hope that melancholy burden bore
Of 'Never—nevermore'"

But the Raven still beguiling my sad fancy into smiling,
Straight I wheeled a cushioned seat in front of bird, and bust and door;
Then, upon the velvet sinking, I betook myself to linking
Fancy unto fancy, thinking what this ominous bird of yore—
What this grim, ungainly, ghastly, gaunt, and ominous bird of yore
Meant in croaking "Nevermore."

This I sat engaged in guessing, but no syllable expressing
To the fowl whose fiery eyes now burned into my bosom's core;
This and more I sat divining, with my head at ease reclining
On the cushion's velvet lining that the lamp-light gloated o'er,
But whose velvet-violet lining with the lamp-light gloating, o'er,
She shall press, ah, nevermore!

Then, methought, the air grew denser, perfumed from an unseen censer
Swung by seraphim whose foot-falls tinkled on the tufted floor.
"Wretch," I cried, "thy God hath lent thee—by these angels he hath sent thee
Respite—respite and nepenthe from thy memories of Lenore!
Quaff, oh quaff this kind nepenthe and forget this lost Lenore!"
Quoth the Raven, "Nevermore."

"Prophet!" said I, "thing of evil!—prophet still, if bird or devil!—
Whether Tempter sent, or whether tempest tossed thee here ashore,
Desolate yet all undaunted, on this desert land enchanted—
On this home by Horror haunted—tell me truly, I implore—
Is there—*is* there balm in Gilead?—tell me—tell me, I implore!"
Quoth the Raven "Nevermore."

"Prophet!" said I, "thing of evil!—prophet still, if bird or devil!—
By that Heaven that bends above us—by that God we both adore—
Tell this soul with sorrow laden if, within the distant Aidenn[2],
It shall clasp a sainted maiden whom the angels name Lenore—
Clasp a rare and radiant maiden whom the angels name Lenore."
Quoth the Raven "Nevermore."

"Be that word our sign of parting, bird or fiend!" I shrieked, upstarting—
"Get thee back into the tempest and the Night's Plutonian shore!
Leave no black plume as a token of that lie thy soul hath spoken!
Leave my loneliness unbroken!—quit the bust above my door!
Take thy beak from out my heart, and take thy form from off my door!"
Quoth the Raven "Nevermore."

And the Raven, never flitting, still is sitting, *still* is sitting,
On the pallid bust of Pallas just above my chamber door;
And his eyes have all the seeming of a demon's that is dreaming,
And the lamp-light o'er him streaming throws his shadow on the floor;
And my soul from out that shadow that lies floating on the floor
Shall be lifted—nevermore!

[2] Eden

COMMENTS

In composing his peculiar and unforgettable masterpiece, Poe ends the first and third line of every stanza with a pure trochee, but he chooses to end the other lines with truncated trochees (and thus masculine rhymes). "The Raven" is composed of eighteen sestets (108 lines), and it rhymes *abcbbb*, where the *a* line has an internal rhyme (*dreary* and *weary* in the first stanza), and the *c* line not only has an internal rhyme (*napping* and *tapping*), but the rhyme is carried over into the fourth foot of the fourth line (*rapping*)!

In the twentieth century, the most famous example of trochaic meter is the third and final section of Auden's renowned tribute, "In Memory of W.B. Yeats," written in February 1939, a month after the death of the great Irish poet.

Earth, receive an honoured guest:
William Yeats is laid to rest.
Let the Irish vessel lie
Emptied of its poetry.

In the nightmare of the dark
All the dogs of Europe bark,
And the living nations wait,
Each sequestered in its hate;

Intellectual disgrace
Stares from every human face,
And the seas of pity lie
Locked and frozen in each eye.

Follow, poet, follow right
To the bottom of the night,
With your unconstraining voice
Still persuade us to rejoice;

With the farming of a verse
Make a vineyard of the curse,

Sing of human unsuccess
In a rapture of distress;

In the deserts of the heart
Let the healing fountain start,
In the prison of his days
Teach the free man how to praise.

COMMENTS

With the death of Yeats, and the awareness that a second world war was on the verge of breaking out (which it did, in September of that year), Auden writes the final section of his great tribute in memorable tetrameter quatrains, each consisting of two couplets, where all of the final trochees are truncated, and all of the rhymes are solid, except *lie* and *poetry* in the second couplet. The poet uses the unsettling feel of the falling trochees to enhance his concerns about a world that seems to be falling apart and the simultaneous loss of its greatest poetic voice.

[ANAPESTIC POEMS]

Like the trochee, the anapest has also, on occasion, been used to create some exceptional and memorable poems. One of the very best was composed by Byron.

The Destruction of Sennacherib

The Assyrian came down like the wolf on the fold,
And his cohorts were gleaming in purple and gold;
And the sheen of their spears was like stars on the sea,
When the blue wave rolls nightly on deep Galilee.

Like the leaves of the forest when Summer is green,
That host with their banners at sunset were seen:
Like the leaves of the forest when Autumn hath blown,

That host on the morrow lay withered and strown.

For the Angel of Death spread his wings on the blast,
And breathed in the face of the foe as he passed;
And the eyes of the sleepers waxed deadly and chill,
And their hearts but once heaved, and forever grew still!

And there lay the steed with his nostril all wide,
But through it there rolled not the breath of his pride;
And the foam of his gasping lay white on the turf,
And cold as the spray of the rock-beating surf.

And there lay the rider distorted and pale,
With the dew on his brow, and the rust on his mail:
And the tents were all silent, the banners alone,
The lances unlifted, the trumpet unblown.

And the widows of Ashur[1] are loud in their wail,
And the idols are broke in the temple of Baal[2];
And the might of the Gentile, unsmote by the sword,
Hath melted like snow in the glance of the Lord!

COMMENTS

Byron's tightly constructed anapestic tetrameter couplets perfectly exploit their vigorous meter to enhance for the reader a fuller sense of the thundering, advancing army of the invading Assyrians and the swift and supernatural devastation of the "Angel of Death." The basis of the poem comes from 2 Kings 18:13–19:37, where Sennacherib, the king of the Assyrians, has crushed mighty Babylon and is moving toward Jerusalem. The Jews, in desperation, are instructed by the prophet Isaiah to pray for divine deliverance. When they do, an angel appears and instantly destroys the entire camp of the invading army (nearly 200,000 soldiers). The fact that Byron's poem was written in 1815, the year of the Allied success against Napoleon at Waterloo, is no coincidence.

[1]Assyria [2]an idol

Within Byron's poem, the rhymes are solid and the meters are tight, but the poet, in eight different places, initiates various lines with an iamb before once again picking up his distinctive anapestic beat. For example, notice the beginning of line two in the second stanza.

Thăt hóst | wĭth thĕir bán | nĕrs ăt sún | sĕt wĕre seén:

In the course of English-language literary history, many of the most well-known poems written in anapestic meter might be more accurately described as poems *dominated* by the anapest. Such poems, like Poe's melodic masterpiece "Annabel Lee," contain numerous iambic substitutions within their overall anapestic meter.

Annabel Lee

It was many and many a year ago,
  In a kingdom by the sea,
That a maiden there lived whom you may know
  By the name of Annabel Lee;
And this maiden she lived with no other thought
  Than to love and be loved by me.

She was a child and *I* was a child,
  In this kingdom by the sea,
But we loved with a love that was more than love—
  I and my Annabel Lee—
With a love that the wingéd seraphs of Heaven
  Coveted her and me.

And this was the reason that, long ago,
  In this kingdom by the sea,
A wind blew out of a cloud by night
  Chilling my Annabel Lee;
So that her high-born kinsman came
  And bore her away from me,
To shut her up in a sepulcher

In this kingdom by the sea.

The angels, not half so happy in Heaven,
Went envying her and me:
Yes! that was the reason (as all men know,
In this kingdom by the sea)
That the wind came out of the cloud, chilling
And killing my Annabel Lee.

But our love it was stronger by far than the love
Of those who were older than we—
Of many far wiser than we—
And neither the angels in Heaven above
Nor the demons down under the sea,
Can ever dissever my soul from the soul
Of the beautiful Annabel Lee:

For the moon never beams without bringing me dreams
Of the beautiful Annabel Lee;
And the stars never rise but I feel the bright eyes
Of the beautiful Annabel Lee;
And so, all the night-tide, I lie down by the side
Of my darling, my darling, my life and my bride,
In her sepulcher there by the sea—
In her tomb by the sounding sea.

COMMENTS

Poe's heavily rhymed poem, using stanzas of varying length, begins with a mix of anapests and iambs.

Ĭt wăs mán | y̆ ănd mán | y̆ ă yéar | ăgó,
Ĭn ă kíng | dŏm bý | thĕ séa,

Thus, the first line consists of three anapests and an iamb, and the second line, given the metrical elevation of the word *by*, contains an anapest followed by two iambs. But as the poem proceeds, Poe gradually increases the number of his anapests, giving more speed and intensity to his lulling melody as the narrative grows more and more tragic—and as the mental state of the narrator grows increasingly melancholic. By the final stanza of the poem, every single foot in the octave is an anapest but one. Can you find it?

Sometimes popular song lyrics use an anapestic meter to reinforce the musical structure of the melody—or vice versa, depending on which is written first. If you know the beautiful melody of the song "Red River Valley," please sing it out loud!

Red River Valley

From this valley they say you are going:
We will miss your bright eyes and sweet smile,
For they say you are taking the sunshine,
Which has brightened our pathway a while.

Chorus

Come and sit by my side if you love me,
Do not hasten to bid me adieu,
But remember the Red River Valley
And the girl that has loved you so true.

Won't you think of the valley you're leaving?
Oh how lonely, how sad it will be,
Oh think of the fond heart you're breaking,
And the grief you are causing me.

Chorus

I have promised you, darling, that never
Will a word from my lips cause you pain;
And my life, it will be yours forever
If you only will love me again.

Chorus

COMMENTS

This justly famous song was originally written in the 1890s about the Mohawk Valley in New York state, but it was eventually transported west and turned into a cowboy lament. In the musical notation for the song, each of the accented syllables of the anapestic lyrics is further emphasized by musical notes of extended duration. For example, in the first line of the song, the *val-* of *valley*, the word *say*, and the *go-* of *going* are all quarter notes, but the other syllables in the line are only eighth notes. Thus, both the meter and the melody of the song combine to emphasize the key words of the lyrics.

Over the years, a number of children's poems have also been composed in the pleasing sounds of the anapest, which clearly dominate the Dr. Seuss classic, *Horton Hatches the Egg*. The book, which is a narrative poem, begins:

> Sighed Mayzie, a lazy bird hatching an egg:
> "I'm tired and I'm bored
> And I've kinks in my leg
> From sitting, just sitting here day after day.
> It's *work!* How I hate it!
> I'd *much* rather play!
> I'd take a vacation, fly off for a rest
> If I could find *someone*, I'd fly away—free...."
>
> Then Horton, the Elephant, passed by her tree.

COMMENTS

I'm hopeful that you know the rest of the story!

As for the meter, beneath his varying line lengths and playful rhymes, the author maintains a markedly anapestic beat to give his narrative its lively and jaunty feel.

Various other forms of light verse also use the anapest, and it may surprise some readers to learn that the limerick is an anapestic poem. The limerick's unique and easily recognizable rhythm comes from a combination of anapests, rhyme, and two truncated lines. Structurally, the limerick is a five-line cinquain poem that rhymes *aabba*. Its first, second, and fifth lines are anapestic trimeter, and its third and fourth lines are anapestic dimeter. Sometimes poets will take the liberty of beginning their limericks with an iamb before initiating the anapestic beat. For example:

> Thĕre wás | ă yŏung lá | dy̆ ŏf Lýnn

(And sometimes a similar iambic substitution is used at the beginning of the truncated lines—lines three and four.)

Here's a sample of limericks (many anonymous) that reveals the form's remarkable cleverness and versatility. As we all know, the limerick has a natural tendency to become "Disorderly, drunk, and obscene" (see the tenth example below). Nevertheless, the limerick also has the ability to refrain from its vulgar proclivities and still be both witty and pleasurable.

> There was a young lady of Lynn
> Who was so uncommonly thin
> That when she essayed
> To drink lemonade
> She slipped through the straw and fell in.

> There was a young lady from Niger
> Who smiled as she rode on a tiger;
> They returned from the ride
> With the lady inside
> And the smile on the face of the tiger.

> A tutor who tooted the flute
> Tried to teach two young tooters to toot.
> Said the two to the tutor,
> "Is it harder to toot, or
> To tutor two tooters to toot?"

—CAROLYN WELLS

There was a young maid who said, "Why
Can't I look in my ear with my eye?
If I put my mind to it,
I'm sure I can do it.
You never can tell till you try."

A goat on a stroll near a brook
Found an old movie film and partook.
"Was it good?" asked his mate.
Said the goat, "Second-rate!
Not nearly as good as the book!"

—MARTIN BRISTOW SMITH

A decrepit old gas man named Peter,
While hunting around for the meter,
Touched a leak with his light.
He arose out of sight,
And, as anyone can see by reading this, he
also destroyed the meter.

There once was a man from Nantucket
Who kept all his cash in a bucket;
But his daughter, named Nan,
Ran away with a man,
And as for the bucket, Nantucket.

There was a young lady from Spain,
Who was exceedingly sick on a train,
Not once but again
And again, and again
And again, and again, and again.

There was a faith healer of Deal,
Who said, "Although pain isn't real,
If I sit on a pin

And I puncture my skin,
I dislike what I *fancy* I feel."

The limerick is furtive and mean;
You must keep it in close quarantine,
Or it sneaks to the slums
And promptly becomes
Disorderly, drunk, and obscene.

A limerick packs laughs anatomical
Into space that is quite economical.
But the good ones I've seen
So seldom are clean,
And the clean ones so seldom comical.

It took me some time to agree
To appear in a film about me
And my various ex-wives
Detailing our sex lives,
But I did—and they rated it G.

—JOHN CIARDI

There once was an old man of Lyme
Who married three wives at a time.
When asked, "Why a third?"
He replied, "One's absurd!
And bigamy, sir, is a crime."

A maiden at college, Miss Breeze,
Had B.A.s and M.A.s and Litt. D.s.
Said her doctor, "It's plain,
You'll collapse from the strain,
For you're killing yourself by degrees."

Said an erudite Sinologue, "How
Shall I try to describe to you Tao?

It is come, it is go,
It is yes, it is no.
Yet it's neither—you understand now?

—R.J.P. HEWISON

Finally, here's a limerick that my wife has given me permission to include.

There was a young maid from Madras
Who had a magnificent ass,
Not rounded and pink,
As you probably think,
It was grey, had long ears, and ate grass.

COMMENTS

I know. I'm sorry about the last one!

ASSIGNMENT 9

Write two exercises and two poems. (Please note: Use only solid rhymes for all the assignments!)

1. In the fashion of Byron, write a perfect anapestic tetrameter quatrain, consisting of two couplets, that would fit right into "The Destruction of Sennacherib." Try to write a stanza that Byron would like so much that he would insist on including it in his poem. You might, for example, describe the angel of death and insert your quatrain after Byron's third stanza, or you might describe more of the scene of destruction and insert your quatrain after the poem's fourth or fifth stanzas. Try to mimic not only the meter and the rhymes of the original, but also its tone, diction, syntax, etc.
2. Similarly, in the fashion of Auden, write a perfect trochaic tetrameter quatrain consisting of two couplets that would

fit perfectly into Auden's poem about Yeats. You might describe more of the present "nightmare" and insert your quatrain after the second or third stanzas, or you might describe more of the lost powers of the poet and insert your quatrain after the fourth or fifth stanzas.

3. Write two limericks. Avoid iambic substitutions, except, if needed, in the poem's first foot.

CHAPTER 12

EPIGRAMS AND NONSENSE VERSE

[EPIGRAMS]

Epigrams are short, memorable, occasionally elegant expressions of intellectual wit that derive their weight from their marked compression. Many epigrams are maxims or adages, often satiric, and sometimes relying on antithesis. The word *epigram* comes from the Greek word meaning "inscription," referring to the pithy inscriptions carved on ancient monuments and graveyard stones. In Western culture, some of the most famous epigrammatists writing in prose have been Publilius Syrus; François, duc de La Rochefoucauld; Benjamin Franklin; Oscar Wilde; Ambrose Bierce; and G.K. Chesterton.

Poetic epigrams have an even longer history, and some can be found in *The Greek Anthology*. But the best of the ancient practitioners of the epigram were the Romans Catullus and Martial. In English literary history, both John Donne and Robert Herrick wrote notable epigrams in the seventeenth century, but the most celebrated epigram of the period (which some poets and critics consider to be the best epigram in the language) was written a bit earlier by Sir John Harington.

Treason

Treason doth never prosper: what's the reason?
For if it prosper, none dare call it treason.

Eventually, of course, the epigram would truly flourish in the Augustan era, when the couplet, which is naturally suited to aphoristic expression (see chapter seven), dominated poetic practice. The absolute master of the epigrammatic couplet was Pope; and, although almost all of his famous epigrams were parts of larger works (see the selection from "An Essay on Criticism" on page 102), their intention as epigrammatic statements is perfectly clear. For example, the following epigrams are all from Pope's *Imitations of Horace* series.

Satire's my weapon, but I'm too discreet
To run amuck, and tilt at all I meet.

There still remains, to mortify a wit,
The many-headed monster of the pit.

Give me again my hollow tree,
A crust of bread, and liberty.

Sometimes epigrams will extend beyond a single couplet to a quatrain, as in these often-quoted lines from Pope's poem "An Essay on Criticism."

A little learning is a dangerous thing;
Drink deep, or taste not the Pierian spring:
There shallow draughts intoxicate the brain,
And drinking largely sobers us again.

It's often claimed that, excepting Shakespeare, Pope is the most-quoted author in English-language history, and this is certainly the result of his mastery of the couplet. If his thoughts had been expressed, for example, in blank verse, they would not be as striking or sonically memorable.

Sometimes poets writing quatrain epigrams have used rhyme schemes other than the couplet, as in this witty *abab* epigram from "Shorts" by W.H. Auden.

To the man-in-the-street, who, I'm sorry to say,
Is a keen observer of life,
The word *Intellectual* suggests right away
A man who's untrue to his wife.

In this chapter, however, we'll focus on single-couplet epigrams that are not incorporated or embedded in longer works, like this mischievous little poem from Pope.

On the Collar of a Dog

I am his Highness's dog at Kew:
Pray tell me, sir, whose dog are you?

Such epigrammatic poems have a long history in English-language poetry. Here are three more from the pre-modern tradition.

Epitaph: On Peter Robinson

Here lies the preacher, judge, and poet, Peter,
Who broke the laws of God, and man, and metre.

—LORD JEFFREY

Translated From Lebrun

Aegle, beauty and poet, has two little crimes;
She makes her own face, and does not make her rhymes.

—LORD BYRON

Rhyme for a Child Viewing a Naked Venus in a Painting

He gazed and gazed and gazed and gazed,
amazed, amazed, amazed, amazed.

—ROBERT BROWNING

Among the various masters of the twentieth-century couplet poem are Belloc (see page 104 in chapter seven), J.V. Cunningham, John Frederick Nims, and Wendy Cope (see page 109 in chapter seven). Here are samples from the work of Cunningham and Nims.

The Humanist

This *Humanist* whom no beliefs constrained
Grew so broad-minded he was scatter-brained.

— J.V. CUNNINGHAM

Visiting Poet

"The famous bard, he comes! The vision nears!"
Now heaven protect your booze. Your wife. Your ears.

—JOHN FREDERICK NIMS

Finally, here are three contemporary examples of the epigrammatic couplet poem.

With a Book of Robert Frost's Poetry

As you read, remember, from time to time
That another word for "frost" is "rime."

—JOHN HOLLANDER

Your Midlife Crisis

You found yourself—but at an awful cost.
We liked you better when you were lost.

—A.M. JUSTER

Looking Back

I wish I'd been alone
with Dorothy Malone.

—ED ROSSMANN

This delightfully ridiculous trimeter couplet referring to Dorothy Malone (a soulful and rather exotic Hollywood movie star of the forties and fifties), seems a perfectly fitting segue into the subject of nonsense verse.

[NONSENSE POETRY]

Nonsense poetry, of course, doesn't entirely lack sense, but it's naturally illogical, absurd, exaggerated, hyperbolic, and playful. Ostensibly written for the amusement of children, the best nonsense verse is equally appealing to adults. Such poems are highly rhythmic, often short, and they contain action that defies common sense. They will also, on occasion, use invented words (neologisms) which sometimes turn into tongue twisters.

It's a natural compulsion of human beings to amuse each other (and especially children) with silly, ludicrous, ridiculous rhymes, and the most apparent examples in our long tradition are nursery rhymes.

Hey, Diddle, Diddle

Hey, diddle, diddle!
   The cat and the fiddle,
The cow jumped over the moon;
   The little dog laughed
   To see such sport,
And the dish ran away with the spoon.

Though the poem's meaning is uncertain, it's still perfectly pleasing, given its absurdist images of a cow jumping over the moon and a dish running away with a spoon. Nevertheless, despite such a strong element of nonsense in many of our early nursery rhymes, there's a rather limited tradition of nonsense verse in our more literary history—with the obvious exception of the "mad-songs" in some of the Elizabethan plays—like Ophelia's mad-but-meaningful ditties in *Hamlet* (act 4, scene 5), or Edgar's odd little song in *King Lear* (act 3, scene 4). It's not really until the Victorian period that nonsense poetry truly steps forward with authority, beginning with the highly inventive poetry of Edward Lear (initiating in 1846 with *A Book of Nonsense*) and continuing with the poems and Alice books of Lewis Carroll.

A classic example of nonsense poetry, replete with invented words, is Carroll's "Jabberwocky," which he included in *Through the Looking-Glass*, his sequel to *Alice's Adventures in Wonderland*.

Jabberwocky

'Twas brillig, and the slithy toves
   Did gyre and gimble in the wabe:
All mimsy were the borogoves,
   And the mome raths outgrabe.

"Beware the Jabberwock, my son!
The jaws that bite, the claws that catch!
Beware the Jubjub bird, and shun
The frumious Bandersnatch!"

He took his vorpal sword in hand:
Long time the manxome foe he sought—
So rested he by the Tumtum tree,
And stood awhile in thought.

And, as in uffish thought he stood,
The Jabberwock, with eyes of flame,
Came whiffling through the tulgey wood,
And burbled as it came!

One, two! One, two! And through and through
The vorpal blade when snicker-snack!
He left it dead, and with its head
He went galumphing back.

"And hast thou slain the Jabberwock?
Come to my arms, my beamish boy!
O frabjous day! Callooh! Callay!"
He chortled in his joy.

'Twas brillig, and the slithy toves
Did gyre and gimble in the wabe:
All mimsy were the borogoves,
And the mome raths outgrabe.

Although both Humpty Dumpty and Carroll himself glossed some of the poem's neologisms (*mimsy* means "flimsy and miserable," for example, and *borogoves* are shaggy birds that look like mops), even this rather opaque nonsense poem still carries more than enough "sense" within its quite comprehendible narrative.

Lear, who also helped popularize the limerick, wrote many different kinds of nonsense verse in his various books, but surely his most memorable accomplishment is this beautifully melodic poem (an exquisite blend of iambs and anapests) about a love affair between an owl and a pussy-cat!

(Please read aloud!)

The Owl and the Pussy-Cat

The Owl and the Pussy-cat went to sea
In a beautiful pea-green boat,
They took some honey, and plenty of money,
Wrapped up in a five-pound note.
The Owl looked up to the stars above,
And sang to a small guitar,
"O lovely Pussy! O Pussy, my love,
What a beautiful Pussy you are,
You are,
You are!
What a beautiful Pussy you are!"

Pussy said to the Owl, "You elegant fowl!
How charmingly sweet you sing!
O let us be married! too long we have tarried:
But what shall we do for a ring?"
They sailed away for a year and a day,
To the land where the Bong-tree grows;
And there in a wood a Piggy-wig stood,
With a ring at the end of his nose,
His nose,
His nose,
With a ring at the end of his nose.

"Dear Pig, are you willing to sell for one shilling
Your ring?" Said the Piggy, "I will."
So they took it away, and were married next day
By the Turkey who lives on the hill.

They dined on mince, and slices of quince,
Which they ate with a runcible spoon;
And hand in hand, on the edge of the sand,
They danced by the light of the moon,
The moon,
The moon,
They danced by the light of the moon.

Another excellent, but less well-known, nonsense poem is this amazing narrative in octaves written by Charles E. Carryl (1841–1920), whose work was inspired by Lewis Carroll. This is my daughter's favorite nonsense poem, and she has impeccable taste! Please read aloud!

The Walloping Window-blind

A capital ship for an ocean trip
Was *The Walloping Window-blind*;
No gale that blew dismayed her crew
Or troubled the captain's mind.
The man at the wheel was taught to feel
Contempt for the wildest blow,
And it often appeared, when the weather had cleared,
That he'd been in his bunk below.

The boatswain's mate was very sedate,
Yet fond of amusement, too;
And he played hop-scotch with the starboard watch
While the captain tickled the crew.
And the gunner we had was apparently mad,
For he sat on the after-rail,
And fired salutes with the captain's boots,
In the teeth of the booming gale.

The captain sat in a commodore's hat,
And dined, in a royal way,
On toasted pigs and pickles and figs

And gummery bread, each day.
But the cook was Dutch, and behaved as such;
For the food that he gave the crew
Was a number of tons of hot-cross buns,
Chopped up with sugar and glue.

And we all felt ill as mariners will,
On a diet that's cheap and rude;
And we shivered and shook as we dipped the cook
In a tub of his gluesome food.
Then nautical pride we laid aside,
And we cast the vessel ashore
On the Gulliby Isles, where the Poohpooh smiles,
And the Anagazanders roar.

Composed of sand was that favored land,
And trimmed with cinnamon straws;
And pink and blue was the pleasing hue
Of the Tickletoeteaser's claws.
And we sat on the edge of a sandy ledge
And shot at the whistling bee;
And the Binnacle-bats wore water-proof hats
As they danced in the sounding sea.

On rubagub bark, from dawn to dark,
We fed, till we all had grown
Uncommonly shrunk,—when a Chinese junk
Came by from the torriby zone.
She was stubby and square, but we didn't much care.
And we cheerily put to sea;
And we left the crew of the junk to chew
The bark of the rubagub tree.

This poem is a tour de force of sound and rhyme. It has a rather astonishing rhyme scheme of *abcbdefe*, where the *a*, *c*, *d*, and *f* lines rhyme internally on the second and fourth feet. For example, *ship* and *trip* in the first line:

A capital ship for an ocean trip

We will now follow these longer samples with a group of shorter nonsense poems by various authors.

Antigonish

As I was going up the stair
  I met a man who wasn't there!
He wasn't there again today!
  I wish, I *wish* he'd stay away.

—HUGH MEARNS

Circles

The things to draw with compasses
Are suns and moons and circleses
And rows of humptydumpasses
Or anything in circuses
Like hippopotamusseses
And hoops and camels' humpasses
And wheels on clownses busseses
And fat old elephumpasses.

—HARRY BEHN

I Wish That My Room Had a Floor

I wish that my room had a floor;
I don't care so much for a door,
  But this walking around
  Without touching the ground
Is getting to be such a bore!

—GELETT BURGESS

This last poem is, of course, a limerick (see page 171 in chapter eleven), which can appropriately lead us to several other poetic formats that typically serve for humorous and, sometimes, nonsensical verse.

THE CLERIHEW

The clerihew was invented in 1890 by Edmund Clerihew Bentley when the poet was eighteen years old. The poem consists of two couplets (*aabb*) where the first line of the poem is generally the name of a famous person; the second line is some kind of outrageous predicate; and the final two lines often call up some historical fact or fantasy about the subject. Since Bentley was rather loose about his line lengths (as well as his iambics), there's no set format regarding the number of feet to a line.

Here are two well-known examples from Bentley, followed by a more recent example of the form by Lee R. Parks.

Lord Clive

What I like about Clive
Is that he is no longer alive.
There is a great deal to be said
For being dead.

—EDMUND BENTLEY

George III

George the Third
Ought never to have occurred.
One can only wonder
At so grotesque a blunder.

—EDMUND BENTLEY

Christopher Smart

Christopher Smart
Had a big heart
And a cat named Geoffrey
And a bat in his belfry.

—LEE R. PARKS

THE DOUBLE-DACTYL

This enjoyably frustrating form is a 1951 invention of Anthony Hecht and his friend Paul Pascal. In 1966, Hecht and John Hollander published *Jiggery-Pokery: A Compendium of Double Dactyls*. The poem consists of a pair of quatrains in which each line is composed of two dactylic feet (see page 21 in chapter two)—although the final foot in the final line of each quatrain is truncated to land the poem's tumbling rhythm on a single stress. A double-dactyl always begins with a line of nonsense (like *Higgledy-piggledy*) followed by some kind of name in the second line. As for the second line in the second quatrain, it's always a six-syllable, double-dactylic word (a didaktyliaios); and, ideally, no didaktyliaios used in any previous double-dactyl poem should ever be repeated—thus driving the form's practitioners crazy! Also, lines four and eight rhyme!

Here are two examples.

Thomas Stearns Eliot

Prickly pear prickly pear
Thomas Stearns Eliot
Asked about Pound by a
Friend at the bank,

Answered, "I think him a
Megalomaniac—
Miglior fabbro but
Rather a crank."

— PATRICK NIELSEN HAYDEN

Career Move

Hollywood covergirl
Starlett O'Plasticene
turned to a surgeon to
boost her appeal;

now she's a knockout and
oxymoronically
begs for a chance to have
parts that are real.

— JAN D. HODGE

LITTLE WILLIES

In 1899, the British author Harry Graham, under the pseudonym Col. D. Streamer, published a little book entitled *Ruthless Rhymes for Heartless Homes*. The book was very successful, but Graham didn't write a sequel (*More Ruthless Rhymes*) until 1930. As his titles promised, the poems in Graham's books were ruthless little black-humor poems, which often included violence or death, often at the expense of children. Graham's fiendish poems, which clearly poked fun at both British reserve and human insensibility, delighted the British public. Here are some samples.

Calculating Clara

O'er the rugged mountain's brow
Clara threw the twins she nursed,
And remarked, "I wonder now
Which will reach the bottom first?"

Mr. Jones

"There's been an accident!" they said,
"Your servant's cut in half; he'd dead!"
"Indeed!" said Mr. Jones, "and please
Send me the half that's got my keys."

Surely the most influential of all of Graham's gruesome little poems was the following.

Tender-Heartedness

Billy, in one of his nice new sashes,
Fell in the fire and was burnt to ashes;

Now, although the room grows chilly,
I haven't the heart to poke poor Billy.

This little poem spawned countless imitations, and (like the limerick) the numbers of Little Willie poems wax and wane over the years, often catching on for periods at different colleges and universities. Oddly enough, the original character's name switched at some point from "Billy" to "Willie," and the poems, always composed of two tetrameter couplets, begin with "Little Willie" or just "Willie." Here are two anonymous examples.

Full of Hell

Little Willie full of hell
Pushed his sister in the well
Said his mother drawing water
"It's so hard to raise a daughter."

Father's Tea

Willie poisoned father's tea.
Father died in agony.
Mother was extremely vexed—
"Really, Will," she said, "what next?"

BRATS

A number of well-known contemporary poets—including Nancy Willard, Richard Wilbur, and X.J. Kennedy—have written successful children's poetry. Kennedy, in the tradition of the Little Willie poems, has written three books of "brat" poems about perfectly intolerable little children. The first line of these couplet poems (usually composed in quatrains) generally contains the name of the bratty child who, within the next three lines, faces the music.

Stephanie

Stephanie, that little stinker,
Skinny-dipped in fabric shrinker,

We will find her yet, we hope,
Once we buy a microscope.

Kennedy claims that the best of the brat poems was actually written by his son, Josh, who was twelve years old at the time. Josh had heard a number of his father's brat poems, and while his parents were shopping for bedding in a department store, the bored young boy passed the time by composing the following.

Stupid Little Lucy Wankett

Stupid little Lucy Wankett
Washed her automatic blanket
While the thing was still plugged in.
Notify her next of kin.

ASSIGNMENT 10

Write four epigrams or a nonsense poem. Or both!

1. Write four single-couplet epigrams on any subject.
2. Or write a six-stanza (or more) nonsense poem in the demanding rhyme scheme of Carryl's "The Walloping Window-blind."
3. Use solid rhymes!
4. Also, why not try some clerihews, double-dactyls, Little Willies, or brats?

CHAPTER 13
OTHER ENGLISH FORMS

There are hundreds of poetic forms for the English-language poet to use and, in this chapter, we'll look at a few that have not been previously discussed, but that have had a significant impact on the history of English-language verse. We'll begin with two well-known quatrains that differ from common measure and hymnal measure, the two quatrains already discussed in chapter three.

THE IN MEMORIAM QUATRAIN

This iambic tetrameter quatrain, rhyming *abba*, was used by Tennyson in 1850 for his famous long poem *In Memoriam*. The stanza, which rhymes like the first four (as well as the second four) lines of the Italian sonnet's octave, is called an *enveloping stanza* because the *b* rhymes are surrounded by the *a* rhymes. As a result, the quatrain's final rhyme is a sizable distance from its companion rhyme in the first line, which gives the quatrain a lighter feel and creates a comfortable flow from stanza to stanza. Here's a sample excerpt from Tennyson's long masterpiece.

XXVII

I envy not in any moods
  The captive void of noble rage,
  The linnet born within the cage,
That never knew the summer woods:

I envy not the beast that takes
  His license in the field of time,
  Unfetter'd by the sense of crime,

To whom a conscience never wakes;

Nor, what may count itself as blest,
  The heart that never plighted troth
  But stagnates in the weeds of sloth,
Nor any want-begotten rest.

I hold it true, whate'er befall;
  I feel it, when I sorrow most;
  'Tis better to have loved and lost
Than never to have loved at all.

COMMENTS

Despite the poet's pain at the loss of his good friend, Arthur Hallam (see the discussion of "Ulysses" on page 46 in chapter four), the narrator still has no desire to be like the inexperienced "linnet," the unthinking "beast," the uncommitted person who "never plighted troth," or the insensate individual. Rather, he's willing to accept the pain since "'Tis better to have loved and lost / Than never to have loved at all." Tennyson, realizing the power of these lines (which are among the most famous in English literature), repeated them at various other places in his long tribute to his deceased friend.

THE RUBAIYAT STANZA

This iambic pentameter quatrain, rhyming *aaba*, was made popular by Edward Fitzgerald's 1859 translation of "The Rubáiyát," a collection of poems attributed to twelfth-century Persian poet Omar Khayyám. Rather appropriately, the Persian word *rubáiyát* actually means "quatrain," and the cynic Khayyám uses his quatrains to encourage his readers to enjoy life and all its sensual pleasures while there's still time. The most famous line in Fitzgerald's long translation occurs in the seventh quatrain, where Khayyám's sense of fleeting time is expressed as "the Bird is on the Wing."

Here's the poem's opening quatrain.

Wake! For the Sun who scattered into flight
The Stars before him from the Field of Night,
Drives Night along with them from Heav'n, and strikes
The Sultán's Turret with a Shaft of Light.

RIME ROYAL

The most famous and popular seven-line stanza in English literature is also known as the Chaucerian stanza since Chaucer used it for several of the tales in *The Canterbury Tales* as well as for his long romance poem *Troilus and Criseyde*. The iambic pentameter lines of the stanza rhyme *ababbcc*; thus each septet has a strong couplet resolution. Shakespeare used rime royal for *The Rape of Lucrece*, and it was later used by Milton (with some variation) and Wordsworth, but since the seventeenth century, the stanza has seldom been used—with W.H. Auden being one of the exceptions.

The following sample is the opening stanza of Milton's well-known "Ode on the Morning of Christ's Nativity," a fairly long poem that begins with four Chaucerian stanzas. Note that Milton, for emphasis and variety, chooses to end his rime royal stanzas with a hexameter rather than a pentameter.

This is the month, and this the happy morn
Wherein the Son of Heaven's Eternal King
Of wedded maid and virgin mother born,
Our great redemption from above did bring;
For so the holy sages once did sing
That He our deadly forfeit should release,
And with His Father work us a perpetual peace.

OTTAVA RIMA

Ottava rima, which consists of iambic pentameters rhyming *abababcc*, is the most common octave in English poetry. Used by Boccaccio and Torquato Tasso, it's the "national stanza" of Italy, and it has a remarkable versatility, being appropriate for lyrics, narratives, and even humorous poems. The English-language masters of ottava rima are Byron (who used it for *Don Juan*) and Yeats, who used it for some of his most famous and complex poems like "Sailing to Byzantium," "The Municipal Gallery Revisited," "The Circus Animals' Desertion," and "Among School Children." The difficulty in writing ottava rima is the extensive rhyming on the *a* and *b* rhymes. Yeats, in the twentieth-century fashion, occasionally uses slant rhymes in his ottava rima poems, as we can see in the last stanza of his difficult poem "Among School Children," which concludes with one of the most memorable couplets of the century.

> Labor is blossoming or dancing where
> The body is not bruised to pleasure soul,
> Nor beauty born out of its own despair,
> Nor blear-eyed wisdom out of midnight oil.
> O chestnut-tree, great rooted blossomer,
> Are you the leaf, the blossom or the bole?
> O body swayed to music, O brightening glance,
> How can we know the dancer from the dance?

SPENSERIAN STANZA

This nine-line stanza was invented by Edmund Spenser for his masterpiece, *The Faerie Queene*. The stanza rhymes *ababbcbcc*, and all the lines are iambic pentameter except the last line, which is always a hexameter. Despite its length and complexity, the Spenserian stanza's interlocking rhymes pull it forward, creating a sense of driving rhythm that poets have used for narration, description, analysis, and even reflection. Despite its versatility, it can, nevertheless, seem a rather exhausting experience for the reader, and Shapiro and Beum in *A Prosody Handbook* claim that the Spenserian stanza is "almost the largest stanza the mind can grasp as a whole."

Despite these potential pitfalls, the stanza has been used very effectively by a number of the Romantics, including Byron (*Childe Harold's Pilgrimage*), Keats ("The Eve of St. Agnes"), and Shelley (*Adonais*). Here's the opening stanza of Keats's "The Eve of St. Agnes," as the poet begins his romantic narrative of Madeline and Porphyro with carefully chosen descriptions.

> St. Agnes' Eve—Ah, bitter chill it was!
> The owl, for all his feathers, was a-cold;
> The hare limped trembling through the frozen grass,
> And silent was the flock in woolly fold:
> Numb were the Beadsman's fingers, while he told
> His rosary, and while his frosted breath,
> Like pious incense from a censer old,
> Seemed taking flight for heaven, without a death,
> Past the sweet Virgin's picture, while his prayer he saith.

ODES

Despite the ode's misappropriation by youthful versifiers who believe that anything poetic can be called an ode, the term has very specific meanings. An ode is an elaborately structured, rhymed poem which is exalted, elevated, and sometimes enthusiastic in tone. Even modern odes have a classical feel and an appropriate air of decorum. Nevertheless, despite these general characteristics, there are no set rhyme schemes or stanzaic patterns for the ode. As a result, they are usually classified into three somewhat overlapping groups: (1) the highly elaborate and structurally repetitive Pindaric odes; (2) the still regular but more adaptable Horatian odes (like Keats's odes, for example); and (3) the more irregular but still rhymed and metrical Cowleian odes (named for the seventeenth-century English poet Abraham Cowley).

Again, it should be emphasized that even a Cowleian ode, like Wordsworth's elaborate, eleven-part "Intimations of Immortality From Recollections of Early Childhood," will reveal meticulously rhymed and metrical stanzas of various length. Keats's well-known odes, as mentioned above, are even more tightly structured, and his "Ode to a Nightingale," for example, consists of eight ten-line stanzas of iambic pentameter (with a trimeter in line eight) that rhyme *ababcdecde*. This sample (stanza seven) includes Keats's famous reflection about the Biblical character Ruth.

Thou wast not born for death, immortal Bird!
No hungry generations tread thee down;
The voice I hear this passing night was heard
In ancient days by emperor and clown:
Perhaps the self-same song that found a path
Through the sad heart of Ruth, when, sick for home
She stood in tears amid the alien corn;
The same that oft-times hath
Charmed magic casements, opening on the foam
Of perilous seas, in faery lands forlorn.

NONCE FORMS

Many times, poets, in the act of composition, will create their own formal patterns. This might involve the rhyme scheme, the meter, the stanza length, the length of individual lines, refrains, etc. Sometimes it's not possible to know if one's new form is truly new, but this kind of variation and experimentation is natural for poets, and it can create some memorable poetry. Thomas Hardy is a perfect example of a great poet who used, along with the traditional forms, many nonce forms in his work. His famous poem about the 1912 sinking of the *Titanic*, "The Convergence of the Twain," uses oddly constructed triplets (numbered with roman numerals) that rhyme *aaa*, where the first two lines of the tercets are heavily indented iambic trimeters, and the final line is a hexameter. Here, for example, is the eighth stanza.

VIII

And as the smart ship grew
In stature, grace, and hue,
In shadowy silent distance grew the Iceberg too.

Does the stanza look like a little ship? Whether it does or not, Hardy's idiosyncratic nonce form works very effectively in his celebrated poem about vanity and disaster. On the other hand, it's still worth mentioning the obvious: The traditional and popular poetic forms (which have carried the bulk of English-language poetry) have been used over and over again because they work!

OTHER FORMS

Modern poets have also been attracted to a wide range of less-common poetic forms, which are described and delineated in numerous poetry handbooks. There are hundreds of these forms, many of which have provided the basis for successful poems in English. They include, for example, Sapphics from the ancient Greeks, the various Welsh forms, the Malayan pantoum, numerous sonnet variants (like Hopkins' curtal sonnet), the Spanish quintilla, the French terzanelle, and many others. Such forms create interesting possibilities for poets who have adequately developed their craft.

"INTENDED" FORMS AND "FINDING" FORMS

Many modern formalist poets begin writing their poems with just their initiating idea (an incident, a phrase, a sound, etc.); and then, as their original idea begins to formulate on the page, they find or "discover" the form that they feel the poem wants to be. This form might be one of the standard formats, like a sonnet or a poem in quatrains, or it might be a nonce form. Other poets will begin their writing process with a form specifically in mind, like the sonnet, and then develop their initiating idea within the strictures of the intended form.

Some contemporary poets seem almost ashamed to admit that the form was there at the very beginning—as if beginning with a specific form in mind might suggest an inhibition of their poetic freedom—despite the fact that the blank verse of Shakespeare's plays, his 154 sonnets, and his rime royal stanzas for *The Rape of Lucrece*, etc., were all, clearly, "intended" formats. At any rate, the good news (actually, the *great* news!) is that both methods work, and both have produced extraordinary poetry. So new writers will have to discover the process that works the best for them—and sometimes they'll find that they're comfortable with both methods.

ASSIGNMENT II

Write a poem of your choice, using any of the forms discussed in this chapter or in any of the previous chapters. Find a form that you feel will be appropriate to your subject.

1. Avoid nonce forms for now.
2. Unless you're using blank verse, use solid rhymes.

CHAPTER 14
OTHER METRICAL SYSTEMS

Let's begin this chapter by looking at four passages of literature and trying to decide if they're prose or poetry. Each piece, whether poetry or not, is placed on the page like prose and concludes with a period. Even if you recognize the samples, examine them closely, attempt to scan the lines, and decide whether you think the writing is prose or poetry. Then, assuming that all of the samples are poetry, try to decide where the line breaks would go. (Please note that in setting up each of these passages, I've made a few minor adjustments of punctuation and capitalization.)

> In a somer seson, whan soft was the sonne, I shope me in shroudes, as I a shepe were, In habite as an heremite, vnholy of workes, Went wyde in this world, wondres to here.

> I, too, dislike it: there are things that are important beyond all this fiddle. Reading it, however, with a perfect contempt for it, one discovers in it after all, a place for the genuine.

> We'd rather have the iceberg than the ship, although it meant the end of travel. Although it stood stock still like cloudy rock and all the sea were moving marble.

> Sorrow is my own yard, where the new grass flames as it has flamed often before but not with the cold fire that closes round me this year.

SAMPLE 1

> In a somer seson, whan soft was the sonne, I shope me in shroudes, as I a shepe were, In habite as an heremite, vnholy of workes, Went wyde in this world, wondres to here.

These lines are the famous opening of William Langland's medieval masterpiece, *Piers Plowman*, which was written in the late fourteenth century. Using normal scansion techniques, we can see that the poem falls into a mix of mostly iambs and anapests without any regular pattern. But Langland, who was writing in a period when the English language was still developing, is actually using a different metrical system that's more appropriate to the language's Germanic roots. This system is called *accentual verse*, and it demands four accents in each line, with an alliteration on at least two of the accented words, and with a heavy (and marked) caesura occurring within each line. Here's how the first stanza of *Piers Plowman* looks on the page.

> In a somer[1] seson · whan soft was the sonne,
> I shope[2] me in shroudes · as I a shepe[3] were,
> In habite[4] as an heremite[5] · vnholy of workes,
> Went wyde in this world · wondres to here[6].

Langland, despite the varying number of syllables in his lines, is still able to create a very clear, four-beat-per-line rhythm by using the words' natural stresses along with his alliterations. In the poem's first line, all four of the accented words (*somer*, *seson*, *soft*, and *sonne*) are alliterated, but in its subsequent lines the more normal pattern is three alliterations. Thus, without any sense of the classical metrical foot, Langland's Anglo-Saxonish poetry, like the earlier *Beowulf*, establishes a clear and powerful rhythm. Nevertheless, after the metrical accomplishments of Langland's younger contemporary, Chaucer (discussed below), accentual verse quickly fell out of favor. In modern times, this mostly forgotten metrical system has been used, on rare occasions, by W.H. Auden and a few contemporary poets like Richard Wilbur and Charles Martin.

[1]summer [2]dressed [3]shepherd [4]clothes [5]hermit [6]hear

SAMPLE 2

> I, too, dislike it: there are things that are important be-
> yond all this fiddle. Reading it, however, with a perfect
> contempt for it, one discovers in it after all, a place for
> the genuine.

Despite its two (rather flat) declarative sentences, this sample is actually taken from a well-known poem entitled "Poetry" by the twentieth-century American poet Marianne Moore. Although the first line begins rather iambically, it soon falls into anapests, and the second line reveals no clear metrical pattern at all. So what kind of poetry is this? It's called *syllabic verse*, and it comes from the French habit of syllable-counting. Since French is not an accentual language, French poets have always used syllable-counting, along with rhyme and other sonic devices, to establish the basic structure of their poetry. For example, the most popular line in French poetry is the alexandrine, consisting of twelve syllables with a caesura after the sixth syllable.

So let's look at how Marianne Moore places the first stanza of her syllabic poem on the page.

> I, too, dislike it: there are things that are important beyond all this fiddle.
> Reading it, however, with a perfect contempt for it, one discovers in
> it after all, a place for the genuine.
>   Hands that can grasp, eyes
>   that can dilate, hair that can rise
>   if it must, these things are important not because a

Yes, the stanza really does end with the word *a*, which enjambs over to the next stanza. Given the excessive length of her first two lines, sometimes when the poem is reprinted, a few of the lines won't fit on the page, so they're carried over and indented. Regardless, the poem's five stanzas are all basically sestets, and the syllable counts for the six lines are 19-19-11-5-9-13, although some of the lines in the subsequent stanzas vary a bit. You will, of course, decide for yourself whether the poet's line breaks are effective, but our primary concern is whether syllabic meter can actually create rhythm—some kind of up-and-down, back-and-forth, ebb-and-flow beneath the line and under the meaning. In a poem like this, the varying syllabic lines do nothing to create a sense of rhythm for the reader. In truth, the only way that a syllabic poem can create some kind of metrical beat or rhythm is if the poem consists of very short lines with a fairly regular syllable count. In that case, a reader might be able to sense the duration of each line as a kind of sonic unit, but there would, of course, still be no underlying beat in the individual lines.

Japanese poets, like the French, also use syllable-counting in their verse, as in their well-known tankas and haiku. The haiku, for example, is a Zen-based poem that consists of three lines with a 5-7-5 syllable count. Translators usually do their best to use the same syllable count when attempting to render Japanese haikus into English. Here, for example, is an English translation of a famous haiku written by Moritake, a sixteenth-century Japanese poet.

> The fallen blossom,
> rising back up to its branch,
> is a butterfly.

Syllabic verse, given its lack of an underlying beat, has not been used very much in our language. Robert Bridges, who was appointed the English Poet Laureate in 1913, and his daughter, Elizabeth Daryush, wrote a number of syllabic poems, but with only limited success. In the twentieth century, the form has been used by Marianne Moore and, sometimes, by Dylan Thomas and John Hollander.

SAMPLE 3

> We'd rather have the iceberg than the ship, although it
> meant the end of travel. Although it stood stock still like
> cloudy rock and all the sea were moving marble.

These lines from "The Imaginary Iceberg" by the distinguished twentieth-century American poet Elizabeth Bishop are easily scannable and easily recognized as poetry. They form the first four lines of her poem's opening stanza, and the line breaks are natural and easy to discern.

> We'd rather have the iceberg than the ship,
> although it meant the end of travel.
> Although it stood stock still like cloudy rock
> and all the sea were moving marble.

These four lines consist of alternating and unrhymed (blank) iambic pentameters and tetrameters, and the powerful beat of Bishop's iambics are not only naturally pleasing, but they're also skillfully used to enforce the meaning of the lines by giving added weight to the most significant words.

This, of course, is what we've been studying throughout this book, and it's called *accentual-syllabic poetry* because it combines the Saxon accent-counting with the French syllable-counting (which now becomes foot-counting). With the exception of *Beowulf*, *Piers Plowman*, and a few other early Germanic poems, our English-language literature really begins with the works of Chaucer, who successfully married the German and French metrical systems to create the accentual-syllabic meter that has dominated English-language poetry.

Here, for example, is Chaucer's well-known description of the knight in *The Canterbury Tales*—a perfect iambic pentameter.

> Hĕ wás | ă vér | răy, pár | fĭt gén | tĭl knýght.

Just as the English language combined the Germanic and the French languages, Chaucer's metric combined their two metrical systems to create an extraordinary rhythmical template for poetic expression that is the envy of the world. It has, as we've seen throughout this book, been the powerful medium for the greatness of Shakespeare, Milton, Pope, Tennyson, Yeats, Frost, and countless others.

SAMPLE 4

> Sorrow is my own yard, where the new grass flames as it has flamed often before but not with the cold fire that closes round me this year.

Despite its lovely poetic language, this sentence is impossible to scan into a regular metrical pattern. Like any piece of English writing—prose or poetry—it contains a naturally "rising" feel, given its iambs and anapests. But this, of course, is simply the natural propensity of the language. As pointed out in chapter two, even English prose consists of nearly 60 percent iambs. Thus, these unmetered lines, written by the twentieth-century American poet William Carlos Williams, are a sample of free verse (nonmetrical verse). These particular lines initiate Williams's twenty-eight-line poem entitled "The Widow's Lament in Springtime," and the author arranges them as follows.

> Sorrow is my own yard
> where the new grass
> flames as it has flamed
> often before but not
> with the cold fire
> that closes round me this year.

The line breaks follow a kind of syntactical logic, and the short lines might be read in such a way as to create a kind of overall "cadenced" rhythm (which one can also create with short-lined syllabic poems), but there is clearly no underlying beat in the poem. This is intentional, of course, and free-verse practitioners, aware of this deficit, often try to enhance their nonmetrical verse with other sonic devices, like alliteration, assonance, the repetition of words, or the repetition of phrases. In the nineteenth century, both Walt Whitman (who tried to create a chant-like rhythmic feel through phrasal repetition) and W.E. Henley wrote nonmetrical poems, but English-language free verse was first written on a regular basis in the wake of Ezra Pound and the Imagists (see appendix

III). In general, free verse is a form of poetic expression that has no set metrical rhythm—as well as no set line or stanza lengths, and a tendency to avoid end-rhyme.

QUANTITATIVE VERSE

It should also be briefly mentioned that there have been serious attempts by Robert Bridges and a few other poets to adapt the classical metrical models to English-language verse, but these experiments have failed. In Greek and Latin poetry, the rhythm is created by a metrical system based on duration (the actual sonic length of the given syllables). But when this is attempted in English, the syllables of duration are invariably overwhelmed by the natural stresses of the language.

IN SUMMARY

There are four ways to compose verse in the English language: (1) using accentual meter, (2) using syllabic meter, (3) using syllabic-accentual meter, or (4) writing nonmetrical (free) verse.

A NOTE ABOUT PUBLICATION

The purpose of writing is to communicate, and the best way to communicate with readers outside your personal circle of family and friends is by publication. Aspiring poets, like all writers, start off small and then progress to larger formats. Thus, poets usually begin by publishing in the literary journals; and then, when they've had substantial journal publication, they'll begin to seek out book publication. Both are difficult to do. Since so many people enjoy writing poetry, the journals are inundated with submissions. As for book publication, since there's little, if any, financial reward for producing collections of poetry, publishers are naturally wary.

Newer poets (as already discussed) need to, above all, read the great works of our literary past. But, eventually, they also need to familiarize themselves with the contemporary milieu by reading the literary journals—usually in college libraries (since college libraries generally carry more journals than the local libraries). In time, when these aspiring poets have completed three poems that they feel are publishable, they can start to submit their work. Sometimes journals give their submission guidelines within the journal itself; sometimes they will mail the guidelines to poets who request them with a SASE (self-addressed stamped envelope); and sometimes they will have them listed on their Web sites. *Poet's Market*, which is updated once a year, is an invaluable source of information about the various publishers of poetry. It lists nearly two thousand journals that regularly publish poetry, and it gives information about what they're looking for, whom they've published, the dates of their reading periods, whether they consider simultaneous submissions (poems that are submitted to more than one journal at the same time), etc.

Obviously, the personal taste of each editor will dictate the policies of the journal; some editors prefer free verse, others are open to both metrical and free verse, and some (like the editors of *Measure*) specialize in metrical verse. As a result, it's wise to familiarize yourself with the different journals before you submit—so you can get a feel for the editors' aesthetic preferences.

Finally, poets (like all writers) need to accept rejection as a natural aspect of the process. *Everyone* has been rejected. The stories we've all heard about poets (like the great Edwin Arlington Robinson) covering their walls with rejection slips are true. Nevertheless, if you have talent, and if you've learned your craft, some editor will eventually recognize and appreciate what you're doing. Poets, as mentioned earlier, need to carefully consider criticism, but they also need to know when to have faith in their own work.

ASSIGNMENT 12

When you feel you're ready, submit your poems to a literary journal.

1. Examine the journal you intend to submit your work to. If it's not available at your local bookstore or library, you may be able to get a recent back-issue through interlibrary loan (or purchase a copy from the editor).
2. Include a very brief, modest, and factual cover letter. Newer poets can mention their education and their profession if they wish. If previously published, mention the names of your three most significant publications.
3. Submit three poems, neatly typed (double-spaced or single-spaced) on individual sheets of standard white paper. Include on each sheet your name, address, telephone number, and e-mail address.
4. Include a SASE for the editor's response and the return of your poems. If you'd rather not have the poems returned, you can mention your preference in your cover letter.
5. Send the submission in a standard business envelope (no. 10) containing the cover letter, the poems, and the SASE (all neatly folded in thirds).
6. Be sure your submission has enough postage (all serious writers eventually get a scale!). Some editors, with perfect justification, simply return submissions that are marked "Postage Due."
7. Be patient.
8. Realize that rejection is a natural fact of life for all writers, so plan ahead. Decide which journal you'll send your poems to next, and if they're rejected, send them out again as soon as possible.

CHAPTER 15

CONCLUDING THOUGHTS AND RECOMMENDED READING

At this point in the semester, my students and I read "Prosody and Period," a brief survey of English-language poetry (from its medieval beginnings through the 1950s) written by Robert Beum and Karl Shapiro for *A Prosody Handbook*. I then conclude the class with some personal and rather opinionated observations about metrical poetry (see below) and some brief facts about Ezra Pound and F.S. Flint, the founders of Imagism. For the purposes of this book, I've included both the Beum and Shapiro survey and my own comments about Imagism, "Pound, Flint, Imagism, and *Vers Libre*," in appendices I and II. I would strongly encourage you to read (and study!) Beum and Shapiro's excellent survey, which reminds us of the remarkable history of English-language poetry and the dominance of metrical verse. Also, if you'd like to read my parting thoughts about Imagism, I hope you'll enjoy them as well.

By now, I'm sure that it's perfectly clear that I much prefer metrical poetry to nonmetered verse, believing that the accentual-syllabic system, which has served all the great poets in the English language from Chaucer to Wilbur, is fundamental to the great and permanent tradition of English-language poetry. As mentioned in chapter one, my own doctoral emphasis was Ezra Pound and Imagism, and thus the foundations of Modernism. At the time, as an aspiring poet, I felt that it was crucial to understand the creation of Imagism and its influential demand for nonmetrical poetry, which had quickly become the dominant mode of the twentieth century. At the present time, given my proclivity for metered poetry, my students will sometimes ask me (or challenge me): "But isn't there *good* free verse?" And the answer, of course, is "of course."

Many intelligent, creative, and talented people have dedicated their lives to writing such verse, and their poems can discuss important subjects, have beautiful lines, contain lovely sounds, be very moving, and so on.

But so can prose.

The real question is whether free verse is the best choice for the practicing poet. In my opinion, all young poets will—and should—eventually experiment with free verse. My own earliest poems were written in free verse, and all of my invaluable teachers (up to Howard Nemerov) wrote mostly nonmetrical verse: William Packard, James Dickey, and David St. John. Personally, I found writing free verse rather easy, and within a year of sending out my work, I was very grateful to be appearing in *Poetry* and many other distinguished journals. Nevertheless, I felt that something was missing, and I knew *exactly* what it was. I knew that my own little attempts to write poetry clearly lacked something that was fundamental to the work of Homer, Dante, and Shakespeare. So I decided to teach myself about metrics, and eventually, with Jim Dickey's blessing, I was able to work with Howard Nemerov at the Bread Loaf Writers' Coference.

Think about it this way: When a writer sits down at his desk, he has a number of things at his service: diction, syntax, the figures, the tradition, his imagination, his experience, his intelligence, etc. But the prose writer *also* has access to each of those writerly things. The poet, however, is even more fortunate because he has another extremely powerful tool at his disposal: poetic meter. And this particular tool (or weapon) has obviously been time-tested, having served Homer, Virgil, Dante, Shakespeare, Milton, Tennyson, Yeats, and Frost. Pound, of course, chose to go in another direction—and he took many talented people along with him—but I finally came to the conclusion that I preferred to follow in the metrical tradition of Homer and the rest.

Today in the United States, despite the current and exciting Formalist revival (see appendix IV), free verse is still the dominant poetic mode. It would be fair to say that more than 90 percent of current English-language verse is written in nonmetrical formats. But as recently as a hundred years ago, aspiring poets didn't even have to ask themselves the crucial question: Will I write metrical or nonmetrical verse? Poe, of course, would have thought the question perfectly ludicrous.

> Contenting myself with the certainty that music, in its various modes of meter, rhythm, and rhyme, is of so vast a moment in poetry as never to be wisely rejected—is so vitally important an adjunct, that he is simply silly who declines its assistance—I will not now pause to maintain its absolute essentiality.

Certainly, if we reflect on it a moment, it does seem rather incautious (if not audacious) to reject meter out of hand when it has been used so effectively (and almost exclusively) by, among others: Chaucer, Spenser, Marlowe, Shakespeare, Donne, Jonson, Milton, Dryden, Pope, Blake, Burns, Wordsworth, Coleridge, Byron, Shelley, Keats, Emerson, Elizabeth Browning, Longfellow, Poe, Tennyson, Robert Browning, Dickinson, Swinburne, Hardy, Hopkins, Wilde, Alfred Housman, Yeats, Robinson, Frost, Ransom, Millay, Owen, Auden, Bishop, Nemerov, Wilbur, and Larkin.

It's certainly something to think about seriously.

In conclusion, I would like to encourage you to continue the development of your poetic craft. Writing poetry, like reading poetry, is one of the most pleasurable of all human activities, and I wish you well. We should, of course, be quite serious about the improvement of our craft; but, on the other hand, we should also have some fun as well!

I'd like to finish this introductory book with an appropriate quote from Samuel Johnson, that great literary genius of the eighteenth century.

> Versification, or the art of modulating his numbers, is indispensably necessary to a poet. Every other power by which the understanding is enlightened or the imagination enchanted may be exercised in prose. But the poet has this peculiar superiority, that to all the powers which

> the perfection of every other composition can require, he adds the faculty of joining music with reason, and of acting at once upon the senses and the passions.

[RECOMMENDED READING]

INDISPENSABLE

Shapiro, Karl, and Robert Beum. *A Prosody Handbook*. New York: Harper & Row, 1965. This exceptional introduction to prosody has been out of print for many years, but Dover is currently planning to reprint the book in 2006.

Steele, Timothy. *Missing Measures: Modern Poetry and the Revolt Against Meter*. Fayetteville: University of Arkansas Press, 1990. The subtitle tells it all. This is one of the most important literary studies of the past hundred years.

Baer, William. *Fourteen on Form: Conversations With Poets*. Jackson: University Press of Mississippi, 2004. This book is indispensable not because of who's asking the questions, but because of who's answering them! Aspiring poets can learn a great deal about the craft of poetry (and many other matters) from these fourteen interviews with contemporary masters like Richard Wilbur, Anthony Hecht, Wendy Cope, etc.

HIGHLY RECOMMENDED

Paul Fussell, Jr. *Poetic Meter and Poetic Form*. New York: Random House, 1965. This classic and excellent book about form and meter came out the same year as *A Prosody Handbook*, and this one, fortunately, is still in print.

Steele, Timothy. *All the Fun's in How You Say a Thing: An Explanation of Meter and Versification*. Athens: Ohio University Press, 1999. An in-depth and always entertaining study of versification. *Everyone* can learn from this book. Even Richard Wilbur found it "instructive"!

Baer, William, ed. *Sonnets: 150 Contemporary Sonnets*. Evansville, IN: University of Evansville Press, 2005. This unique anthology contains carefully crafted contemporary sonnets by ninety-seven poets, including Wilbur, Seamus Heaney, Hecht, and many others.

Bach, Bert C., William A. Sessions, William Walling. *The Liberating Form: A Handbook-Anthology of English and American Poetry*. New York: Dodd, Mead, 1972. This exceptional book about form is sadly forgotten and out of print. Sometimes, copies can still be found on the Internet.

Hungerford, Edward Buell. *Recovering the Rhythms of Poetry: The Elements of Versification*. Chicago: Scott, Foresman, 1964. This is an entire workbook of scansion exercises, using samples from Shakespeare. Many years ago, I used this little booklet when I was teaching myself meter. Even if you don't agree with all of Professor Hungerford's scansions, this exercise book will definitely develop your ear and your sense of poetic rhythm. Long out of print, it can still be requested through interlibrary loan and photocopied!

Saintsbury, George. *A History of English Prosody From the Twelfth Century to the Present Day*. 2nd ed. New York: Russell & Russell, 1961. This legendary study of English versification, though originally published in 1906, is still highly engaging and extremely informative. In 1910, Saintsbury wrote an excellent compressed version, which he entitled *Historical Manual of English Prosody* (New York: Schocken Books, 1966).

Turco, Lewis. *The Book of Forms: A Handbook of Poetics*. 3rd ed. Hanover, NH: University Press of New England, 2000. The standard reference for the various forms available to English-language poets.

Hollander, John. *Rhyme's Reason: A Guide to English Verse*. 3rd ed. New Haven: Yale Nota Bene/Yale University Press, 2001. A little tour de force in which the author good-naturedly illustrates the various forms and types of English-language poetry.

Drury, John. *The Poetry Dictionary*. 2nd ed. Cincinnati: Writer's Digest Books, 2006. A very useful reference book.

APPENDICES

I.
Prosody and Period

BY ROBERT BEUM
AND KARL SHAPIRO

The following is a synopsis, by period, of significant developments in English prosody.

Old English (Anglo-Saxon)—449–1066

The ALLITERATIVE LINE (accentual prosody) for all poetry. *Beowulf*, *Deor*, *Widsith*, *The Seafarer*, *The Battle of Maldon*, runes.

Early Middle English (Anglo-Norman)—1066–1350

Development of ACCENTUAL-SYLLABIC VERSE, the marriage of syllable-counting (the French habit) and stress-counting (the native English habit). Development of IAMBIC AND TROCHAIC METERS, uncertainly and irregularly. Development of RHYME, also uncertainly, as in Layamon's *Brut*. Imitations of Norman rhyming forms. The old alliterative line continues, but is falling into desuetude. Langland's *Piers Plowman* the last important poem to be written in the alliterative meter (c. 1350).

Late Middle English—1350–1500

Chaucer (d. 1400): *The Canterbury Tales*, *Troilus and Criseyde*. This, almost the first regular accentual-syllabic verse, remains among the greatest. Chaucer is also the first Englishman to make the RHYME ROYAL an expressive stanza; in emulation, English poets make it a principal stanza for the next two hundred years.

Early Tudor—1500–1558

The ITALIAN SONNET, OTTAVA RIMA, TERZA RIMA, all introduced by Wyatt (d. 1542). The ENGLISH (SHAKESPEAREAN) SONNET and BLANK VERSE, pioneered by Surrey (d. 1547). Surrey's verse, smoother than Wyatt's, gains the greater favor and sets the fashion.

Elizabethan—1558–1603

Marlowe, Shakespeare, and others develop BLANK VERSE FOR THE THEATER. The SPENSERIAN STANZA, devised by Spenser for his epic allegory *The Faerie Queene* (Books I–VI complete, 1596). Spenser a great prosodic innovator. Much of his early verse looks backward to Chaucer and to the alliterative tradition. Throughout the Elizabethan Age, verse forms of every sort flourish: SONG FORMS and SONNETS especially popular. Prosodic intricacy admired for its own sake: prosody as a form of wit. The Elizabethans were as fond of imaginative and elaborate forms as the Augustans were of the rhymed couplet. Thomas Campion, a musician-poet, disparages rhyme (1602), urges poets to pay more attention to their quantities, and experiments with a kind of quantitative verse. Rebutted by Samuel Daniel in a defense of rhyme (1602).

Jacobean and Caroline—1603–1642

BLANK VERSE continues at a high level in the plays of Ben Jonson, the late plays of Shakespeare, and often in those of John Ford and of Beaumont and Fletcher. The form becomes less regular, and sometimes indistinguishable from prose, in the hands of John Webster, Philip Massinger, and others. John Donne fashions a vigorous, flexible, conversational idiom that retains an iambic basis and regularity of stanza form. Donne, Jonson, and others bring new prestige to the HEROIC COUPLET inaugurated by Chaucer and illuminated by Christopher Marlowe in *Hero and Leander*. Anglican devotional poetry of greatness by George Herbert (d. 1633), often in intricate and sometimes in emblematic stanza forms; Roman Catholic devotional poetry by Richard Crashaw (d. 1649).

Puritan—1642–1660

Milton: ITALIAN SONNETS of great power, sometimes ambitiously onomatopoeic; intricate, resonant BLANK VERSE in *Paradise Lost*; unusual metrical freedom and experimentation in *Samson Agonistes*. Edmund Waller (d. 1687) and John Denham (d. 1669) favor PENTAMETER COUPLETS and make the form still more popular. Great Anglican devotional poetry in both simple and intricate stanzaic forms by Thomas Traherne (d. 1674) and Henry Vaughan (d. 1695).

Restoration—1660–1700

HEROIC COUPLETS for all kinds of verse; John Dryden (1631–1700) the master of the form.

Augustan (Enlightenment, Neoclassical)—1700–1798

The Age of Reason, of Nature conceived as rational and infinitely manipulable, of Baconian optimism. The great and representative figures: Alexander Pope (1688–1744), Jonathan Swift (1667–1745), Samuel Johnson (1709–1784). Much of the period's first-rate poetry is in COUPLETS, much of that in the CLOSED COUPLET, which is now held to be the most rational (i.e., most natural) form. Yet the sway of the heroic couplet has been exaggerated. Swift, for example, favored tetrameter couplets through the very heart of the period; and Matthew Prior turned many a fair quatrain. Satiric and didactic verse are the century's main interests; and couplets, of course, are the most pungent of forms. Very few sonnets, none of any value. Prosodic experimentation toward the end of the age (e.g., Gray, Collins). The status of BLANK VERSE in this period is an interesting paradox to which too little attention has been called. Outside the drama, blank verse had practically disappeared for about half a century (1671: Milton, *Paradise Regained*—1730: Thomson, *The Seasons*). It had never been anathematized, however, and generally it retained a theoretical approval even among poets who preferred the couplet for their own verse. To these more "classical" Augustans (e.g., Swift, Pope, Addison), blank verse was acceptable because it was plain and could be brought close to the manner of prose. To the more romantic Augustans (e.g., Thomson, Shenstone, Young), it was attractive for other reasons: it avoided the polished tone and packaging tendency of couplets; its rhymelessness, diminishing aesthetic distance, not only made possible the prosaic quality that was viable for the more rationalistic temperaments, but also could make for an effect of "naturalness" congenial to the "pre-romantics'" spontaneous enjoyment of meadows, vales, hills, and ruins; also, blank verse connoted Shakespeare and the romantic Elizabethans generally.

Romantic—1798–1832

William Blake (1757–1827), William Wordsworth (1770–1850), and Samuel Taylor Coleridge (1772–1834) are influential in restoring the prestige of a wide variety of forms by restoring the prestige of passion, imagination, exoticism, and strongly asserted individuality. BALLADS regain favor. Wordsworth prizes the ballad stanza for its associations with simple, rustic life; Keats and Coleridge value it more for its associations with an idealized and exotic past. Wordsworth breathes new life into the SONNET. ODE forms are valued, not because of their classical origin, but because they can be employed with a certain looseness and spiritedness, and because they permit patterns of varying line lengths, which in turn can help create an effect of contraction and expansion (rendering unity in variety) once again felt to be admirable in its own right and also felt to resemble the "pulsations" of intense feeling. Blake develops a very free long-lined ACCENTUAL VERSE, and experiments successfully with SLANT RHYME. Blake is a great master of the QUATRAIN. Burns's colloquial SONG FORMS are a splendid achievement. The SPENSERIAN STANZA has exotic and romantic Elizabethan connotations, and attracts Burns, Byron, Shelley, Keats, and others. Keats's *Eve of St. Agnes* is perhaps the finest Romantic poem in this stanza. The later Keats ODES are a great body of controlled lyricism and meditation. Byron revitalizes the OTTAVA RIMA in *Don Juan*. Shelley, in *Ode to the West Wind* and the unfinished *Triumph of Life*, raises the TERZA RIMA to new prestige.

Victorian—1832–1900

Few generalizations about either prosody or taste will stand up. There is an immense variety of verse forms, and much experimentation alongside much conservatism. Imitations of CLASSICAL PROSODY by Tennyson (1809–1892) and Swinburne (1837–1909). WEBSTERIAN BLANK VERSE by Matthew Arnold (1822–1888). Arnold's "Scholar Gypsy" stanza an excellence mysteriously unique. FREE VERSE (of inferior quality) by W.E.

Henley (1849–1903), and (of greatness) by Walt Whitman (*Leaves of Grass*, 1st ed., 1855). Whitman's free verse was deeply influenced by the King James version of the Bible (a book few of his admirers read or recommend); his line tends to be long, end-stopped, and—in this respect like Spenser's—"beautifully redundant." The RUBAIYAT STANZA by Edward Fitzgerald (1809–1883), a remarkable single achievement. Edgar Allan Poe (1809–1849) experiments in unusual, often highly onomatopoeic, forms. Coventry Patmore (1823–1896) experiments with the COWLEIAN ODE, sometimes achieving greatness in the form. Gerard Manley Hopkins (1844–1889; publ. 1913) develops SPRUNG RHYTHM and a highly alliterative, assonantal, and strongly stressed metric; his sonnets, Italian in form, are the best of the period and among the best of any period. His flashing and dithyrambic idiom exerted an enormous influence on many twentieth-century poets; less well known, but equally remarkable, are several poems that are as quiet and as quietly effective as Patmore's usual vein. Robert Bridges (1844–1930), Hopkins' editor, experiments, not very successfully, with imitations of classical prosody, but develops a relatively successful and historically important SYLLABIC VERSE. One of the most significant prosodic developments of the Victorian age is the perfection of CONVERSATIONAL STYLES within the bounds of regular, fixed metrical form.

Modern—1900–

FREE VERSE by Ezra Pound, Amy Lowell, T.S. Eliot, Basil Bunting, H.D., D.H. Lawrence, William Carlos Williams, Richard Eberhart, and a great many others. Free verse not infrequently showing end rhyme: Louis Zukofsky and Robert Creeley. Pound develops a species of free verse which is often sparer and flatter than Whitman's, and usually shorter lined. W.B. Yeats, a great master of the QUATRAIN, also revives the OTTAVA RIMA, writing several remarkable poems in this unlikely stanza. DRAMATIC BLANK VERSE of a very loose type—sometimes free or accentual verse—by William Butler Yeats and T.S. Eliot. More normal blank verse for the theater by Maxwell Anderson; for lyric and narrative poems by Conrad Aiken, Hart Crane, Robert Frost, Edwin Arlington Robinson,

Wallace Stevens. Syllabic Verse made the vehicle of excellent poetry by Elizabeth Daryush, Kenneth Rexroth, Marianne Moore, Dylan Thomas. Elaborate or highly regular verse favored by, for example, E.A. Robinson, Dylan Thomas, J.V. Cunningham, Roy Campbell, Robert Lowell, Richard Wilbur, John Fandel. Freer and more traditional forms seem about equally popular. One of the most striking characteristics of contemporary poetry is its tendency to favor a definite, even rhyming, stanzaic pattern, but to employ a line "played by ear"—a Speech-Cadence Line, usually with iambic overtones. In rhyme, the preference is for Slant Rhyme, although at the time of this writing ordinary rhyme seems to be gaining the ascendancy again. The undisputed masters of slant rhyme are Yeats, Auden, and Dylan Thomas; the tradition goes back to Emily Dickinson and William Blake. Another salient feature of contemporary poetry is the imaginative and sensitive Use of Space on the printed page.

[This survey comprises Chapter 18 of *A Prosody Handbook*, 1965.]

II.
A Brief History of the Sonnet

SICILY—CREATION IN THE HIGH MIDDLE AGES

Although its origins are generally associated with the Renaissance, the sonnet was actually created nearly 800 years ago in the late-Medieval, Sicilian court of Frederick II (1194–1250), the Holy Roman Emperor and King of Sicily. Frederick, nicknamed *stupor mundi* (the wonder of the world), was a great patron of the arts, and his Italianate kingdom extended from the island of Sicily in the Mediterranean to Naples on the Tyrrhenian Sea. To establish order in his Catholic dominions, Frederick maintained a group of fourteen legal officials called notaries at his royal court to draw up legal documents. It was in this group of Sicilian lawyers that the sonnet was first created, as Frederick's well-educated notaries passed around their creations at court. Fifty-eight of these early sonnets still survive, some quite excellent, and some reputedly written by the Emperor himself.

At least twenty-six of the fifty-eight surviving Sicilian sonnets were written by Giacomo da Lentino, later memorialized in Dante's *Purgatorio* (Canto XXIV). Although little is known about da Lentino, various scholars have speculated, without any evidence, that he created the first sonnet, and there are also many related theories about how the sonnet structure first came into being, some associating its proportions to Pythagoras' Golden Mean (despite its different 8:5 ratio) and even the Fibonacci series. The truth is, we have absolutely no idea which of Frederick's notaries first came up with the Sicilian sonnet, and it seems far more probable that its creation was a matter of "inspiration" in the course of composition (as J. L. Borges speculates in his poem "*Un Poeta del Siglo XIII*") rather than some kind of externally imposed mathematical construct. This is especially likely given the fact that the first eight lines (or "octave") of the Sicilian sonnet (which rhymes abababab) are essentially the eight-line stanza known as the *strambotto*, which was commonly used in Sicilian folk songs. It seems highly probable that the unknown originator of the sonnet (*sonetto*, "little song") took the *strambotto* and then added two tercets consisting of six lines (the "sestet," rhyming cdecde) to create the 14-line Sicilian sonnet.

In both subject and tone, these early sonnets set the pattern for the next two hundred years, being essentially love poems, often with a spiritual foundation. Yet despite the court's enthusiasm for these new Sicilian poems, the sonnet would not become widely known until the Renaissance.

MEDIEVAL FLORENCE—DANTE

T. S. Eliot has written that "Dante and Shakespeare divide the modern world between them; there is no third" (*Dante*, 1929), and both of these preeminent literary geniuses found themselves drawn to the irresistible sonnet. In *La Vita Nuova* (1292), the world's first sonnet sequence, Dante Alighieri (1265-1321) composed a series of sonnets, along with supplemental commentary, that expressed his distant yet very personal and emotional love for Beatrice Portinari, a woman he'd first seen when he was nine years old and she was eight, and whom he never knew personally. Within his exquisite sonnets, Dante establishes Beatrice as his earthly ideal who, at first, causes him serious emotional difficulties, but who eventually leads him, as she will in his epic *Commedia* (1321), toward God—serving as a symbol of Christian salvation. These sonnets are deeply felt, personal and psychological, and they prepare the way for Petrarch.

In structure, Dante chooses to use the rhyme scheme reputedly adapted by Guittone d'Arezzo (1230?-1294) from the original Sicilian model. This pattern, known as the Italian sonnet (and later as the Petrachan sonnet), uses a new "enveloping" pattern in the octave, abbaabba, which creates a tighter cohesion in the first eight lines given the new central couplet which fuses the first four lines with the subsequent four and clearly establishes the octave as a seamless unit of thought. Petrarch would later follow this pattern as well, similarly using a number of variants in the sestet (usually cdecde or cdcdcd).

THE ITALIAN RENAISSANCE—PETRARCH

Francesco Petrarca (1304-1374), the greatest literary figure of the Italian Renaissance, was also the most important and influential sonneteer of all time. Unlike Dante, who is always associated with his *terza rima* masterpiece the *Commedia*, Petrarch's reputation rests entirely on his perfection of the sonnet. Petrarch's sonnets, similar to Dante's, express his distant but very real and frustrated love for a young woman he identifies as Laura, who was most likely Laurette de Noves. Given that Petrarch had taken minor orders in 1326 and that Laura seems to have been a married woman, the poems are full of deep personal frustrations. These sonnets, although they have much in common with Dante's, are generally written in a less exalted style, and, being in tune with the new Renaissance humanism, they seem even more personal. In his earlier sonnets, Laura is an ideal but very real presence who inflames him with passionate desire, but the sonnets written after her death in 1348 seem to, as with many of Dante's poems to Beatrice, envision her more as an angelic presence directing his thoughts to God.

Petrarch's mastery of the form and the popularity of the sonnets in his *Canzoniere* ("Lyric Poems") combined with the cultural excitement of the early Renaissance to make the little *sonetto* the most popular and imitated form in Italy and, in time, in all of Europe.

THE EUROPEAN SONNET

In the wake of Petrarch, the sonnet, along with many other Renaissance concepts and attitudes, moved into the neighboring countries of Europe, each of which soon produced excellent sonneteers. In France, Pierre de Ronsard (1524?-1585) was the master of the Pléiade poets, and exquisite sonnets were also written by Joachim du Bellay (1522-1560) and Louise Labé (1524?-1566). In Spain, the sonnets of Juan Boscán (1490-1542) would inspire Garcilaso de la Vega (1503?-1536) and Lope de Vega (1562-1635) to write in the form. In Italy herself, the sonnet tradition was admirably carried forward by Torquato Tasso (1544-1595) as well as his earlier predecessors, Michelangelo Buonarotti (1475-1564) and Baldassre Castiglione (1478-1529). Further west, the Spanish introduced the sonnet into Portugal, the small but important explorer-nation, which produced Luís de Camões (1524-1580), the author of the last great western epic, *Os Lusiadas* (1572), as well as several hundred masterful sonnets. Camões, more than any other poet in the first four hundred years of the sonnet, expanded the little *sonetto*'s subject matter. Although most of his sonnets were love poems (including many that were quite idiosyncratic), Camões also wrote sonnets about myth, history, contemporary politics, nature, religion, and personal despair.

Europe's subsequent dedication to the sonnet can be recognized in the fact that many of her greatest poets from the Renaissance to the modern era were also distinguished sonneteers, including: Goethe, Pushkin, Baudelaire, D'Annunzio, and Mallarmé.

THE ENGLISH-LANGUAGE SONNET

The influence of Petrarch is clear at the very beginnings of modern English literature when Geoffrey Chaucer (1343?-1400) in his *Troilus and Criseyde* (*c.*1385, Book I, 400-420) translated one of Petrarch's sonnets (#132), although Chaucer chose to render the poem in rhyme royal stanzas. The actual sonnet format would not appear in England until two hundred years later, at the beginning of its own Renaissance, when Sir Thomas Wyatt (1503?-1542) began translating some of Petrarch's sonnets using the Italianate rhyme scheme. Wyatt, in both his adaptations and his own sonnets, used the traditional Italian pattern, but he preferred the rarer sestet rhyme-scheme of cdddcc which allowed for the origins of the couplet-ending sonnet in English. Such a pattern was more clearly defined by Wyatt's friend, Henry Howard, Earl of Surrey (1517?-1547), who created what is now known as the English sonnet (or Shakespearean sonnet) -- abab cdcd efef gg.

This new rhyme scheme not only allowed for many new possibilities of internal division within the sonnet (4-4-4-2, or 8-4-2, or 8-6, or 12-2, etc.), but it made composition in the more rhyme-difficult English language much easier. The new form also gave great emphasis and power to its final couplet. Generally, the structure of the asymmetrical, two-part,

Italianate sonnet was seen as a situation-response format: the octave presents a problem or situation, which leads to a turn or "*volta*" in line nine where the sestet comments on or resolves the sonnet's "problem." But now the new English sonnet, with all its various possibilities of internal structure (including the traditional 8-6 format) put tremendous emphasis on its concluding couplet. Since the final couplet of the English sonnet often tends to summation, or aphorism, or wit, the English sonnet was typically seen as a more "analytical" (even more intellectual) structure than the Italianate form, which tended to a more "emotional" but less climatic expression. These, of course, are only basic, though useful, generalizations since both sonnet formats allow for endless possibilities and variants.

Ten years after the death of Surrey (and fifteen years after the death of Wyatt), Richard Tottel published *Songes and Sonettes* in 1557. This collection of lyrics, generally known as *Tottel's Miscellany*, contained many of the sonnets of Wyatt and Surrey, both of whom had adapted the European hendecasyllabic (eleven syllable) line into the sturdy English iambic pentameter which was presently coming into its own. Thus the pioneer sonnets of Wyatt and Surrey laid the groundwork for the great Elizabethan sonnet revival that would begin about twenty-three years after the publication of *Tottel's Miscellany*.

The sudden explosion of the sonnet at the end of the 16th Century resulted in a number of lengthy English sonnet-sequences, including Sir Philip Sidney's *Astrophel and Stella* (1591), Edmund Spenser's *Amoretti* (1595), and William Shakespeare's *Sonnets* (1609). The publication of Shakespeare's elegant, passionate, and intelligent sonnets represents a crucial moment in the history of the form, and it's fair to say that even if Shakespeare had never written his masterful blank verse plays, he would still be regarded as one of the greatest poets in human history.

In the wake of Shakespeare, although the sequence format fell out of favor, the sonnet itself became the most popular fixed form in English literary history -- a history replete with distinguished sonneteers who used the formats of both the English and Italian sonnets, as well as numerous variations and combinations, to create a long list of lyric masterpieces. With the exceptions of the Neoclassicists of the 18th Century (Johnson, Pope, and Swift), who seemed suspicious of the unpredictable and inductive nature of the sonnet, the list of English sonneteers includes the names of almost all of the great writers in the history of the language, including John Donne, John Milton, William Wordsworth, Percy Bysshe Shelley, John Keats, Alfred Lord Tennyson, Elizabeth Browning, Gerard Manley Hopkins, and Oscar Wilde. Similarly, this irresistible attraction for the sonnet also manifested itself in America where excellent sonnets were written by Henry Wadsworth Longfellow, James Russell Lowell, and Edwin Arlington Robinson.

THE MODERN SONNET

Despite the 20th Century's obsession with "experimentation" and Pound's dictum to "make it new," the traditional rhymed sonnet continued, throughout the entire century, to attract the best writers in Western civilization. Even a short list is extremely impressive, if not daunting: Yeats, Valéry, Frost, Rilke, Machado, Lorca, Borges, Neruda, and Auden. In America, there was an unfortunate period late in the century where the sonnet came under attack by a number of writers who claimed that the poem was somehow an unwanted symbol of a restrictive past. Nevertheless, the traditional sonnet was still used with remarkable success by such distinguished poets as Howard Nemerov, Richard Wilbur, and Anthony Hecht, and now, at the beginning of the 21st Century, the little *sonetto*, nearly 800 years old, is in the throes of a great and exhilarating English-language revival.

III.
Pound, Flint, Imagism, and Vers Libre

In 1914, Ezra Pound published *Des Imagistes* and initiated English-language Modernism. One of the most significant consequences of *Des Imagistes* was its successful promotion of *vers libre*. In the previous century, two talented metrical poets, Walt Whitman and W.E. Henley, had experimented with nonmetrical verse, but Whitman produced no real followers (and few admirers, excepting Ralph Waldo Emerson), and Henley's nonmetrical verse was obviously substandard and was essentially ignored. In France, some of the later Symbolists (particularly Arthur Rimbaud) had also experimented with *vers libre*, which, as Stéphane Mallarmé pointed out, was supposed to be, at most, a small, experimental "side chapel" in the great "cathedral" of metered poetry.

In 1914, Pound changed all that.

POUND (BRIEFLY)

Born in Hailey, Idaho, in 1885, Pound began college at the age of fifteen at the University of Pennsylvania, and he finished in 1905 at Hamilton College in upstate New York. After a master's degree at Penn, and a trip to France, Italy, and Spain to study the troubadour poets, Pound briefly taught at Wabash College in Indiana, where he was fired as a "Latin-Quarter type" for breaking the curfew rules. Unconcerned, the ambitious, talented, and flamboyant Pound sailed on a cattle boat for Europe, where he passed himself off as a tour guide to wealthy Americans in Spain and Italy, and where he also self-published for eight dollars his first collection of poems, *A Lume Spento* (1908). He was now ready to go to England.

The following year, after the death of George Meredith and Algernon Swinburne, the ever-confident William Butler Yeats declared, "And now I'm king of the cats." Regardless of Yeats's bravado, it was true, and Pound *knew* it was true in 1908 when he arrived in London, where the Irish poet was currently living. At the time, the British capital was the "where it's happening" place for aspiring English-language poets like Pound, and he quickly made alliances with young British poets, like F.S. Flint and Richard Aldington, and with American expatriates, like Hilda Doolittle (whom he'd known in the States) and William Carlos Williams. Convinced that he needed to revive English verse, which he felt was stuffy, diffuse, and worn-out, Pound (along with Flint) created Imagism. It had three key principles:

1. Direct treatment of the "thing" whether subjective or objective.
2. To use absolutely no word that does not contribute to the presentation.
3. As regarding rhythm: to compose in the sequence of the musical phrase, not in sequence of a metronome.

In 1914, Pound published the first Imagist anthology, *Des Imagistes*. Two years earlier, in Chicago, Harriet Monroe had begun publishing a new poetry journal called *Poetry*, with Pound serving as her foreign correspondent. Thus, Imagism and its practitioners had great influence at the new poetry journal. Nevertheless, within a year of *Des Imagistes*, Pound had abandoned his new movement to another American expatriate, Amy Lowell, and he quickly moved on to create Vorticism, referring disparagingly to Imagism as "Amygism." Certainly, the Imagist emphasis on carefully crafted images did help to revive a visual specificity in English-language poetry. But most of the poems were short, with little substance, and with the unfortunate air of pretentiousness about them. Whatever one's response to the more famous of the Imagist poems, it's hard not to appreciate Howard Nemerov's dismissal of Imagist poems as "costume jewelry."

F.S. FLINT

Since Pound was essentially a medievalist (the troubadour poets), then where did Imagism really come from? Despite some borrowings from

T.E. Hulme and the sinologist Ernest Fenollosa, it came mostly from F.S. Flint, who was an expert on French Symbolism, which became (along with Asian poetry) the primary theoretical model for Imagism. In 1908, six years before *Des Imagistes*, Flint had written an article in *The New Age* about the similarities of method between Mallarmé and the Japanese poets. It's quite significant that Frost (who was in London at the time, rejecting Pound's enticements to become an Imagist) and Edward Dahlberg both claimed that Flint was the true "founder" of Imagism.

MORE POUND

Pound, of course, had no interest in abiding by the limitations of his own Imagist constraints, so he quickly moved on to other kinds of verse. In 1920, he would again dramatically alter the history of modern English-language poetry by drastically editing the poetic fragments of his American protégé T.S. Eliot. The resulting poem, *The Waste Land*, was eventually published in *The Criterion* in 1922. It is impossible, of course, to overestimate the impact of both Imagism and *The Waste Land*. But Eliot's poem, unlike most of the little Imagist pieces, was highly literate and intellectual, and its disjunctive construction and its countless literary allusions created immense literary interest, especially among young poets and young professors (always readily attracted to the "new," especially when it has some "theoretical" basis). As a result, nonmetrical verse soon became the currency of the times.

AFTERMATH

The renowned British poet and historian Robert Conquest has discussed the results in his lecture, "But What Good Came of It at Last? An Inquest on Modernism," which he read at the General Meeting of England's Royal Society of Literature in 1979:

> As to free verse, once it ad established itself in the 1920s in England it became pervasive. No more than a decade later school magazines of expensive girl's schools—always keener on "creativity" than boy's schools—were full of

vague pieces of chopped up prose with vaguely emotional content. This may remind us that one notoriously bad effect of "free" verse is that large numbers of people educated during the last half century no longer understand the structure of real verse.

W. H. Auden was to remark in his later years:

> I cannot settle which is worse,
> The Anti-Novel or Free Verse ...

The truly astonishing discovery made by free versifier and anti-novelist alike was how much they could get away with. People have taken seriously, in recent times, novels consisting of loose pages in a box which the reader is invited to shuffle in any order he likes. It was of such things, and the many worse ones which will be familiar to all of you, that Philip Larkin writes, "The adjective 'modern,' when applied to any branch of art, means 'designed to evoke incomprehension, anger, boredom, or laughter'" and defines modernism as "tending towards the silly, the disagreeable, and the frigid."

In a fuller context the same writer tells us:

> I dislike such things not because they are new, but because they are irresponsible exploitations of technique in contradiction of human life as we know it. This is my essential criticism of modernism, whether perpetrated by Parker, Pound, or Picasso: it helps us neither to enjoy nor endure. It will divert us as long as we are prepared to be mystified or outraged, but maintains its hold only by being more mystifying and more outrageous: it has no lasting power.

Certainly Larkin's comments, cited approvingly by Conquest, are rather incendiary. But Larkin (1922-1985), who is often considered the best English poet of the latter half of the twentieth century, raises important questions that need to be seriously considered. Are free verse poems "irresponsible exploitations of technique"? And, is it possible that free verse "has no lasting power"? Regarding the second question, there have been, ever since the publication of *Des Imagistes*, numerous predictions of doom for the free verse poetics. Maybe the most persuasive case was made by A.D. Hope in his 1950 essay entitled "Free Verse: A Post-Mortem." Hope (1907-2000), possibly Australia's most distinguished poet of the twentieth century, predicted that free verse had run its course and would eventually be seen as a historical anomaly. But this was before the Beats, the New York School, the Black Mountain poets, and the many other new groups that developed in the fifties and used free verse for their various purposes and thus encouraged the use of nonmetrical verse. This was further encouraged by the development of creative writing programs in American universities, which hired American poets (most of them practitioners of free verse) as teachers. As a result, free verse increased its popularity among university-trained writers and became the dominant poetic mode, the status quo.

Nevertheless, these undeniable facts really don't adequately address Larkin's claim about "lasting power," since he wasn't writing about whether free verse would continue to be written. Larkin was, instead, claiming that free verse poems, because they lacked an underlying beat, would, as a consequence, also lack literary "staying power." This question will, naturally, be best answered several centuries from now, but the fact remains that after nearly a century of free verse domination, almost all of the most highly regarded English-language poets were metricists: Thomas Hardy, Edwin Arlington Robinson, William Butler Yeats, Robert Frost, and W.H. Auden. Pound and Eliot, of course, are special cases, especially since Eliot wrote much of his later work in various meters. A few decades ago, William Carlos Williams was generally regarded as the preeminent free verse poet of the twentieth century, but his reputation has clearly diminished.

Another interesting fact is that some of the most anthologized work by free verse poets is actually metrical. Examples include such indestructible poems as "We Real Cool" by Gwendolyn Brooks and "Traveling Through the Dark" by William Stafford. Stafford's gentle and evocative poetic touch made him the most imitated poet of the 1970s and 1980s, and a virtual free verse icon. Yet, this kindly man's most famous poem is basically blank verse (iambic pentameter). It begins:

> Traveling through the dark I found a deer
> dead on the edge of the Wilson River road.
> It is usually best to roll them into the canyon:
> that road is narrow; to swerve might make more dead.

As for Larkin's other charge—that free verse poems are "irresponsible exploitations of technique"—it might be more useful to ask if such verse is rather a mode that *lacks* a crucial technique. If human beings like rhythm, and if meter offers a species of rhythm that people have enjoyed since Chaucer, is it wise to eliminate it? Frost had no doubts, and he gave the world his famous analogy that free verse is "like playing tennis with the net down." We hear this comment so often that we seldom stop to consider how carefully constructed Frost's analogy actually is. Frost's free verse tennis players still have their racquets; they still have the same court boundaries; they still score in the same way; etc., but they are lacking one particular element of the game that seems fundamental. They have lowered the net. Now it might seem that a better analogy would portray the players competing on the court with the net actually removed, but even here Frost is accurate. If the net is rhythm, then the free verse players can still use various other sonic devices to create certain rhythmic effects. They will also have the natural "ghost" of meter that exists in all English-language writing, given the language's predominance of iambs. So the net is down. The meter is disrupted. And very few people would go to Wimbledon to see such a game of tennis.

POUND AGAIN

In the immediate aftermath of Imagism and Vorticism, Pound became disgusted with the metrical irregularity that he'd done so much to promulgate. He later explained his reactions in a famous essay that appeared in *The Criterion*.

> That is to say, at a particular date in a particular room, two authors, neither engaged in picking the other's pocket, decided that the dilution of *vers libre*, Amygism, Lee Masterism, general floppiness had gone too far and that some counter-current must be set going. Parallel situation centuries ago in China. Remedy prescribed "Emaux et Camées" (or the Bay State Hymn Book). Rhyme and regular strophes.
>
> Results: Poems in Mr. Eliot's *second* volume not contained in his first (*Prufrock*, Egoist, 1917), also "H. S. Mauberley."
>
> Divergence later.

As Pound recollects, he used both rhyme and (rough) meters in much of his famous poem "Hugh Selwyn Mauberley" (1920), which included quatrains that were clearly based on the hymnal measure of the Bay State Hymnal. While Eliot progressed with his own metrical studies, poems, and verse dramas, Pound clearly diverged "later," returning to a free verse of an even wilder construction for his epic poem, the *Cantos*.

In 1920, Pound moved to Paris, eventually migrating south to Rapallo, Italy, in 1925. While living in Italy, Pound not only supported the Fascist regime of Benito Mussolini, but he actually broadcast over Radio Rome a series of rather incomprehensible attacks against the United States, encouraging the American G.I.s to throw down their weapons. Thus, the most influential poet in the world had become a kind of fascist Tokyo Rose.

When the war ended, Pound was arrested for treason and placed in a restraining cage in the city of Pisa, and the following year, after being brought back to America, he was committed "of unsound mind" to St. Elizabeths mental institution in Washington, D.C. Despite his behavior during the war and his blatant anti-Semitism, countless American poets visited Pound at the hospital, and his influence continued. In 1958, due to the intercession of a number of well-known poets (including Eliot, Archibald MacLeish, and even Frost), Pound was released from St. Elizabeths, and he set sail for Italy. As soon as he arrived, he gave a fascist salute, called America "an insane asylum," and continued to mistreat his wife and avoid his son.

RECONSIDERATIONS

But, eventually, Pound's guilts—both literary and personal—caught up with him. In 1962, he admitted that he was "wrong, wrong, wrong. I've always been wrong." The following year he claimed, "Everything that I touch, I spoil. I have blundered always." In 1966, he admitted that his "opus," the *Cantos*, "don't make sense," and he dismissed his 803-page poem as "stupidity and ignorance." He called all of his work "a botch," saying, "I picked out this and that thing that interested me, and then jumbled them into a bag. But that's not the way to make a work of art."

And what of F.S. Flint, the co-creator of Imagism? Flint stopped writing poetry after 1920, claiming in a 1932 article for *The Criterion* that his own verse made him feel "physically ill." More importantly, in an interview in the 1950s, Flint claimed that, at the beginning, no one took Imagism "very seriously," admitting that it had been "a joke" started by a bunch of lively young people in London. Pound himself had admitted, back in 1915, that "the whole affair was started not very seriously chiefly to get H. D.'s [Hilda Doolittle's] five poems a hearing without its being necessary for her to publish a whole book."

These comments and later doubts by the founders of Imagism do not, of course, necessarily negate their founding principles, specifically free verse, but they should encourage all aspiring writers to carefully consider their choices. It's interesting, although some might consider it irrelevant, that Picasso had similar misgivings about his own iconoclastic work. In 1951, he told the Italian author Giovanni Papini:

> In art the mass of the people no longer seek consolation and exaltation, but those who are refined, rich, unoccu-

> pied seek what is new, strange, original, extravagant, scandalous. I myself, since Cubism and before, have satisfied these masters and critics with all the changing oddities which have passed through my head, and the less they understood me, the more they admired me. By amusing myself with all these games, with all these absurdities, puzzles, rebuses, arabesques, I became famous and that very quickly. And fame for a painter means sales, gains, fortunes, riches. And today, as you know, I am celebrated, I am rich. But when I am alone with myself, I have not the courage to think of myself as an artist in the great and ancient sense of the term. Giotto, Titian, Rembrandt were great painters. I am only a public entertainer who has understood his times and exploited them as best he could.... Mine is a bitter confession, more painful than it may appear, but it has the merit of being sincere.

Like Picasso, the founders of Imagism came to disavow their methods. It's a true story that, unfortunately, is not often told to young aspiring writers. Certainly, serious poetic artists need to experiment, but not all experiments are necessarily useful or permanent. Even in the seventeenth century, Milton, on rare occasions, experimented with a looser metric, as did later poets like Blake, Dryden (surprisingly), and Christopher Smart. Nevertheless, Smart's contemporary, Samuel Johnson, in his famous dictionary, still defined poetry as "metered language," and prose as "unmetered language." Oddly enough, even now, after nearly a hundred years of *vers libre*, the current *Random House Webster's* still defines poetry as "literary work in metrical form" and prose as "the ordinary form of spoken or written language, without metrical structure, as distinguished from poetry or verse." Johnson, like most poets in the great tradition, believed that meter was "indispensably necessary to a poet." As he explained:

> However minute the employment may appear, of analysing lines into syllables, and whatever ridicule may be incurred by a solemn deliberation upon accents and pauses, it is certain, that without this petty knowledge no man can be a poet; and that from the proper disposition of single sounds results that harmony that adds force to reason, and gives grace to sublimity; that shackles attention, and governs passion.

Tennis anyone?

IV.
The Formalist Revival

A BRIEF HISTORICAL NOTE

For many decades, American poetry has been dominated by free verse. It fills the literary journals; it's taught in the classrooms; and it's the most common form of poetic expression. Yet, at the present time, there's a sizable and active Formalist community within the larger world of American poetry. Although various people have claimed credit for this revival, it was essentially a logical reaction against the limitations of free verse that affected disparate members of the baby boom generation. These poets realized that the contemporary poetry of the sixties and seventies had abandoned something of great value—meter—which had powerfully enhanced the great poetic works of the past.

THE FIFTIES, SIXTIES, AND SEVENTIES

Despite the fact that a number of distinguished poets—like Howard Nemerov, Richard Wilbur, Anthony Hecht, and James Merrill—continued to write and publish formal poetry, the dominant trend in the late 1950s, the 1960s, and the 1970s was for short, free verse lyrics, often autobiographical. The emergence of various groups like the Beats, the Black Mountain poets, the New York School, the Deep Imagists, and others encouraged this trend, as did the fact that free verse quickly became the lingua franca of the newly forming creative writing programs in the American universities. With the exception of some metrical poetry written by certain established poets, by the 1970s, very little formal verse was being published in the literary journals, and both meter and rhyme were considered, at best, an outdated aspect of the literary past, or, much worse, a debilitated form of bourgeois or capitalist control. Occasionally, these attacks, at their worst and most shrill, even descended into fantastic charges that formal poetry was actually "fascist" (as William Carlos Williams once delineated the sonnet), in spite of the fact that most of the best poets of the twentieth century had used poetic forms, and that even leftists like Federico García Lorca and Pablo Neruda (a Communist) had also used forms.

In 1972, X.J. Kennedy and his wife Dorothy initiated a short-lived journal called *Counter/Measures*, and they received an "enormous volume" of interested mail. Kennedy, born in 1929, was a member of the generation between the senior poets (like Nemerov) and the baby boomers. Kennedy, along with other established poets like Miller Williams, Lewis Turco, James Whitehead, and Dick Allen, did not abandon poetic forms despite a sometimes hostile environment.

Despite this environment, various younger poets of the baby boom generation, often in isolation, began writing in meter, forms, and rhymes. The influence of Yvor Winters at Stanford led Timothy Steele to attend graduate school at Brandeis, where he studied with Winters's former student, J.V. Cunningham. Similarly, at Louisiana State University, another of Winters's former students, Donald E. Stanford, had an important influence on a number of young poets, including Wyatt Prunty, David Middleton, and John Finlay. At Harvard, the influence of Robert Fitzgerald and several other professors encouraged poets like Rachel Hadas, Dana Gioia, Brad Leithauser, and Mary Jo Salter. Nevertheless, there was no true center for the gradually reviving Formalism, as many isolated young poets in various parts of the country began experimenting with meter and rhyme.

So where does the revival begin? People can debate this endlessly. It's certainly significant that Rachel Hadas's first chapbook, *Starting From Troy*, was published by Godine in 1975; Charles Martin's first book, *Room for Error*, was published in 1978; and Timothy Steele's first collection, *Uncertainties at Rest*, appeared the following year.

THE EIGHTIES

The 1980s were the decade of formation for the Formalist revival. Many of the new metrical poets published their first books in this decade, and others wrote articles and essays defending the practice of formal poetry. From 1979–1982, Frederick Turner and Ronald Sharp served as the editors of the newly revived *The Kenyon Review*, in which they published both poems and literary essays by the new generation of poets. At the same time, Brad Leithauser was writing several excellent essays for *The New Criterion*, particularly "Metrical Illiteracy," which appeared in January 1983. Two years later, Frederick Turner and Ernst Pöppel published their seminal and award-winning essay, "The Neural Lyre: Poetic Meter, the Brain, and Time," in *Poetry*. This in-depth essay discussed new scientific evidence for the neurological foundations of the human pleasure response to regular rhythm.

Thus, gradually, the larger literary world began to take notice of the new metrical poets, who were dubbed "the New Formalists" in a negative article entitled "The Yuppie Poet" written by Ariel Dawson for the *AWP Newsletter* (May 1985). Nevertheless, a number of the mainstream literary journals began to include metrical poetry within their pages, including *The Southern Review*, *Poetry*, *The Paris Review*, and *The Hudson Review*. Later in the decade, two valuable anthologies appeared that highlighted contemporary formal poetry by writers of all generations: *Strong Measures: Contemporary American Poetry in Traditional Forms* (1986), edited by Philip Dacey and David Jauss; and *The Direction of Poetry: An Anthology of Rhymed and Metered Verse Written in the English Language Since 1975* (1988), edited by Robert Richman.

Also particularly significant at mid-decade was the creation of Story Line Press by Robert McDowell in 1985. In subsequent years, McDowell would publish many of the new voices in the Formalist revival, especially through the press's annual Nicholas Roerich Poetry Prize (now called the Frederick Morgan Poetry Prize in honor of the late founding editor of *The Hudson Review*). McDowell was also the co-editor, with Mark Jarman, of *The Reaper* (1981–1989), a journal of narrative poetry that further expanded contemporary poetic possibilities beyond the free verse lyric. At the end of the decade, the poet Wyatt Prunty, a professor at the University of the South in Sewanee, Tennessee, became the founding director of the extremely influential Sewanee Writers' Conference. The intensive poetry workshops at this annual summer gathering were taught by senior faculty members (like Howard Nemerov, Mona Van Duyn, Donald Justice, or Anthony Hecht) along with a member of the Formalist revival (such as Charles Martin, Rachel Hadas, Andrew Hudgins, or Mary Joe Salter).

THE NINETIES

The year 1990 saw the publication of the first issue of *The Formalist: A Journal of Metrical Poetry* (which I edited); the publication of Timothy Steele's masterful critical study, *Missing Measures: Modern Poetry and the Revolt Against Meter*; and the initial issue of *Hellas: A Journal of Poetry and the Humanities*, edited by Gerald Harnett. In 1994, *Sparrow*, edited by Felix Stefanile, rededicated itself entirely to the sonnet, and several other formalist-friendly journals were initiated: *The Edge City Review* (1994); *The Dark Horse* (1995); the revived *Pivot* (1995); *The Tennessee Quarterly* (1995), and *Janus* (1996).

The early nineties also saw the publication of important critical works by two of the leading figures in the Formalist revival: Wyatt Prunty's *"Fallen From the Symboled World": Precedents for the New Formalism* (1990) and Dana Gioia's *Can Poetry Matter?: Essays on Poetry and American Culture* (1992). Four years later, Story Line Press published *Rebel Angels: 25 Poets of the New Formalism*, an anthology edited by Mark Jarman and David Mason; and, in 1998, the University of Evansville Press initiated the Richard Wilbur Poetry Award, an annual book competition that has created further publishing possibilities for Formalist poets.

At mid-decade, Dana Gioia and co-director Michael Peich initiated another extremely important writers' conference. The Exploring Form and Narrative Poetry Conference began in the summer of 1995 at West Chester University in Pennsylvania; and it provided, among other features, specialty writing workshops conducted by such revivalist poets as Timothy Steele, Emily Grosholz, and R.S. Gwynn. Within a few years, the annual West Chester gathering was the largest summer poetry conference in America.

THE TWENTY-FIRST CENTURY

At the present time, the Formalist revival is ever-expanding and as vibrant as ever. The pleasures, challenges, and rewards of writing metrical poetry are constantly attracting serious poets from the younger generations. Despite some residual complaints from the free verse orthodoxy, formal poetry is generally accepted as a viable poetic option, and the anathematizing attacks of the previous decades are fewer in number and essentially insignificant.

In the meantime, two new journals have stepped forward to replace those that have been discontinued: *Iambs & Trochees* (2001) and *Measure* (2006). In 2000, Kevin Walzer founded Word Press in Cincinnati, which has published many books by poets associated with the Formalist revival. Also, several new and exciting poetry prizes that include book publication are currently underway: the Donald Justice Poetry Award, directed by Michael Peich at West Chester University; the Anthony Hecht Poetry Prize, directed by Philip Hoy at England's Waywiser Press; and the Anita Dorn Poetry Prize, directed by Alfred Dorn of New York City.

In retrospect, the current Formalist revival has many similarities with the great Romantic revival of the early nineteenth century. Both revivals breathed new and passionate life into the traditional poetic forms while simultaneously emphasizing the contemporary idiom. While it's certainly true that contemporary Formalism is still a literary subset of the overall poetry world, it proudly traces its roots back to Chaucer (and to Homer as well), seeing itself as the natural extension of the great tradition of English-language poetry.

V.
50 Quotes About Meter, Form, and Rhyme

Aristotle

Thus prose should be rhythmical, but not metrical; otherwise, it will be a poem.

—RHETORIC, BOOK 3

William Shakespeare

(Hamlet on his love poem)

O dear Ophelia, I am ill at these numbers;
I have not art to reckon my groans: but that
I love thee best, O most best, believe it. Adieu.

—HAMLET, ACT II, SCENE 2

Samuel Johnson

Versification, or the art of modulating his numbers, is indispensably necessary to a poet. Every other power by which the understanding is enlightened or the imagination enchanted may be exercised in prose. But the poet has this peculiar superiority, that to all the powers which the perfection of every other composition can require, he adds the faculty of joining music with reason, and of acting at once upon the senses and the passions.

—THE RAMBLER, NUMBER 86

However minute the employment may appear, of analysing lines into syllables, and whatever ridicule may be incurred by a solemn deliberation upon accents and pauses, it is certain, that without this petty knowledge no man can be a poet; and that from the proper disposition of single sounds results that harmony that adds force to reason, and gives grace to sublimity; that shackles attention, and governs passion.

—THE RAMBLER, NUMBER 88

(To James Boswell, July 14, 1763)

Sir, I was once in company with [Adam] Smith, and we did not take to each other; but had I known that he loved rhyme as much as you tell me he does, I should have hugged him.

—THE LIFE OF JOHNSON, 1791

Immanuel Kant

It is advisable, however, to remind ourselves that in all the free arts there is yet a need for something in the order of a constraint, or, as it is called, a mechanism. (In poetry, for example, it is correctness and richness of language, as well as prosody and meter.) Without this, the spirit, which in art must be free and which alone animates the work, would have no body at all and would evaporate completely. This reminder is needed because some of the more recent educators believe that they promote a free art best if they remove all constraint from it and convert it from labor into mere play.

—CRITIQUE OF JUDGMENT, 1790
TRANSLATION: WERNER S. PLUHAR

Thomas Jefferson

It is the business of the poet so to arrange his words as that, repeated in their accustomed measures, they shall strike the ear with that regular rhythm which constitutes verse.

—"THOUGHTS ON ENGLISH PROSODY," 1786

Henry Wadsworth Longfellow

Form is so much in poetry!

—A LETTER TO JAMES E. HEWITT, 1875

Edgar Allan Poe

Contenting myself with the certainty that music, in its various modes of meter, rhythm, and rhyme, is of so vast a moment in poetry as never to be wisely rejected—is so vitally important an adjunct, that he is simply silly who declines its assistance—I will not now pause to maintain its absolute essentiality.

—"THE POETIC PRINCIPLE," 1850

George Santayana

Like the orders of Greek architecture, the sonnet or the couplet or the quatrain are better than anything else that has been devised to serve the same function; and the innate freedom of poets to hazard new forms does not abolish the freedom of all men to adopt the old ones.

—THE "PREFACE," POEMS, 1925

Versification is like a pulsing accompaniment, somehow sustaining and exalting the clear logic of the words.

—THE "PREFACE," POEMS, 1925

W.B. Yeats

Alas the inspiration of God, which is, indeed, the source of all which is greatest in the world, comes only to him who labours at rhythm and cadence, at form and style, until they have no secret hidden from him. This art we must learn from the old literatures of the world.

—UNCOLLECTED PROSE, VOLUME 1, 1970

Robert Frost

Writing free verse is like playing tennis with the net down.

—MILTON ACADEMY ADDRESS, MAY 17, 1935

The possibilities for tune from the dramatic tones of meaning struck across the rigidity of a limited meter are endless.

—"THE FIGURE A POEM MAKES," 1939

I.A. Richards

That the art of responding to the form of poetry is not less difficult than the art of grasping its content—its sense and feeling—will be evident to anyone who has glanced through Part II. And since half perhaps of the feeling that poetry carries comes through its form (and through the interaction of form and content) the need for better educational methods, here also, will be admitted. ... A large proportion of even a picked public neither understand the kind of importance that attaches to the movement of words in verse, nor have any just ideas of how to seize this movement or judge it.

—PRACTICAL CRITICISM, CHAPTER FOUR, 1929

We shall never understand metre so long as we ask, "Why does temporal pattern so excite us?" and fail to realize that the pattern itself is a vast cyclic agitation spreading all over the body, a tide of excitement pouring through the channels of the mind.

—PRINCIPLES OF LITERARY CRITICISM, 1924

Yvor Winters

I cannot grasp the contemporary notion that the traditional virtues of style are incompatible with a poetry of modern subject matter; it appears to rest on the fallacy of expressive form, the notion that the form of the poem should express the matter. This fallacy results in the writing of chaotic poetry about the traffic; of loose poetry about our sprawling nation; of semi-conscious poetry about semi-conscious states. But the matter of poetry is and always has been chaotic; it is raw nature. To let the form of the poem succumb to its matter is and will always be the destruction of poetry and may be the destruction of intelligence. Poetry is form; its constituents are thought and feeling as they are embodied in language; and though form cannot be wholly reduced to principles, there are certain principles which it cannot violate.

—BEFORE DISASTER, 1934

W.H. Auden

I cannot settle which is worse,

the Anti-Novel or Free Verse.

—"DOGGEREL BY A SENIOR CITIZEN," 1969

I have always been a formalist.

—THE NEW YORK QUARTERLY, 1970

The formal structure of a poem is not something distinct from its meaning but as intimately bound up with the latter as the body is with the soul.

—"THE VOICE OF THE POET," 2004

Speaking for myself, the questions which interest me most when reading a poem are two. The first is technical: "Here is a verbal contraption. How does it work?" The second is, in the broadest sense, moral: "What kind of a guy inhabits this poem? What is his notion of the good life or the good place? His notion of the Evil One? What does he conceal from the reader? What does he conceal from himself?"

—"MAKING, KNOWING AND JUDGING," *THE DYER'S HAND*, 1962

... my only complaint when I am reviewed is the critic's lack of knowledge. The one thing I am vain about is my knowledge of meters. I do think a reviewer should know his job. I look to see how a poem is made before I think what it says. Then I begin to read.

—*THE NEW YORK QUARTERLY*, 1970

A.D. Hope

The truth about free verse is that it is not free and it is not verse. It is not free because it has no discipline by which its freedom may be assessed. It is not verse because it has neither measure nor metre.

—"FREE VERSE: A POST-MORTEM," *QUADRANT*, 1965

Karl Shapiro and Robert Beum

... few even of the most ardent "unrhymers" would want to dispose of practically the whole tradition of English lyric verse; few would suggest that Shakespeare or Chaucer would have been better off without it. How seriously dare we take a man who would exclude all rhyme from his theory of the good and the beautiful?

—*A PROSODY HANDBOOK*, 1965

Laurence Perrine

And finally, there is in all form the pleasure of form itself.

—*SOUND AND SENSE*, 1956

Robert Conquest

Someone once said that American poets no longer see the need for meter and rhyme. Geoffrey Grigson commented that if that's the case, then American poets aren't poets in any sense known to civilization for the past three thousand years.

—THE FORMALIST, FALL/WINTER 1997

Primo Levi

It has too many virtues; it is too beautiful to disappear.

—"RHYMING ON THE COUNTERATTACK," 1989

Howard Nemerov

Jan Castro: Did the iambics come naturally?

Howard Nemerov: I talk that way.

—WEBSTER REVIEW, FALL 1980

I never abandoned either forms or freedom. I imagine that most of what could be called free verse is in my first book. I got through that fairly early. I am not at all clear what free verse is anymore. That's one of the things you learn not to know.

—THE SOUTHERN REVIEW, SUMMER 1979

I think there was a revolution in poetry, associated chiefly with Eliot and Pound; but maybe it is of the nature of revolutions or of the nature of history that their innovations should later come to look trivial or indistinguishable from technical tricks.

—POETS ON POETRY, 1966

It is part of the delight in poetry, too, that there are formal problems; going at these relieves you of a certain pretentiousness connected with what you are supposed to be saying; you let it say itself, if only because you are so blessedly busy getting things to fit.

—JOURNAL OF THE FICTIVE LIFE, 1965

Richard Wilbur

There is a goofy argument going around, to the effect that metrical writing tempts one to make strong closures, and that strong closures are fraudulent in an age of doubt and confusion. To which I can only say that poets are not bound to conform to anyone else's notion of the age, and that a few iambs and trochees never led an able poet to say more than he meant.

—CONVERSATIONS WITH RICHARD WILBUR, 1990

I've heard some poets say they don't use rhyme because it makes them say things that they didn't mean to say. That's ridiculous: it's as if a sculptor should object to the hardness of stone; or, as John Nims said, it's as if a hurdler should object to there being hurdles in his path. Rhyme and meter present difficulties which, if overcome, turn into added force; and any poet who can't use them on occasion, and at the same time pursue his thought, is in the wrong racket.

—NATIONAL ARTS CLUB LECTURE, FEBRUARY 1994

The hope that something may endure is based on a sense that it is well-made and useful.

—CONVERSATIONS WITH RICHARD WILBUR, 1990

Philip Larkin

I haven't anything very original to say about metre. I've never tried syllabics; I'm not sure I fully understand them. I think one would have to be very sure of oneself to dispense with the help that metre and rhyme give, and I doubt really if I could operate without them.

—THE LONDON MAGAZINE, NOVEMBER 1964

Anthony Hecht

No one would dream of trying to be a Metropolitan basso or soprano if one were born tone-deaf, or without years of painstaking private practice. But no such decent humility deters great hordes of poets who could not, to save their lives, compose some formal neck-verses.

—CORRESPONDENCE, 1989

Paul Fussell, Jr.

Poetic forms are like that: they tend to say things even if words are not at the moment fitted to their patterns. As Louis MacNeice has said, "In any poet's poem the shape is half the meaning."

—POETIC METER AND POETIC FORM, 1965

Donald Justice

Let us concede that the effects of the meters are mysterious, from moment to moment imprecise, often enough uncertain or ambiguous. Like Coleridge's incense or wine, however, their presence may "act powerfully, though themselves unnoticed."To which he adds an interesting comparison to yeast—"worthless," as he says, "or disagreeable by itself, but giving vivacity and spirit to the liquor" in right combination.

—"METERS AND MEMORY," 1978

Maxine Kumin

I believe that writing in a rhyme scheme startles you into good metaphor. At least, it works that way for me. It's the form in which to pour the cement of the poem.

—TO MAKE A PRAIRIE, 1979

X.J. Kennedy

When you write in rhyme, it's as if you're walking across a series of stepping stones into the darkness, and you can't really see what's at the far end of the stepping stones. So you're led onward, often to say things that surprise and astonish you. As Rolfe Humphries once put it, rhyme leads you to say much better things than you could have thought of all by yourself.

—THE FORMALIST, FALL/WINTER 2000

Many today dismiss the sonnet and other traditional forms as drab boxes for cramming with words. But to me the old forms are where the primitive and surprising action is. Writing in rhythm and rhyme, a poet is involved in an enormous, meaningful game, not under his ego's control. He is a mere mouse in the lion's den of the language—but with any luck, at times he can get the lion to come out.

—CONTEMPORARY AUTHORS, 1993

Snodgrass says that in travailing over the poem he gets closer to what he really feels and did not know at the start that he felt. Formality is a way of achieving sincerity. But it can be sincerity only for a man who has made formality his true medium. If such a requirement excludes those who have not worked to shape their abilities—the would-be musicians full of passion who never learned to play an instrument—then that is a necessary exclusion. No man gets to be a poet except by preparing himself to be one.

—SATURDAY REVIEW, MAY 20, 1972

Derek Walcott

The imagination wants its limits and delights in its limits. It finds its freedom in the definition of those limits.

—THE PARIS REVIEW, WINTER 1986

In truth, all you can really do at a young age is apprentice yourself to the craft. And the total absence of that apprenticeship in this country has made most of the verse unbearable.

—THE FORMALIST, SPRING/SUMMER 1994

I teach classes, and most of the young writers have never had any training in meter and have been told, horribly enough, you mustn't be too musical, rhyme is dead, etc. It is horrible that there are poets, young poets, who are taught this as almost an American law.

—THE KENYON REVIEW, SPRING 2001

Joseph Brodsky

In my opinion a regular meter and exact rhymes shaping an uncomfortable thought are far more functional than any form of free verse. Because in the former case the reader gets a sense of chaos being organized, while in the latter a sense of dependence on and being determined by chaos.

—THE AMERICAN POETRY REVIEW, 1972

Douglas Dunn

Metre, rhyme and stanza can be isolated as the groundwork of a poet's craft, as well as the skill with which vocabulary can be harvested. There exists what I would like to call a secret interplay between the poet and technique, between the instinctive and the deliberated.

—THE POET'S VOICE AND CRAFT, 1994

Timothy Steele

Today, one almost hesitates to say that most poets write unmetrically: such a statement suggests that they know what meter is, which does not appear to be the case. Rather, it seems that versification, as it has been understood for millennia, is for the majority of contemporary poets an irrelevant matter.

—MISSING MEASURES, 1990

It seems terribly simple-minded to say of a medium that allowed for the poems of Homer and Virgil and Dante and Shakespeare that it is a strait-jacket.

—MISSING MEASURES, 1990

Brad Leithauser

The exploding population of poets, the dizzying diffusion, the sense of open opportunities—clearly these conditions will little profit us so long as a belief persists that a person who is not a decent prosodist can be a decent poet. Or so long as we fail to recognize that metrical illiteracy is, for the poet, functional illiteracy.

—"METRICAL ILLITERACY," THE NEW CRITERION, 1983

A

B

C

F

G

H

I

J

K

L

M

N

Q

R

PERMISSIONS

"If I Could Tell You" from *Collected Poems* by W.H. Auden. Copyright 1945 by W.H. Auden. Reprinted by permission of Random House.

"In Memory of W.B. Yeats" from *Collected Poems* by W.H. Auden. Copyright 1945 by W.H. Auden. Reprinted by permission of Random House.

"Circles" from *The Little Hill* by Harry Behn. Copyright 1949 by Harry Behn. Reprinted by permission of Marian Reiner.

"Daniel Boone" by Stephen Vincent Benét, from *A Book of Americans*. Copyright 1933 by Rosemary and Stephen Vincent Benét. Reprinted by permission of Brandt & Hochman Literary Agents.

"Prosody and Period" from *A Prosody Handbook* by Robert Beum and Karl Shapiro. Copyright 1965 by Robert Beum and Karl Shapiro. Reprinted by pemission of Robert Beum.

"One Art" from *The Collected Poems 1927-1979* by Elizabeth Bishop. Copyright 1979, 1983 by Alice Helen Methfessel. Reprinted by permission of Farrar, Straus & Giroux.

"It took me some time to agree" by John Ciardi, from *Limericks* by Isaac Asimov & John Ciardi. Copyright 1978 by W.W. Norton & Company. Reprinted by permission by W.W. Norton & Company.

"Variation on Belloc's 'Fatigue'," "Poem Composed in Santa Barbara," and "Two Cures for Love" from *Serious Concerns* by Wendy Cope. Copyright 1992 by Wendy Cope. Reprinted by permission of Faber and Faber and Wendy Cope.

"The South Bank Poetry Library, London" by Wendy Cope is reprinted with the permission of Wendy Cope.

"#30" from *The Poems of J. V. Cunningham* by J.V. Cunningham. Copyright 1997 by Jessie Cunningham. Reprinted by permission of Ohio University Press.

"Cleared Away" by Dana Gioia, from *The Gods of Winter*, Graywolf Press. Copyright 1991 by Dana Gioia. Reprinted by permission of Dana Gioia.

"The Road" by Dana Gioia, from *Sonnets: 150 Contemporary Sonnets*, University of Evansville Press. Copyright 2005. Reprinted by permission of Dana Gioia.

"At the Center" by R.S. Gwynn, from *No Word of Farewell: Selected Poems 1970-2000*, Story Line Press. Copyright 2001 by R.S. Gwynn. Reprinted by permission of Story Line Press.

"Super Nivem" from *Halfway Down the Hall: New and Selected Poems* by Rachel Hadas. Copyright 1998 by Rachel Hadas. Reprinted by permission of Wesleyan University Press.

"Thomas Stearns Eliot" by Patrick Nielsen Hayden. Published by permission of Patrick Nielsen Hayden.

"Career Move" by Jan D. Hodge. Published by permission of Jan D. Hodge.

"With a Book of Robert Frost's Poetry" by John Hollander, from the Spring/Summer 2000 issue of *The Formalist*. Reprinted by permission of John Hollander.

"To Zelda" by Lauren Hroblak. Published by permission of Lauren Hroblak.

"Your Midlife Crisis" by A.M. Juster. Published by permission of A.M. Juster.

"1" from *The Collected Poems of Weldon Kees* by Weldon Kees. Copyright 1975 by University of Nebraska Press. Reprinted by permission of the University of Nebraska Press.

"Stupid little Lucy Wankett" by Josh Kennedy, from *Brats*, Atheneum. Copyright 1986 by X.J.

Kennedy. Reprinted by permission of Josh Kennedy.

"Stephanie, that little stinker" by X.J. Kennedy, from *Brats*, Atheneum. Copyright 1986 by X.J. Kennedy. Reprinted by permission of Curtis Brown.

"At the Last Rites for Two Hotrodders" by X.J. Kennedy, from *Cross Ties: Selected Poems*, University of Georgia Press. Copyright 1985 by X.J. Kennedy. Reprinted by permission of Curtis Brown.

"Death Will Do Nothing" from *Starting from Sleep: New and Selected Poems* by Charles Martin. Copyright 2002 by Charles Martin. Reprinted by permission of Overlook Press.

"Last Chance at Reconciliation" by Joshua Mehigan from *The Optimist*. Copyright 2004 by Joshua Mehigan. Reprinted by permission of Ohio University Press.

"The Ballad of Charles Starkweather" by Robert Mezey and Donald Justice is reprinted by permission of Robert Mezey.

"Visiting Poet" by John Frederick Nims, from *Of Flesh and Bone*. Copyright 1967 by John Frederick Nims. Reprinted by permission of Bonnie Nims.

"Death and the Maiden," "Moment," and "Two Girls" by Howard Nemerov from *The Collected Poems of Howard Nemerov*, University of Chicago Press. Copyright 1977 by Howard Nemerov. Reprinted by permission of Margaret Nemerov.

"Striders" by Howard Nemerov, from *Inside the Onion*, University of Chicago Press. Copyright 1984 by Howard Nemerov. Reprinted by permission of Margaret Nemerov.

"Christopher Smart" by Lee R. Parks from the Fall/Winter 1998 issue of *The Formalist*. Reprinted by permission of Lee R. Parks.

"The Funerals" from *Unarmed and Dangerous: New and Selected Poems* by Wyatt Prunty. Copyright 2000 by Johns Hopkins University Press. Reprinted by permission of the Johns Hopkins University Press.

"Ballad of Birmingham" by Dudley Randall, from *Cities Burning*. Copyright 1968 by Dudley Randall. Reprinted by permission of Broadside Press.

"Looking Back" by Ed Rossmann, from the Fall/Winter 1997 issue of *The Formalist*. Reprinted by permission of Ed Rossmann.

"Contract Murder" by Joseph S. Salemi, from *Formal Complaints*, Somers Rocks Press. Copyright 1997 by Joseph S. Salemi. Reprinted by permission of Joseph S. Salemi.

"Dutch Interior" from *Collected Poems 1930-1973* by May Sarton. Copyright 1974 by May Sarton. Reprinted by permission of W. W. Norton.

"The Ballade of the Hanged" by Marion Shore, from the Fall/Winter 2000 issue of *The Formalist*. Reprinted by permission of Marion Shore.

"Hades Welcomes His Bride" by A.E. Stallings, from *Archaic Smile,* University of Evansville Press. Copyright 1999 by A.E Stallings. Reprinted by permission of A. E. Stallings.

"Cleo" by Amanda Sykes. Published by permission of Amanda Sykes.

"Do Not Go Gentle Into That Good Night" from *The Poems of Dylan Thomas* by Dylan Thomas. Copyright 1952 by Dylan Thomas. Reprinted by permission of New Directions.

"The Psychic" by Gail White, from the Fall/Winter 2003 issue of *The Formalist*. Reprinted by permission of Gail White.

"Parable" by Richard Wilbur, from *New and Collected Poems*. Copyright 1988 by Richard Wilbur. Reprinted by permission of Harcourt, Brace, & Jovanovich.